TANKERMAN

Capt. Dick Williams

TANKERMAN
A seafarer's recollections of a life afloat with "Shell"

First published by Bernard Durnford Publishing
The Old Museum, Bramber, West Sussex BN44 3WE
England.
1999

A catalogue record of this book
is available from the British Library

ISBN 0 9535670 1 X

Format, design and cover by StewART

Printed and bound by, Antony Rowe Ltd
Bumper's Farm, Chippenham, Wiltshire.

TANKERMAN
A seafarer's recollections of a life afloat with "Shell"

CAPT. DICK WILLIAMS

Published by

Bernard Durnford Publishing

PREFACE

These memoirs cover the time between 1945 and 1984. They recount my experiences during 39 years of seafaring, from Deck Apprentice through the ranks, culminating in 18 years as Master. The period was probably the most important and productive in the history of the British Merchant Navy.

During the 1920's and 1930's, the industry was badly affected by the Great Depression and subsequently decimated during World War II, with appalling losses in men and ships. These two factors had a telling effect upon those who had survived both these terrible experiences, with attitudes and morale moulded by the hardships and suffering sustained by the survivors of these two cataclysmic periods in the history of the Merchant Navy.

I went to sea at the end of 1945 as an Apprentice with the Anglo-Saxon Petroleum Company Limited, the British arm of what became the biggest commercial maritime enterprise the world had witnessed: Shell International Marine. Together with the rest of the national fleet, Anglo-Saxon had suffered grievously during the war - 42 ships lost (40% of the total) and an untold toll in brave men.

Before beginning my life under the Pecten (the well known commercial symbol - the 'Shell' that everyone recognises), it seems appropriate to write something about my background.

I certainly was not your usual sailor! Typically he was from a seafaring nursery where tradition pointed youngsters in the direction of ships. Such nurseries were inevitably coastal towns and villages. Taking a broad brush one could generalize and describe Anglo-Saxon as a Geordie (Tyneside) company with a substantial minority from north and west Wales - this was such a well known fact that the company was fondly referred to as the 'Anglo-Geordie Paraffin Oil Company!

I was brought up in Merthyr Tydfil, a medium sized town at the head of the Taff Valley in Glamorgan. During my formative years, Merthyr was in decline. The iron and steel works at Cyfarthfa and Dowlais (during the 19th Century, these two enterprises, together with a smaller third, produced the greatest volume of metals the world had known, surpassing Pittsburgh in size) either had closed or closed during my childhood. The population suffered badly from the effects of these desertions and subsequently from the decline in the coal industry.

I count myself fortunate however, for my upbringing. Merthyr, for all its industrial deprivation and malaise, is situated in an area of unsurpassing beauty. Education figured prominently in the local government's policy at that time. The Borough possessed three first-class grammar schools, enabling the majority of young people to enjoy this level of education - which in the 1930's and 1940's was not the national expectation.

We, as a family of four (including a younger brother), lived in a typical South Walian terraced house where people of modest means reared their families. Both my parents were bank clerks, my mother came from a farming background near Brecon, whilst my father was the son of an industrial chemist, employed in the Cyfarthfa Steel Works.

My upbringing was strict but secure. My brother and I were expected to behave exemplarily because of my father's position at Lloyds' Bank, where ostensibly, any impropriety on our part would reflect adversely upon the bank's reputation! I had a conventionally undistinguished academic history, eventually achieving matriculation. My sporting prowess was equally modest except for an unexpected talent in speed swimming.

Why, one might wonder, would a boy from such a background, with no affiliation to seafaring whatsoever, choose to go to sea? Even more remarkable was the fact that apart from the heartbreak of family partings and the sometimes almost impossible burdens placed upon one's loved ones, it was a career in which I exalted! We are all products or victims of the age within which we live. Over the years I have analysed the motivation that propelled me on the course I took. Apart from those outstandingly different among my peers, the average boy or girl of my era seemed to aim for education as a livelihood - be a teacher or 'preacher'.

My generation was moulded by unique influences. To be a boy between thirteen and seventeen during wartime was to be a youth in conflict. Boys little older than oneself had left school, been conscripted into one of the armed forces and had, subject to their survival, become men and heroes almost instantly. A very powerful and compelling motivation for boys of my age. I recall when I was fifteen years old, one of my older acquaintances had joined the Royal Navy via the auspices of a university entrance procedure known as the 'Y' Scheme. He returned to Merthyr on one of his leaves and gave a 'talk' to we Sea Cadets (he too, had been a member of our unit some eighteen months earlier) about his experiences in command of a small coastal craft. All of nineteen years of age, thoughtfully sucking on his manly pipe, regaling us with breathless exploits he concluded his chat with the reflection "You see lads, you have to work hard and play hard in this game!" This was a very emotive and disturbing experience for a pimply-faced youth such as I - everything was so near, yet so impossibly far!

We grew up in an atmosphere of jingoism and patriotic fervour where one's thoughts were about equally divided between sex and wishing to throw oneself into the front line - be it at Alamein, in a Spitfire over Kent or a midget submarine at Trondheim. Small wonder, with such powerful forces creating a turmoil within some of us, that academia took a back seat!

I suppose if I were to try to objectively single out the most signifi-cant trait that steered me through life, it would be enthusiasm. As a boy I was an ardent patriot who would willingly and unthinkingly have joined any armed enterprise to prove myself. I yearned to be part of the great sacrifice which young men and women were making in the name of patriotism. However, I was too young. At sixteen I was sick with frustration! I too wanted to thoughtfully suck upon a Sherlock Holmes pipe after delivering a polished, daring-do lecture in a fashionably crumpled naval officer's uniform - complete with polo neck sweater!

My association with the sea started with the Sea Cadet Corps. I was a member of the ship's company of Training Ship "Tydfil" rising through the ratings from ordinary seaman to a three badge petty officer during a three year period prior to my going to sea. The Corps nominated and funded me at a monthly course in the Outward Bound Sea School at Aberdovey, in 1944. Nowadays, the Outward Bound Trust is widely known throughout the world, then however, it was relatively unknown. Based on principles evolved at Gordonstoun School, it offered young men, from all walks of life, a month's rigorous training in seamanship, sports and expedition work. It was there that I discovered the Merchant Navy. Perhaps more importantly I met a number of Deck Apprentices - a hitherto quite unknown form of sea-life! They were variously labelled Cadets and Midshipmen, depending upon the shipping company with whom they were indentured, but generally they were Apprentices. I have never forgotten those elegant boys (some little older than I) who were decked in naval uniform with lapel tabs - so worldly and assured. That was it, nothing else would do!

With the utmost difficulty, which included parental disapproval in the early stages and ignorance of the application process, I secured a berth as deck apprentice with the Anglo-Saxon Petroleum Company Limited. Success did not come easily - there were many boys throughout Britain who were as determined as I - with acceptance only achieved after competitive interview and a satisfactory report from the nautical department at Cardiff Technical College, where I spent three months undergoing training. Indentures were signed on November 27th 1945.

By the time I went to sea, I was relatively old at seventeen and a half and had received my call-up papers for the armed forces. The war was over - so the original raison d'etre no longer applied. However I had become too interested and almost enchanted by the ethos of the service, so there was to be no change of mind at this stage. I really had found what I wanted to do. So began a career that spanned 39 years, 57 ships and 1258 port visits. Barring some notable periods of despair and disenchantment and the ever present sense of guilt and heartbreak of leaving one's loved ones, I cherished every minute of those years.

Seafaring is a vocation, not a job. Throughout this account the reader should be aware that from 1946, one year after joining my first ship, I was influenced by the steadfast support of Joan Morris who became Joan Williams in 1952. Apart from her beauty, her humour and her warm heart, it was her understanding of my need to fulfil my career successfully that enabled us, as a family, to make a 'go' of it. Joan had the intellect (university trained, a violinist of note and a teacher by profession) to sustain a seafaring marriage. She raised a lovely daughter, suffered untold loneliness with occasional desolation in her role as sailor's wife. I was also enormously helped by her parents, who relished the whole concept and lifestyle their daughter had accepted. Edward (Ted) Morris, probably had a greater influence on me than anyone, apart from his daughter. He too, possessed a superior intellect, was also a fine violinist. In his reading of travel books, Ted Morris knew more about the world than I, despite never having left the shores of Britain. He was stone deaf.

I have dwelled upon the family, because it was only with their support and pride, that my life and career meant anything. However, in any recounting of a life, particularly a seafaring life, there are victims. In my case it was my daughter Rhiannon, who, although she had a matchless mother, missed the fullness of a complete family with my being absent so much, and that is an abiding regret that I will carry to my grave.

INTRODUCTION

I am no diarist. I did, however, keep a record of all the ports I visited and some of the officers with whom I sailed. It was this 'wee book' (as many of my colleagues termed it) that provided the bare bones of my account.

The original purpose of writing recollections of a life seafaring was to provide my grandchildren with a story of what the old fella did in those far-off days.

Two fellow 'Shell' retirees: Captains Alec Dickson and Bob Allen have written of their experiences during wartime - which make for exciting reading. I was somewhat reluctant, therefore, to follow on in their footsteps given the prosaic life I led by comparison. However, to my knowledge, no one has written about tanker life in the period I cover - which I believe to be a significant chapter in the history of the British Merchant Navy.

RJW

Elora, Ontario
January 1999

ACKNOWLEDGEMENTS

I should like to thank Lloyd Lewis, my son-in-law, for urging me to take this project on - and for his comments during the writing. Thanks, also, to Bonnie and John Smiley, Jeremy Smith and Dick Nightingale for their help and suggestions throughout the year it has taken me to compile these memoirs. Above all I wish to record my deep gratitude to my helpmate, Joan, who has had to put up with a lot in this time, but particularly for her guidance and countless hours spent in 'marking' my work!

DEDICATION

For Caitlin and Owen,
from Taid

CONTENTS

FOREWORD

It would be difficult to find a man better qualified to write memoirs such as these. Dick Williams methodically kept records of places, people and ships in a way which many of his colleagues now wish they had done. As a master, Dick was a delight to sail with. He took constructive criticism on board with the same enthusiasm with which he loaded Shell cargoes. He had the ability to see that there might just be more than one point of view than that enjoyed from God's right hand! His unflagging interest in everything that went on in his ship provoked an involvement from all on board which led to teamwork which was not always evident at sea. The period which he covers was one in which, laying aside the hardship of being separated from one's loved ones, seafaring was a joyous adventure. That there were men like Dick to share it with just added icing to the cake. How I wish it was all starting again.

Ken Hart, MBE,
Paphos, Cyprus

April 1999

CHAPTER ONE
NEW HEART AND PF4

My first ship was "Neocardia". During my farewell visit to the local Sea Cadet unit, the padre, Canon Pugh, took me aside and said "Williams, you know what "Neocardia" means, don't you?" "No, Sir!" said I. "New Heart lad, New Heart! Let's hope it's prophetic!" On Tuesday, 4th December 1945, I reported to the shipping agents, Brinings, at 0900 in their office located in the Liver Building in Liverpool. My father who was serving in the Army, obtained leave to see me from home to ship. My mother, predictably, was distraught at losing me, particularly as I had assumed my father's mantle of 'man of the house' during his Army sojourn. So his presence was a solace to us all. After a wrenching parting, he and I travelled to Liverpool, the day prior to my reporting.

The Liver Building was one of Britain's more commanding provin-cial office buildings and probably still is. My father and I were ushered into an oak panelled conference room where the Captain and his officers were assembled, wearing dark suits or naval uniform, to "sign-on" before the Shipping Master. A most impres-sive scenario! We were both overawed, or at least I was! After talking to the Captain and officers, my father left, convinced that I was in good hands, his having been assured by them, and by the Chief Officer in particular, of their sincere concern for apprentices' welfare. What a travesty this impression was to prove!

Neocardia was anchored at the Mersey River Bar anchorage, waiting to go alongside Dingle Oil Jetty. As there wasn't a vacant

14

berth until the following day, the joining crew had a free day in Liverpool. We stayed in Atlantic House, a hostel for seafarers operated by the Stella Maris organization. My fellow apprentice was a Derby lad named Archer, also a first tripper. He had undergone two years' training at the University of Southampton sea school, an immeasurable advantage! We hit it off immediately and thoroughly enjoyed our day and night on the town! Donned in naval officer's uniform, we had a great day in this city of seafarers. Although we chatted up girls I was too excited at the prospect of joining the ship to follow-up any encounter with the opposite sex! This was man's stuff in those far-off days! I wish I could convey the brimming exuberance I felt at the threshold of a career I so wanted, and, the release from parental control.

Our ship anchored off the Liverpool Stage the following morning, 5th December, expressly to change crews. We left the Stage by tug and tender (the latter carrying our luggage and ship's stores), excitement rising as we moved into the river in thick fog. I don't know quite what I expected to see. What I saw was a dim, grim, grey, rust-streaked outline of a ship shrouded in mist! She was in full wartime garb: naval grey; eight guns; a spar deck (for carrying aircraft across the Atlantic); plastic armour sheathing across the bridge front and weird minesweeping equipment at the bow. Not a graceful sight, rather a formidable, no-nonsense image for this young man, perhaps even intimidating in its functional appearance. As we clambered up the accommodation ladder, the smell of gasoline and aviation spirit permeated the main deck, a flower garden of valve wheels (the only colours other than grey and rust) with pipelines everywhere. Unmistakably this was a modern operational tanker. Neocardia was to be my home for the next eleven months, I loved the whole ambience and was particularly impressed with the standard of the apprentices' accommodation. The departing crew had been aboard for a year or more, and we had about an hour with the lads from whom we were taking over. They plied Archer and myself with tales of exotic ports and amorous conquests, adding to my almost frenetic excitement. Life seemed too good to be true. Forgotten were family and Merthyr Tydfil; ahead the world beckoned with promise and allure. Disillusion came in short order!

On completion of discharge of cargo at Dingle, Neocardia put to sea on 7th December 1945. Voyage instructions were "Key West for orders", which meant nothing specific other than that the ship was to head for this point initially until firm instructions were sent to the Master en route. Key West lies on the southern tip of Florida so the ship could be directed to either the Caribbean or the Gulf of Mexico to load a cargo for virtually any port in the world. These two areas were the main oil distribution zones in the Western Hemisphere, the former had oil terminals in Trinidad, Venezuela, Columbia and the Netherlands Antilles, whilst the latter embraced numerous oil ports throughout Texas and Louisiana.

Having received our voyage instructions, Neocardia headed for the Azores. It was the favoured voyage plan of practically all masters in those days to follow this route, as it usually meant better weather with the ship reaching warmer climes sooner than the shorter, colder and rougher great circle route which took ships well north of the Azores. It was always a debatable issue, which was the more economic route. There was little doubt that crews preferred the Azores track! Either way in December was uncomfortable with a ship in ballast (just a few tanks filled with water to submerge the propeller, and prevent the bow pounding) heading into the prevailing westerly winds and ubiquitous Atlantic swell.

My first week at sea was wretched! I was sea-sick for six days until we reached the Azores. This condition was not viewed with the slightest sympathy by any of the officers, and, as luck would have it, my fellow apprentice, Alan Archer was unaffected! To compound my misery I was gauche, naive, un-coordinated and wholly credulous and after six days completely lacking in self-esteem! I was the target for what all first-trip youngsters are subjected - a sort of daily 'April Fool Day'! It seemed to me, in my jaundiced state of mind, that the height of amusement and entertainment among merchant seamen was to enjoy the embarrassment and humiliation of a first tripper! Having diligently followed instructions to bring a can of green oil for the starboard navigation light from the Lamp Room (issued with straight faced gravity by the Deck Storekeeper) to the Bridge and told to top up the oil reservoir, only to discover a light bulb therein! The ensuing mortification would have been painful had it not caused such hilarity! There were numerous other japes played upon me until I became street-wise! Whereas I had had an academic course at Cardiff Tech prior to going to sea, nothing had prepared me for the practicalities, it is perhaps best summed up by the Mate who said one morning "Williams, you're neither use nor ornament!" So, it was a hard, and often miserable learning process. During these initial days we worked a minimum of eight hours, every day, including weekends, doing work that was sheer drudgery: scrubbing decks; washing paintwork; cleaning brass (with colza oil and bathbrick, none of your Brasso nonsense!) and joy-of-joys, cement washing fresh water tanks behind the engine room boilers, in fearful heat!

In spite of all the doom and gloom, youth is irrepressible! With the swells easing, the temperature rising and the sun shining, the spirits soared. The sight of the island of Pico in the Azores, with its towering peak, was my first, unforgettable sight of foreign soil which gave me huge pleasure. Life took on a brighter hue with the prospect of working outside, perhaps even getting a sun tan and, above all, feeling well again after the ghastly days of nausea. I was determined to get my act together, however difficult it was going to be. This gave me a sense of endeavour to counter the palpable hostility the Chief Officer (aka the Mate) was showing towards me, and, as an apprentice, he was the most important man in my life aboard ship - my boss. However, life had many compensations! The feeling of independence, the metamorphosis from schoolboy to that of a young man, the discipline of wearing correct uniform when not working all gave one a sense of dignity and set a certain standard in a life that was developing into one where accepted civilized precepts were rapidly disappearing! Eating meals in the Officers' Saloon and being treated as officers by stewards was a civilizing interlude, as was the use of the Officers' Smoke Room for recreation. Our personal accommodation was of a high standard and a source of pride to Archer and myself. Duty-free cigarettes were unbelievably cheap, there was a Seafarers' Education Service library which consisted of about 100 books which was changed every three months and provided enormous pleasure to the ship's company. In many respects we were well blessed. Such could not be said for the standard of catering! The food was appallingly bad, both in quality and presentation. Nor could one say anything about our standard of training - it was non-existent in the early months - in fact no one gave this responsibility any consideration whatsoever! We were, quite literally, the cheapest of cheap labour, and boy! did they take advantage of that!

With better weather, our work went outside. Arch (as he was known to all) and I teamed with two Royal Naval ratings, I remember them as Taff and Ginger. As mentioned earlier, Neocardia still possessed her wartime outfit, which included eight guns for defensive purposes (one four inch naval gun on the Poop, a twelve pounder on the Fo'cas'le Head and six Oerlikon machine cannons, housed on armoured platforms, ranged along the sides of the well decks and Bridge wings). With the advent of peace, all merchant ships were disarmed. However this process had to be staged and whilst equipment remained on board, RN ratings maintained the guns. These men spent a fraction of their time caring for the weaponry so they were employed by the ship, at overtime rates, to carry out shipboard maintenance. They were very keen to work as much as they could, and, being non-unionized labour, could be employed to do anything! Of course, the apprentices, were also in that category working for sixteen shillings and eight pence plus five pounds 'danger money' per month (danger money was paid because of the existence of unswept minefields in many parts of the globe), a pittance compared with the deck ratings. A team of four coolies, no less!

The prime reason for the carrying of Deck Apprentices was that they were to be trained in the arts and crafts of a Deck Officer which naturally included the very important aspect of ship maintenance. As indicated above, there was no training of any conceivable kind in the first period of my service aboard Neocardia. We apprentices were virtual slaves! To the extent that we had to do the Mate's dhobi (washing and ironing) for nothing in our spare (!) time, on occasion serve in the Saloon as stewards when the catering ratings were diagnosed with social diseases - a travesty of the agreement implicit in our indentures. Character building, you might suggest? Maybe. However, I felt then, and I feel equally strongly to this day, it was demeaning and soul destroying! Paradoxically, I still enjoyed the life, despite the humiliation and grinding work.

Apprentices had to provide all their apparel, uniforms and working clothes. Prior to joining one's first ship one was guided by a list issued by the shipping company to advise one's parents on what to purchase to cover all eventualities. This was a total nonsense! Obligatory were three sets of Number Tens - these were white uniforms for use in tropical climes consisting of long trousers, brass button-up front jackets and white shoes! Totally unsuited as wear aboard a tanker. The list of working clothes had apparently been compiled by an idiot! Two boiler suits were among the stipulations, when six would have been nearer the requirement for the work we were about to undertake! Our fond imaginings of working on deck with a pair of shorts and developing a tan were swiftly quashed when the Mate decided to give the apprentices and gunners the job of coating the spar and main decks with a substance which gloried in the simple name of PF4! To anyone who served aboard Shell ships on deck, these three symbols when mentioned to a deck man generated various reactions, none of them favourable, varying from instant loathing to resigned despair! PF4 was a viscous tar-like liquid, an end product of the refining process, marketed to the marine arm as a protective coating for steelwork. Its rust inhibiting properties were non-existent, its decorative qualities dismal and adhesive ability pathetic (except, it should be pointed out in all fairness, to the human body where it stuck with remarkable tenacity!). Shell, in its infinite wisdom and superb range of petroleum products, came a cropper with this stuff! Anglo-Saxon used this 'paint' for coating decks and ships' sides for decades with ruinous effect upon appearance and protection. Anyway, the four of us became intimately acquainted with PF4 and whereas crew members would apply the substance with brushes, we had to use pieces of cloth (tank flannel). The spar deck had been erected over the main and fore decks to carry aeroplanes from the USA to Britain during the war, it was a forest of rusting girders. Imagine then dipping pieces of flannel into the noxious liquid and coating the girders by bare hand. At the end of a day's work, a boiler suit would stand up on its own, it was sheet hard! Our hands were cut to ribbons by the shards of rust, our hair congealed and matted, eyes red and burning. At the end of the day, we had to clean-up and change into white uniform and eat in the Saloon - talk about contrast! After the meal we had, somehow, to clean the day's boiler suit, dissolving the PF4 in kerosene, hand washing with bar soap and drying the garment in the Boiler Room. After a few days our skin, under the boiler suits, became red, blotched and itching! Boy! What work for a well brought-up young man! To add to our job satisfaction, the ship had inherited a mascot from the previous crew - a German shepherd who used the main deck as his personal toilet, resulting in many a bare hand grasping mounds of dog waste. Vigilance was the order of the day when we coated the decks!

After leaving the Azores, we received instructions to go to Curaçao to load for Rotterdam. Despite everything, this was an exciting prospect. The weather was beautiful, we passed through the Sargasso Sea with its inexplicable rafts of weed (Sargasso weed) stretching as far as the eye could see - each raft having myriads of small fish around it and occasionally, a turtle. Our second landfall, the British island of Sombrero on the eastern side of the Anegada Passage, presaged our arrival in the Caribbean. What a magical experience! Calm blue sea, balmy weather, clear starlit nights, exotic scents carried by off-shore breezes with the imminent prospect of my first visit to a foreign place! Despite PF4, impossible treatment, lousy food, I was still a happy, if somewhat chastened, lad. I looked forward with great antic-ipation, on the premise that nothing lasts forever!

Some words about tanker preparation in the late forties. Neocardia was classed as a white oiler - a ship that carried aviation fuels, motor gasolines, kerosene, gasoil and cleaning fluids. If the forthcoming cargo was similar to the previous, cleaning was a rudimentary affair. Each tank was gasfreed with a windsail (a canvas tube strung from a wire runner which had an open mouth at the top with wings either side of the mouth to catch the wind to blow out the tank) followed by hand hosing the tank surfaces, and, if necessary the lifting of rust accumulation. Pipelines were flushed through with sea water and drained. The ship presented itself at the loading port gasfree and clean, ready to load as soon as the ballast had been discharged into the harbour. So it was with Neocardia on Sunday, 23rd December 1945.

We arrived at Curaçao on that day, a peerless morning in brilliant sunshine, light breezes, an azure sky and clear aquamarine sea. The impression was etched on my mind for all time. The approach to the port entrance at Willemstad was spectacular with its confection of pastel coloured buildings and orange roofs on either side of the passage through the town. An unique motorized pontoon bridge straddled the entrance which swung open to allow ships to pass .As we sailed through the town, we absorbed the picture of the colourfully clothed inhabitants promenading on this Sunday morning with the cacophony of American car horns in the background; all creating an unforgettable image and such a contrast from drab, war torn and weary Britain!

Curaçao is the main island of the Netherlands Antilles, a group of three islands lying some 50 miles off the Venezuelan coast. The islands are sometimes referred to as the ABC islands, Aruba, Bonaire and Curaçao. Aruba to the west and Bonaire east of Curaçao, the main centre, with the administrative capital at Willemstad . Curaçao possesses one of the finest natural deep water harbours in the Western Hemisphere and together with Aruba were flourishing entrepots in those days. Crude oil was imported from Venezuela, refined and exported worldwide. Shell had its biggest refinery (at that time) in Curaçao whilst arch rival, Esso, had its refinery at San Nicholas in Aruba. Crude oil was transported from ports in Lake Maracaibo to the two refineries by small, shallow draft tankers known as mosquito boats or jitneys. These were very busy little craft, bustling back and forth across the sea area between Venezuela and Curaçao/Aruba, creating almost a constant stream of ships, virtually a floating mobile pipeline. Deep sea tankers exported the refined products, ranging from the finest industrial spirits, lubricating oils to bitumen (at the other end of the scale) to ports all over the world. As described above, the colonial administration had created an outstanding amalgam of Dutch architecture with Caribbean colour and a definite Venezuelan flavour. The population was no less colourful, arguably the supreme interracial mixture to be found anywhere. Predominantly Afro-Caribbean with European, South American, Chinese, sub-continental Indian, Malay and Carib Indian strains mixed by intermarriage to produce some outstandingly good-looking people! They spoke an unique language called Papiemento, a blend of English, Dutch, Spanish and Carib. What an interesting place to visit, especially for one's first port!

The main port in Curaçao is Emmastad, a ship reaches this deep water harbour via a channel that dissects the town of Willemstad, so every ship berthing at the oil terminals passes through this channel (Sta. Anna Baai) en route to load, returning through, in the opposite direction, when outward bound. Believe me when I tell you it is one of the most attractive harbour steaming experiences a tanker man encounters. Port operations were controlled from Fort Nassau which lies atop a hill overlooking the sea approach, Willemstad and the inner harbour at Emmastad - an ideal command situation.

The inner harbour berths were all occupied so Neocardia made fast alongside an American naval tanker at the mooring buoys, to await a vacant loading jetty. This was another hugely impressive experience for me! The American ship was in immaculate condition, not a rust streak in sight, the crew attitudes so totally different from the Brits, on board were a swimming pool, an outdoor cinema, soft drink dispensers and fridges everywhere not to mention individual showers and wc's in every cabin! The naval tanker quit the buoy mooring soon after we arrived so we were alone until a loading berth became available on Boxing Day. So my first Christmas at sea was spent in almost an ideal situation - moored to buoys with no cargo operations being carried out. Arch and I continued on Christmas Eve to PF4 the spar deck, but we were told by the Chief Officer that if we did well we could have Christmas Day off! We were slavishly grateful!

In the course of my seafaring career I spent 25 out of 40 Christmas Days aboard ship! Without exception, catering staffs on every ship, as if inspired by divine prompting, produced excellent fare on that particular day! We had a whale of a time on this, our first Christmas away from home. Unfortunately, shore leave was not allowed at the buoy moorings - in case of emergency, nevertheless we, Arch and I, had a good time.

We went alongside on Boxing Day and commenced the business of the ship earning its bread. All tanks were inspected and passed, deballasting commenced as soon as we berthed and cargo hoses were connected to our pipelines. Traditionally, each watchkeeping officer had the assistance or hindrance of an apprentice. As there were only two of us, we accepted that we would work watch about (six hours on and six off), what we had not anticipated was the plan the Mate had in mind! We were made to work on on shipside painting, loading stores and provisions in our 'watch below' (ostensibly our free time) during the day. When it came to our going ashore, we had to seek permission from the Mate (quite properly) to do so, but this man never graciously granted permission. One of the quite bizarre stipulations was that we had to don Number Tens to do so - so from almost Dickensian urchins on board, to a couple of operetta-like naval officers ashore, complete with PF4 under our finger nails! Of course Arch and I could not go ashore together because one of us was always on duty, and we were ominously warned not to consort with any member of the crew, so it meant we went alone if no other young officer was available. But, hey! Who cared? Once down that gangway, it felt like release from prison! I thoroughly enjoyed myself wandering the streets of Willemstad stopping at the odd café for a coca-cola and buying fruit flavoured chewing gum (neither of which I had tasted before) from elderly ladies who sold candies from trays. Balmy, scented nights gazing at the most interesting people, mixing with seafarers from many nations, it was magical! A piece of reality, of which I was quite innocent and ignorant, faced me on one of my trips ashore. An American stopped me and asked directions to the nearest whorehouse - I was dumbstruck! I was so flabbergasted I just couldn't give a coherent answer - it shows just how naive I was! Although I had read Hank Jansen, I wasn't entirely convinced that such establishments existed!

Whereas a tanker's time in port was considered too short by our dry-cargo and passenger ship brethren, the pace in those days was much more leisurely than it became in later years, when time really was money. We spent two and a half days loading a part cargo of motor gasoline in Emmastad before moving to Bullen Baai, an installation along the coast where the 'dangerous' products were kept - away from the main population centre. We completed loading cargo with aviation spirit and set sail for Rotterdam on New Year's Day 1946.

CHAPTER TWO

"THINK OF THE STARVING PEOPLE IN EUROPE"

The biggest difficulty I have had in compiling my memoirs has been in relating the experiences, objectively, during my first year. The reader should not be discouraged if he or she should find the narrative depressing, be assured that the remainder of the story is much more heartening! The year 1945 was not the best to choose to begin a seafaring career. The Merchant Navy had suffered severe losses in ships and personnel during the War. Those who survived had been sorely tested. Survival, in some cases, meant having undergone unbearable stress and physical strain of telling magnitude. However strong-minded men may have been, the psychological scars took a long time to heal. The healing process manifested itself occasionally in disturbing ways, often associated with heavy drinking. On this voyage aboard Neocardia, we had three officers who had recently been released from a German prisoner-of-war camp. They weren't happy men, and, I suspect, were resented by those who had served the whole term of hostilities. Aboard this sombre ship, eager, naive, pimply-faces boys were not suffered readily!

"THINK OF THE STARVING PEOPLE IN EUROPE"

The Master (Captain) was a dour Yorkshireman, a singularly humourless man, ponderous and unsmiling, yet efficient and dignified. A man not to be trifled with! It seemed that one of his aims in life was to feed his crew with the minimum amounts at the minimum cost! His catch phrase was "Think of the starving people in Europe!" whenever he caught us (the Apprentices) eating a sandwich. This caused no end of mirth, Arch and I used to paraphrase it into "Think of the starving apprentices aboard Neocardia!" in an exaggerated Yorkshire accent!

They say an army marches on its stomach. Apprentices, renowned, for their voracious appetites, dwelled upon the subject of food, perhaps inordinately, as is a young man's wont! As indicated earlier, in the last chapter, the food served aboard this ship was poor. Again this was the consequence of the War, experienced cooks were just not available and our Chief Steward outmatched our Captain in melancholy, possessing an active hatred of humanity and apprentices in particular! We were introduced to such seafaring delicacies as 'bergoo' (oatmeal porridge made with chlorinated water) so that at the start of breakfast one was nearly overcome by chlorine before tasting the vile mixture! Breakfast specials usually consisted of variations on dried egg concoctions accompanied by a square foot of rock hard ox-liver. Then there was 'duff' - the chef's version of steamed pudding, accompanied by a bright yellow slime (euphemistically called custard!). Boy! that was some culinary experience! They (the cooks) managed quite successfully, to murder the remainder of the food served up! You would all love the bread the 'baker' made, that's if your teeth survived the initial onslaught!

Neocardia a motorship built during the War, was of a ship-type known as the 'three twelves' i.e., twelve thousand tons deadweight (the weight she could carry of cargo, bunkers, water and stores), a service speed of twelve knots with a daily consumption of twelve tons of diesel fuel. This class of ship was the workhorse of Shell's post war trading. The Americans, with their genius for mass production, built an entirely different ship, generically known as the T2. This was a bigger, more powerful craft, propelled by a turbo-electric engine with a daily consumption of forty tons of fueloil and a speed of sixteen knots. Shell acquired some twenty odd T2's between 1946 and 1948, but more of that later. Two altogether different concepts, the British ship was slower and smaller than the American, but infinitely more flexible in cargo carrying capability. The T2 had a much more powerful cargo pumping system but was limited in the number of grades of oil it could handle. These two classes dominated the immediate post war tanker scene.

The disadvantages of the motorship were the need for more main engine maintenance and its inherent unreliability. This led to both scheduled and unexpected stops at sea. A scheduled stop would invariably occur in tropical, calm waters where engine maintenance could be handled safely, changing cylinder heads or pistons being the usual operation. The reason I'm describing this feature is that whereas it was the engineers' misfortune, it was often an occasion for 'sport' for the remainder of the crew! Shark fishing, no less!

Actually this was never a sport because the creatures were hooked without the slightest skill and I now regard it as a barbarous business, however as a seventeen year old, I wasn't beset with moral constraints! All that was needed was a stout line and a meat hook with a chunk of raw meat as bait. Once the ship had stopped moving through the water, sharks would soon appear around the stern area, their silvery shapes discernible about twenty feet down. The meat and hook were lowered just below the surface and within minutes a shark would nuzzle the bait and after a while grab it! That was the creature's nemesis. It was hauled up to the top of the hand rails where occasionally it would grip the top rail with its fearsome jaws and score the metal but usually it landed on the deck and thrashed around until it died. Man's innate cruelty came to the fore, they disembowelled the beasts, they cut out their hearts which would beat for hours on the deck (legend had it that they would pulse until sunset). The remains would be thrown overboard and we would watch other sharks go into a feeding frenzy, a thoroughly gruesome affair, but it afforded a bit of excitement!

The voyage to Rotterdam took eighteen days, this included half a day stopped for engine overhaul. The weather was typically North Atlantic for the time of the year. We took a great circle track north of the Azores (the shortest distance between any two points on the Globe) and although the seas and swells were huge, they came up behind the ship and were not as damaging as they might have been. The motion of the ship was most uncomfortable but having conquered seasickness I no longer cared, I felt a real sailor! Arch and I were now getting used to the type of work we were doing and accepted the regime as our lot. In all fairness we were allowed time off at week-ends because there was little advantage in working in such weather as I have described. So this journey back to Europe was a settling-in period where routines were established and 'skills' learned. The most onerous 'skill' was that of washing clothes - something our mothers had done hitherto! No washing machines, no soap powder and often dirty water, made keeping standards a little difficult, especially as we had to wash the Mate's gear too! We started our correspondence courses and began to learn the 'Articles'. These were the International Regulations for the Prevention of Collisions at Sea or more commonly known as the 'Rules of the Road'. There were some thirty rules, each varying in length and complexity which had to be memorized exactly - Article 9 was pages long! As far as our familiarizing ourselves with navigational equipment, we were allowed to go to the Bridge to clean the brasswork and to hand scrub the decks!

Those were the days when difficulty was invariably experienced in establishing a position as the ship neared the Western Approaches. Overcast weather precluded celestial fixing and radio direction fixing was very approximate at best. Radar for commercial ships was in the developmental stage whilst position fixing systems like Decca and Loran were also in their infancy. The most reliable indication was water depth, and as luck would have it, our echo sounding machine packed in at the crucial time. Arch and I were given the job of operating the patent sounding machine - our first meaningful navigational task. This instrument measured the depth with a weight lowered on a fine wire, controlled by a small hand winch. We felt almost important! Anyway, we were able to provide a 'line of soundings' which gave a fairly good indication of our position, in conjunction with D.F. bearings.

As soon as we reached the English Channel, Arch and I were put on 'six on and six off', the watch about system already described. We were employed as additional look-outs and general runabouts. At least we were on the Bridge! We soaked up every bit of knowledge we could, however the only proficiency we achieved was in making tea! I loved every minute of it although it was taxing working this demanding routine until we cleared the English Channel, outward bound, some ten days after our passing Lands End inward. Our hearts were in our mouths as we navigated the NEMEDRI routes, swept paths, marked by buoyed channels, in the minefield areas at the approaches to European ports. It didn't do to stray outside these channels-particularly as it was our job to sight the buoys ahead, a little difficult in reduced visibility.

The contrast between two ports, Curaçao and Rotterdam, could not be more dramatic! Apart from the obvious difference in climate, the dissimilarity was startling. Whereas everything in the Caribbean had been so bright and colourful, the opposite applied to our passage up the River Maas and into the oil harbour at Pernis (the Shell refinery, later to become the World's biggest). It has to be remembered that Holland was recovering from the ravages of war which had ended less than a year back and that fact was evident in practically every aspect during our stay. Although Arch and I had joked about the Old Man's burbling "Think of the starving people in Europe", the harsh fact was there before us - the people of Rotterdam were still starving. Men came aboard prepared to give anything for any item of food or cigarettes, they even took away our Galley refuse to extract usable items of food! I don't think we joked about it again, even to we seventeen year olds, it was upsetting. It took us four days to discharge our cargo and in that time I was able to go ashore and savour the atmosphere of Vlaardingen, the nearest town. In many respects a pretty town, as indeed all Dutch towns and villages seemed to be - they, the Dutch, seem to have a genius for turning a flat featureless landscape into an attractive man-made environment, as appealing as any country I have visited. We apprentices were warned that under no circumstances should we visit any hostelry or drink alcoholic beverages anywhere. However, once ashore, it was akin to ignoring one's parents' ground rules - you forgot them! So the place to go was called "Café Sports" where one indulged in youthful revelry and consorted with young crew members - both activities expressly forbidden! Two lasting impressions linger in my mind: one was of a huge coal fired stove in the centre of the café and the other was of young women with shaved heads! These girls, it transpired, had had their hair shorn at the end of the war because they were suspected of having fraternized with German troops during the occupation. It appeared that this fact did not trouble the consciences of Neocardia's lads and they eventually had souvenirs to prove this!

I have written in fair detail about my first voyage, it would be very tedious to continue in such vein, so I hope to cover the next few months with more dispatch.

We sailed from Rotterdam on the 23rd January 1946, on a bitterly cold day, again bound for Key West for orders. Once we cleared the English Channel, Arch and I reverted to day-work and of course to the same mind-numbing work, PF4 and all that! Within a week of our departure from Rotterdam, crew members were showing the symptoms of venereal disease, first gonorrhoea then, some time later, a few succumbed to syphilis - Ginger, one of the R.N. ratings, had fallen deeply in love with his girl, contracted a 'full house'! This was sad, because he really had become very attached to her, his disillusion was touching. As a consequence of this minor epidemic, the two Saloon stewards had to be laid off from handling food until their condition was stabilized. Guess who became stewards? Right first time! Archer and Williams! This was something I have never mentioned in my curricula vitae! So it was, we served our fellow officers at table for about five or six days until the catering ratings were fit to return to work. So apart from this interlude in our routine (when we continued to work on deck outside meal times) the pattern was similar to that of our first voyage. This time we had instructions to load a cargo at San Nicholas in Aruba, for delivery, again, to Rotterdam.

At a point in this narrative I thought I should explain to the uninitiated, the purpose and role of a Deck Apprentice. The concept of training artisans by apprenticeship derived from medieval times and became a well-known method for young men to acquire the skills of a particular trade, a hands-on means of education rather than a theoretical one. It thus became the technique, until very recently, of training Britain's Merchant Navy deck officers. In short, a boy was indentured to a shipping company for a period of four years, during which time he would be cared for in a responsible way, and, in return the apprentice was expected to work diligently, both practically and educationally, and to behave in an officer-like manner. At the beginning of the four year period "Indentures" were signed which provided rules and guidelines for training, conduct and responsibilities for both parties. A fine water-tight arrangement one might surmise. Ha! It was the shipboard inter-pretation that oft times made a mockery of the system! Most shipboard managements carried out, more or less, the requirements of the training and behavioural regimes, so that at the end of the apprentice-ship a young man would be adequately prepared to undertake a Third Officer's responsibilities. As the reader will have discovered, such was not the case aboard this vessel!

The place of a deck apprentice in a ship's hierarchy was a delicate one. Small wonder that the term for apprentices' accommodation was called the Half Deck, it could well have been described as the Demi-Monde! There were so many contradictions, many of which I'm sure, you the reader, will have already gleaned. Life was a dichotomy - there were always two ways to go - but you had better choose the right one! As an example, it was forbidden to fraternize with crew members, yet it suited the Mate to give us the most menial and degrading tasks, work that crew members would have refused to carry out, and then we were expected to be aloof! We often worked under the direction of the Bosun (deck crew foreman) and on completion of the workday we were obliged to ignore him! Association with the officers was often difficult because of age and experience and this particular Mate frowned upon that as well! We should have had time off for study, cleaning our cabin and especially to wash the Mate's clothes - we did not. Despite everything we continued to enjoy ourselves

The navigation of this voyage was almost identical to that of the previous crossing, except that departure points were different. The huge plus this time was that I no longer experienced seasickness, consequently I felt very different. We had a change of scene during this trip, at least for a couple of days anyway (away from PF4, that is!) we went 'tank diving'. This was the expression used to describe hand cleaning of cargo tanks. Once the tanks had been hosed down with seawater and blown gas free, gangs would enter tanks, sweep stringers and cross beams and finally shovel up rust and residue from the tank bottoms. Now this wasn't entirely unpleasant! As one stirred up the tank bottom residue, gas was liberated from the mixture and occasionally men became intoxicated. Whenever one suspected a man was affected, he was immediately ordered up ladder with someone behind him to prevent his falling and ordered to rest in the fresh air until his system cleared. This happened to us all in varying degrees and at different times, some almost succumbed if they were not spotted early enough, it was the habit to have someone at the first stringer level keeping surveillance of those working beneath and to spot anyone who was becoming tipsy. It was jolly work! Everyone sang bawdy songs with a great sense of camaraderie and time passed pleasantly enough. Another pastime was swimming in the clean ballast tanks (a 'clean' tank was one that had been washed and descaled and filled with clean seawater), the level of the tank was lowered well below the deck so that a swimmer would not be trapped under the deckhead and safely above the first stringer. This became strictly taboo in later years for obvious reasons. There was also a wooden framed canvas lined swimming box available on the main deck - subject to the Mate sanctioning its erection. It was even more dangerous than tank swimming! One was liable to be ejected bodily out of this contraption on to the main deck if there was a swell running, one man had nearly been thrown overboard. Anyway, to we dogs (a term used, by some, for apprentices) it was exhilarating stuff!

I have described the minutia of the work, atmosphere and activities aboard Neocardia in order to give the reader a sense of the life I led in those early months. From now onwards I shall highlight any unusual events or changes in the routines and accelerate my tale, otherwise I should need volumes if I were to continue in such detail throughout my time at sea!

Aruba is quite different from Curaçao. The loading port of San Nicholas is at the eastern end of the island with berths clearly visible from seaward, the refinery was owned by Largo, an affiliate of Esso. One of the features we liked about this refinery was the Commissary Store, it was the oft reviled company store - we, as visiting seamen, were treated as company employees and allowed to buy at the store at much reduced cost. I remember buying stocks of tinned food and other comestibles to take home for my mother because Britain continued to suffer strict rationing. I bought some really 'cool' American working clothes and a fountain pen for my father (who used it all his working life!) After three days, we departed once more for Rotterdam on 12th February 1946.

Apart from experiencing very heavy weather during our crossing, there's nothing significant to relate, nor was there anything exceptional about our second visit to Rotterdam other than that already described. Once again we set sail for Key West and on this occasion we were stemmed for Houston, Texas. This caused great anticipation in the Half Deck! All our young lives, in wartime Britain, we had read and heard about the wonders of America, emulated the life style of the people and, particularly, their music. Glenn Miller, Benny Goodman, Artie Shaw, Harry James and the Dorsey brothers were household names to Arch and myself. We had heard of the

Apprentices Club in New York, exclusively for the use of apprentices, and understood that there was a similar place for us in Houston. We were not disappointed! It was a great experience for us, in that we were able to visit this club (I forget its name) in the city. There we met nice young ladies, of good family, to talk to and drink coke, play table tennis and the like. Everything was properly conducted with mothers never far away! On a more prosaic level we had the pleasure of eating all our meals ashore. At most refineries, in those days, the ship's plant was shut-down whilst loading high octane products. This meant that electrical power and steam were provided by the shore installation. Our Galley was oil-fired, so no cooking could be carried out on board. At the Caribbean refineries there were shore galleys at the end of a set of jetties, so that cooking could take place near the ship. Not so in Houston - thank goodness! We went ashore in relays by bus and taxi to Pasedena, a small town nearby where the local short order restaurant had the contract to feed us during our stay. I had never tasted the like! We had the most fantastic breakfasts - exotic cereals, gallons of orange juice, lashings of bacon, eggs (in any mysterious manner you wished, such as sunny-side-up or easy-over) hash browns, sausages, wonderful toast and all the coffee you could drink! What a revelation it all was, with steaks, roasts, french fries, corn cobs, surf'n'turf et al, for the other meals!! The sandwiches delivered aboard for our night use were fabulous! Undoubtedly, it was apprentices' heaven!

There was great excitement when we left Houston because we received instructions that on completion of cargo discharge, Neocardia was to proceed to Falmouth for repairs. Our port of destination was Isle of Grain, a British Petroleum installation on the River Medway in Kent.. We were carrying industrial alcohol, which was to be the first of three such deliveries to Isle of Grain in the forthcoming months. The Medway lies south of the Thames with the naval port of Chatham at the head of the river. In those days, Isle of Grain was a quiet port near the village of Stoke - a lovely little hamlet with a small but beautiful church. Really, one couldn't have asked for a nicer place to return to in Britain. However, we were impatient for Falmouth! Girls loomed large in our thoughts and expectations!

I have made reference to standards among shipboard personnel in late 1945, of the difficulties in recruiting people of acceptable calibre in a reputable company such as the Anglo Saxon Petroleum Company, because of immediate post-war shortage. You will have gathered that I was somewhat disenchanted with my early experiences, many of which I cannot relate because they were disgusting. These first impressions of Jolly Jack proved to be untypical, but in April 1946, I was neither content with the treatment I had had meted out nor was I at ease with the type of crew member with whom I had been associated. For all my enthusiasm, I felt I was at cross roads so early in my chosen career. It bothered me greatly. During our stay at Falmouth I had been allowed to go home on dry-dock leave - this I might add, had been reluctantly granted by the Mate, who constantly threatened to stop my going on leave until, in the end, he relented. Whilst I was at home I confronted my parents with my predicament and sought their advice as to whether I should continue my career or not. Unequivocally, my father (who had been so impressed by his meeting with the officers at Liverpool) flatly refused to countenance any change of occupation, "You've made your bed, lie in it!" My mother was more sympathetic and troubled by what I told them. She would have supported my quitting seafaring but counselled me to give it another go. I'm so glad I did! Hence forward, everything changed for the better.

When I returned from home leave, I discovered that two other apprentices had joined. One, a senior lad of some three years service, Tommy Hetherington (who tragically died at a young age), who came from the same town as the Mate and was experienced in the ways of ships and the Half Deck in particular. The other, Stephen Hanbury-Sparrow straight from Shrewsbury School, a charming young man whose mother used to launch ships! (This latter snippet of information impressed us all, except the Mate). Immediately our lot improved, Tom was used to handling Mates and as Senior Apprentice, our immediate boss, he fended for his charges well! I suspect that being a townie of the Mate's, had a certain leverage! Suffice to say, that for the most part, the heat came off me and landed squarely upon poor old Sparrow's shoulders! Our stay in Falmouth was memorable! I remember well it was the time of the Cup Final and the University Boat Race and amongst the pleasures, I visited the Helston Floral Dance. I met a local builder's daughter and had great fun in her company - I think I was but one in a string of apprentices with whom she had consorted, teasing me that British

Tanker Company boys were much more attractive! On a technical note, the dratted spar deck and all naval equipment was removed, giving the ship a cleaner, less cluttered appearance. We received peace time paints to replace the drab grey of wartime, the hull had been scraped and coated with PF4 (!) and the ship's side looked tolerable for a few days. We said good-bye, sadly, to Taff and Ginger. We set sail, refreshed and expectant, at the end of May, bound for Houston once more.

The arrival of new people - both officers and crew members had a dramatic effect upon the atmosphere of the ship. To begin, we were four and not two in the Half Deck and fortunately we got along with one another very well. The greatest impact was a new Third Officer called Robinson. This young man devoted untold hours in tutoring us during the following months, he gave us direction, aims and targets to attain. His teaching capabilities were remarkable and his interest in our professional advancement truly encouraging. I really began to enjoy my life. As I have already said, Sparrow became the Mate's whipping boy much to my secret relief! The food changed dramatically for the better and we were learning, and, magically, we were having time off for studying and cabin cleaning - thanks, no doubt, to Tom Hetherington's standing up to the Boss! Mr Robinson influenced the senior officers so that we had structured training for the first time, it made such a difference to my outlook and self-confidence.

Neocardia made two more deliveries from Houston to Isle of Grain, and during the latter visit we had part cargo for Saltend on the Humber, which, incidentally, was the longest tanker jetty in Britain. We continued to carry industrial alcohol. A couple of clowns in one of the crews decided to lace their lemonade with a soupçon of cargo and nearly died as a result - they had to be landed for hospitalization. Fortunately for them they did the business in the English Channel so ports were close at hand, otherwise they would have perished. Returning to the U.K. each voyage meant that crews were changed, so we had a variety of faces. However, most men so enjoyed visiting Houston that they were quite prepared to sign on for further voyages. This, inevitably, came to an end. In September we loaded at San Nicholas, Aruba, for Monrovia in Liberia and Lagos in Nigeria. Whilst in Aruba I had the unnerving experience of meeting up with a rabid dog! Fortunately I was able to outpace the animal because its hind quarters were paralysed - the sight upset me. We delivered a part cargo of gas oil to the Firestone rubber plantation in Monrovia. This operation took about five days because we unloaded into barges whilst anchored off the coast. A substantial swell ran for most of the time, but one could only be highly impressed by the Kru men (a seafaring tribe) in their handling of the barges under difficult conditions - they are superb seamen. Lagos was next, or more precisely, Apapa - on the western side of Lagos harbour. The oil jetty was next to a slaughter house! The noise and screams of the dying animals was awful to hear not to mention the sight of blood and offal passing the ship from the abattoir discharge pipe. Equally upsetting was the sight of animals being killed in full view of the ship.

My time aboard Neocardia was soon to end, although at the time I didn't know it. The contractual period of service between furloughs, at that time, was two years for all staff (Master, officers and apprentices). This was an inordinately long term, however old timers would remind us just how lucky we were! Pre-war, a service period was three years! This was apparent in the Anglo-Saxon nurseries, viz., Tyneside and New Quay, where children were born at three year intervals in the 1930's. On the return from Lagos to Aruba, I began to suffer from infected sinuses caused, it transpired, by swimming in the ballast tanks. I was so seriously affected on arrival at Aruba that I was hospitalized at Orangestadt for observation and treatment. I was 'paid-off'(a seafaring term for leaving a ship) on 30th October 1946 and spent twelve days ashore before joining an Eagle Oil Shipping Company vessel, m.s. San Virgilio as a DBS. These letters signified 'Distressed British Seaman', a ploy used by the shipping industry to repatriate seamen discharged abroad for hospitalization, for men who missed their ship at sailing time and those the victims of shipwreck. I had a very relaxed voyage back to Rotterdam, I did some work to justify my keep but it was light and pleasant. It was interesting to note the differences in standards and attitude between the two companies, when boiled down they didn't amount to much. The ship arrived in Rotterdam exactly one year to the day I had signed indentures, 27th November 1946. I had to wait a few days to secure a berth on the cross channel ferry to Harwich, so I stayed in a seamens' mission (a hostel for seafarers) where the food was very Dutch and took some getting used to! I went home to what was to prove a defining time in my life.

THREE MORE YEARS...

My return to Merthyr Tydfil after nearly one year's absence marked the beginning of another phase in my life. During my time in the Sea Cadet Corps, I had the responsibility of training the local branch of the Sea Rangers (nautical Girl Guides) in marching, signalling and the Morse Code. The Rangers were divided into two 'watches', one of which was led by Bosun Joan Morris. She was in charge of the port watch to which I was assigned, as instructor. It seemed that she and I were forever in mild conflict, no doubt I was aggressive and abrasive while she was intelligent and very good-looking! We never quite resolved our differences, especially when her team beat us in a Morse Code competition! Secretly I admired her. Our occasional encounters happened some years previously so she hadn't figured large in my life's calculations thus far. All was about to change! I went to a Christmas party at my old school as a guest and who served me with green jelly? Joan! I loved her from that day to this. She became my lifelong companion, my dear wife, a wonderful mother and my very best friend. Little did she realize the huge commitment she was making, however without the slightest doubt, she made me into whatever I became. Much to her chagrin she admitted to still being in school but expected to go to university the following year. I now became a young man with a purpose and a responsibility for another- if only to show constancy and respect for this girl's affection.

Anglo-Saxon Petroleum Company which later became Shell Tankers, named their ships after shells. They were not necessarily sea shells, but most were. The origin of the 'Shell' name and symbol dated back to Victorian times, when Marcus Samuel transported sea shells from the East Indies to British homes, subsequently his sons created a fleet of oil tankers, each named after a shell, which became the Anglo-Saxon. In my time the different classes of ship were named after shells beginning with the same letter (the Greek or Latin name), thus we had the "N";"D";"T" & "L" classes in those early days of my career. There were other ships that didn't conform to a class, so they had names starting with a different letter. Admittedly, there were some tongue twisters! Mostly, though, the names were beautiful and distinctive. Witness the names of the ships upon which I served for the remainder of my apprenticeship: Miralda, Alexia, Dorcasia and Hyalina - the words just rolled off the tongue! An example of the shell that a particular ship was named after was displayed in the officers' saloon. Sometimes the shell was so rare, a facsimile had to be made. These shells varied enormously in size, some were so small they had to be magnified, others, such as Spondilus were housed in a case a metre long! Years later I served as first Chief Officer of Arianta, the inscription inside the case of her shell was " 'arianta something', a mollusc occasionally found in Belgian hedgerows." The company always had a conchologist to allocate names to ships and petroleum products. When a ship ended its days, the shell was always removed and returned to London.

At the end of a wonderful leave, I had to say good-bye to my new love - the first of so many farewells. Partings never became any easier as the years passed, in fact the opposite was the case. I travelled from Cardiff to Newcastle-on-Tyne at the end of January 1947 in the midst of the worst winter Britain had experienced for many years. I joined Miralda at Hebburn on the south side of the river. The ship had been lying for months whilst it was 'demacked'. Miralda and a number of other similar ships had been converted to what were known as MAC ships during the war. These letters stood for Merchant Aircraft Carriers (refer to Captain Bob Allen's "Wartime with Shell" for the fullest description). Basically, they had flight decks plonked down over the fore and main decks terminating at the stern, the 'midships accommodation block was trimmed down together with slicing off the funnel to receive the flight deck. The success of this conversion is also recounted in Bob's book. Their entry onto the Battle of the Atlantic was significant and crucial to the war's outcome. Post - war, repair yards were booked to restore the ships to their commercial form, usually returning to the places where the original conversion had taken place. I joined this dark, dank vessel late at night, snow feet deep everywhere, no accommodation heating or cooking facilities, bone chilling and miserable!

I had many great friends in the course of a lifetime at sea, I shall, of course, make reference to each of them as my story unfolds. First among this band of men was one Douglas Carr, who died a few months ago. He was Chief Officer of Miralda, his first ship in this capacity. I was a second-year apprentice, he was second-in-command of the ship! The age disparity was not nearly as great as our difference in rank, he was 25 years old I was 18. He was a charismatic young man. Bright, humorous, efficient and kind - such a contrast from my previous boss, I would have jumped over the moon for this officer! Our paths crossed many times in later years, and always, we had the same rapport. I began to bloom with all the good fortune that was coming my way: my meeting Joan and now a kindly, fair and respectful Mate to work for.

I was fortunate to go home for a few days prior to the ship going on sea trials. Although Joan and I were only able to spend a day together, it was such a happy one, it cemented our relationship. She was studying for her higher school certificate and later in the year went to Aberystwyth University. Paradoxically, meeting me gave her an element of stability despite our not seeing one another again, for many months. We maintained and strengthened our bond by letter writing - many thousands of letters were subsequently written to each other over the next thirty-seven years, we wrote practically every day of our lives apart, this was such an important factor in our courtship and marriage.

I returned to the ship refreshed and happy. Geoff Moat was my fellow apprentice, a first tripper from Essex. As senior apprentice I suddenly began to move up the scale! After what amounted to an exercise in survival in our first days, the ship was now powered and warm. Soon after my return we went on sea trials and a little later we sailed for Curaçao in late February 1947. Miralda was a 'black oil' tanker, one which carried anything from diesel and fuel oils to crude oils (the stuff that came straight out of the ground!).With Mr

Carr, our work was interesting and constructive, he gave us time-off when we were entitled to it, we had study time and a happy social life. Mr.Carr would invite Geoff and myself to his cabin on Saturday nights, after he had come off watch at 2000, to listen to the Voice of America Jazz Hour with Willis Carlova. We also had a beer each! A very enjoyable evening.

We loaded fuel oil at Caracas Bay in Curaçao for Bahia in Brazil and Montevideo in Uruguay. These were fabulous ports! Bahia was a two tier town and to get from the harbour you took a funicular railway to the upper town, a quite spectacular sight to look down on the ship. Montevideo has remained in my mind as the most impressive port I have visited! Now whether that is youthful imagination creating such a notion in my memory or not, I wouldn't like to say! Nevertheless, I have never forgotten the graceful tree-lined avenues, the luxurious shops and the superb restaurants. Of course, together with my fellows, the favourite meal was steak, egg and chips - but what a steak! These South American ports were so friendly towards seafarers, one felt very much at home - and apparently the senoritas added to the welcome! Whenever a Shell ship discharged at a River Plate port, on completion she invariably went to an area known as Banco Chico to load a cargo of river water . The river water was discharged at Curaçao for refinery use, as there wasn't a fresh water source in the island, domestic supply being supplied by desalination. We arrived back in Curaçao in early May, discharged the fresh water, re-loading another cargo for Montevideo and La Plata in Argentina.

Negotiating the coast of the eastern side of South America, and to make the most economic passage, navigating teams had to study the coastal currents carefully to take advantage of favourable flows and to avoid adverse currents. The dividing point where the South Equatorial Current split itself into north and south components was at the eastern tip of the continent near Natal. Seasoned navigators in these waters could make routing decisions that had a significant effect upon voyage performance. The practical art of navigation was a source of great satisfaction if one assessed conditions correctly, on the other hand frustration often accompanied failure!

On both our passages into the River Plate, we passed the stranded wreck of the pocket battleship, Graf Spee, a monument to the Battle of the River Plate when three Royal Navy cruisers: Exeter, Achilles and Ajax overcame the much more powerful German warship in the early days of the war. We discharged part cargo at Montevideo and went across the mouth of the Plate to La Plata, later to be Eva Peron and subsequently reverting to La Plata! This was the port of 'Frigerificos'. Cattle came in at one end and tinned corned beef came out the other. I share the ambivalence that many feel when it comes to the slaughter of animals. Conducted tours were arranged for crew members, I found the experience quite traumatic, and to this day I pass abattoirs with a sense of profound unease - mainly because of my hypocrisy.

Another cargo of river water and return to Curaçao. A change of scene took us to Lisbon to discharge a cargo of fuel oil and from there we went to Trinidad to load bunker fuels for Las Palmas in the Canary Islands. We loaded at Point Fortin in the Gulf of Paria, it was July and very hot and humid. Crossing the Atlantic in summer, particularly going to ports in more southern latitudes, was very pleasant - so different from the winter passages to northern Europe. There is something about the climate in Gran Canaria that maintains cars in pristine condition! I well remember beautifully preserved models of Mercedes, Alfa Romeos and other makes in spanking condition yet they were, in some cases, twenty years old! Las Palmas was a very important bunkering port in the 1940's and 50's. Royal Mail and Union Castle Lines constantly used the port, the former with passenger ships en route to South America, the latter similarly to South Africa. Of course this form of international travel was later superseded by air lines. Miralda next loaded at Curaçao for Vado on the Italian Riviera, it was there that I tasted vermouth and made myself horribly ill as a result! Never liked the stuff since. This was my first experience of the Mediterranean Moor. A favoured way in most open Mediterranean ports was to berth the ship stern - on to the jetty using both anchors to hold the ship in position, the cargo was pumped along a stern line to the poop where the flexible hose from the shore was connected. From Vado we headed towards Port Said and the Suez Canal.

The passage through the Suez Canal was always an enjoyable interlude in a seafarer's life, particularly if the ship was south bound. Each vessel moored to buoys at Port Said while the ship was measured or checked for payment of canal dues. In this time we were visited by bum boats which were, in effect, floating shops. The reputable shipping lines had assigned bum boat merchants and ours went under the name of Abdullah (!) This was an acceptable arrangement in that the merchant had an assured market, in return, he provided a reasonably honest service to the ship. There were hoards of other characters however! Gilli Gilli men - sleight of hand artists who would perform the most spectacular conjuring tricks. Thieves and vagabonds abounded so that one had to be very careful that one's cabin was locked and that all useful ship's equipment was secure. There were even men who would remove corns from people's toes by using a mouth suction tube! North bound, ships anchored off in Suez Bay to measure up so there wasn't much in the way of trade done. On a professional note, it was interesting and a good exercise for we apprentices, particularly steering the ship during the canal passage. Each ship, in those days, lifted a portable searchlight at the bows which illuminated the canal banks during night transit, also we shipped two canal boats and four boatmen, who would tie the ship to the canal bank if orders were received to suspend transit for scheduling or poor visibility (in sand storms, visibility was reduced to zero, everything being choked and caked and totally covered!) Ships moved in convoy, one south bound, another north bound. They passed each other in the Bitter Lakes, which separated the north and south sections of the canal. This afforded the opportunity to swim in the very saline waters of the lake. The British Army was stationed at Ismahlia, we envied their life of sun drenched indolence - or so it appeared to us . The canal banks were lined with suntanned families watching us go by, naturally we watched them too - particularly the nubile females! Usually, the south bound convoy anchored whilst the north bound ships proceeded without stopping. South of the canal we proceeded down the Gulf of Suez into the infamous Red Sea, thence to the Indian Ocean and finally the Persian Gulf.

Our destination was Fahaheel, later to become the huge oil port of Mina al Ahmadi in Kuwait. However we had to call at Bahrein for bunkers, en route. Fahaheel, in those days, was an open buoy berth, well off-shore with just a sandy shoreline visible in the distance, a loading port, the likes of which I hadn't seen before - so different from Caribbean/USA loading ports. We weren't there long fortunately. This was the first experience I had had of Middle East Crude, an odour with which I was to become well accustomed to, later in life! Our destination was Le Havre and Rouen on the River Seine. We passed through the Suez Canal at the end of October 1947 and put into Gibraltar for engine repairs prior to our arrival in France on Armistice Day. We lightened to a river draft for Rouen at Le Havre. Perhaps one of the most beautiful river transits is the passage up the Seine to Rouen. The ship enters the city of Rouen, turns around in a swinging basin and proceeds seaward to berth at Petit Couronne, a few miles west of Rouen. Beautiful, the river may be, but it is a trial for ships berthed to its banks! The problem is the twice daily tidal bore. The ship has to be on stand-by, cargo hoses disconnected, engines at the ready with crew at mooring stations to deal with the sudden surge as the bore lifts the ship bodily. Mooring lines go taut then slacken as the ship careens up and down the jetty face, so the ship has to be re-berthed at each passing bore. On completion of discharge we sailed to the North Sea to tank clean prior to dry-docking at Wallsend, on the north bank of the River Tyne. I went home on arrival for 25 days furlough.

This my third return to my home town, in many ways such a happy visit tinged with heartache. Joan and I had allowed our courtship to flower with regular letter writing, so we knew a lot about one another. By this time she had been at Aberystwyth University for one term, and my return clashed with her first end-of-term examinations. I spent a few days at Aber, staying at the Marine Hotel. I was so grateful for the time she was able to spend with me because I knew the stress any interruption in her studies would cause. So I returned to Merthyr to await her arrival home for the Christmas vacation. Eventually she arrived, a day or so later I was introduced to her parents and almost immediately on 22nd December had to join my third ship! A very testing time for both of us, it seemed so unfair to be parted for Christmas. It was our first taste of the vagaries of a seafaring relationship, an introduction to many more difficult times we would surmount in the years to come.

I joined m.v. Alexia at Falmouth. She too had been 'demacked' (refer to Miralda). In command was Captain W. S. Atkinson, later to become Commodore of the fleet. This was his first stint as Master. I was now a relatively experienced seafaring chap with two years service under my belt! Again I was one of two apprentices, the other was James Cormack, a shy, softly-spoken, first trip lad from near Aberdeen. We spent Christmas Day in dry-dock, so I went to Grampound Road for Christmas lunch with friends - a pleasant family affair. The others had a tolerable meal aboard, under difficult circumstances in the repair yard. We sailed for Curaçao on 28th December 1947, arriving there on 14th January 1948. The voyage pattern was very similar to that of Miralda, viz., Curaçao - Las Palmas - Curaçao - Santos - Aruba - Stanlow - Aruba - Rotterdam. One recollection I think is worth recording. I, together with other officers, was invited to the British Club in Santos where we had afternoon tea followed by gins and tonic. It's worthy of note because there was this enclave of pure Britishness in this Brazilian port city, where everyone dressed as though it was a country club in the South of England. It was my first gin and tonic, the beginning of a pleasant, lifelong association with this beverage!

Stanlow, Shell's biggest refinery in the United Kingdom, is situated near Chester and served by the Manchester Ship Canal. The refinery had its own berths in a dock system as an extension of the canal. Visiting tankers were probably the biggest ships to transit the canal although passenger liners belonging to Manchester Liners used to go as far as Manchester itself, but their draft would not have been as great as that of the tankers. The system of pilotage was unique. A pilot and helmsman would take charge of the ship as soon as the vessel entered the lock at Eastham. The helmsman was really a trainee pilot who would, one day, be upgraded to Pilot, in what was termed 'dead men's shoes'. It seemed to me to be a typically British institution in that one waited for promotion regardless of one's capabilities. There was no doubt, however, that these men were expert ship handlers in the restricted confines of this port system. The interplay between pilot and helmsman was, to say the least, singular, in that they had almost a confidential language, which they used to convey instructions and responses. This probably arose from their being a team who understood one another's nautical patois, to the exclusion of the bridge officers! They used to say that if anyone fell in the canal, one would die of poisoning - such was the level of contamination! Wags would rejoin that that was not the case, in fact one would die of concussion on hitting the water!

We left the Mersey on 21st April 1948, bound for Aruba. We had a kindly, incompetent Chief Officer! He had been master with the

43

Royal Fleet Auxiliary and it was soon apparent why he had left the RFA and was now sailing as Mate with Anglo-Saxon. He had a magisterial manner, affected a plummy accent and was a total alcoholic. One of his outstanding physical features was a veined, bulbous nose! He said to me, whilst I understudied him on watch (!) that the only way to cure a red nose was to drink gin and turn it purple! Actually, being on watch with him gave me experience in both navigation and cargo work that otherwise I would have missed - because I had to perform all the duties! He was a lovable old chap so people used to cover for him. He was an example of the parlous position in which shipping companies found themselves in their endeavours to man expanding post-war fleets. Frankly he should never have been employed. I met him, some eleven years later, in a Sunderland pub, huddled in a corner, unshaven and dishevelled but still with all the aplomb he had acquired in earlier, happier years.

I had managed, up until this point, to maintain a steady study programme, having latterly been given adequate time-off to pursue my academic work. I really loved the work, so it was no hardship for me. The Company organized and paid for the King Edward VII Nautical School to dispatch correspondence courses to each apprentice, these, in turn, were completed and returned to the school for marking and assessment. Every year the Merchant Navy Training Board, a national body formed by the then Chamber of Shipping, set examinations for each of the four years an apprentice served. These exams were conducted under strict supervision, usually in the Master's cabin. Certainly Anglo-Saxon expected their apprentices to be properly trained, if they weren't, it was the fault of the ships' management.

We loaded in Aruba and discharged our cargo at Rotterdam, thence to Falmouth for an emergency repair. Falmouth was the favourite repair port for Companies and crews. One of Europe's finest natural, deep water harbours, it is situated on the south coast of Cornwall right on the routes for all loading areas. The surprising feature about Falmouth was that once outside the dockyard, one was in an attractive seaside resort with fine hotels and great hostelries, carefree visitors and all the fun of the fair! Small wonder it was every sailor's favourite! One drawback was the remoteness to the remainder of the U.K. As soon as Alexia arrived at Falmouth on the 6th June 1948, the Chief Officer, James Cormack and I were transferred to Dorcasia which was at Barry in South Wales, undergoing refit. Little more than an hour from my home, I was able to visit Merthyr for a night or two prior to sailing on the 12th June. There was no way I could see Joan because she was in Aberystwyth, and as far as meeting, she might as well have been in John O'Groats!

Dorcasia was under the command of a senior master from West Wales. The reader will perhaps be unfamiliar with the divisions and prejudices that exist within the Principality. The usual urban versus rural rivalry is compounded by language. The South Wales valleys are urban and English speaking with the exception of pockets of Welsh speaking districts. Swansea, Port Talbot and Llanelli also urban, but Welsh speaking. The remainder of Wales, in general terms, is rural and Welsh speaking. It would be fair to say that there is little love lost between these diverse cultures. You will now, perchance, understand a measure of the disdain poured upon the writer by the Captain. My second nemesis! More of this later.

The most radical change, for me, after having served aboard three British crewed ships, was that Dorcasia was manned by a Chinese crew. Pre-war, Anglo-Saxon had manned its ships exclusively with Chinese crews - a tradition with which, I suspect, the Company was more comfortable. Wartime obliged them to crew about half their fleet with British seamen (or White crews, as they were termed in those days). Historically, senior staff had little experience with British crew standards but were well versed in the ways of our Chinese friends. The balance of approximately half British and half oriental crewing continued throughout my career with Shell. On this month of June 1948, I was fascinated to enter this entirely new seafaring world, it was truly a revelation! One immediately had to learn to speak pidgin English, the lingua franca in communicating with the crew. In those days crews were assembled in Singapore and were known as 'Singapore crews'. There were three departments aboard any ship, viz., Deck, Engine Room and Catering. Although all crew members came from China, each department was manned by men from different parts of that vast country. Without exception, the Deck Department was staffed by Foo Chow people, the Engine Room by Cantonese and the Catering Department (officers' cooks and stewards) by men from the island of Hainan. The heads of these squads were powerful men indeed! The Bosun headed the Deck crew, Number One Fireman the Engine Room team and the Chief Steward the boss of the Catering staff. Strange as it may seem, most of these ratings, from the disparate geographical areas, could scarcely communicate with another from a different part of the country! The three departments spoke separate and distinct languages, ate different food and looked different. The men from the northern province of Foo Chow were taller and better built than the others, neither were they as sophisticated as their shipmates. Cantonese and Hainanese were quite similar and readily understood each other. Cantonese came from the area of Canton (as the name implies), adjacent to Hong Kong, whereas Hainan is an island off the south coast of China in the Gulf of Tonkin. An almost feudal employment system obtained! The heads of each department recruited their own men from their families and friends at their home villages, the Lord only knows what inducements came the way of Bosuns, No.1's and Chief Stewards, in their selection of their crew! These crews travelled 'en bloc' from their area of China, via Hong Kong, to Singapore and stayed in crew boardinghouses awaiting appointment to a ship. The shipping companies that employed this type of crew dealt directly with the departmental heads whenever they needed a new crew. Neat and effective. Invariably, crews sailed with one company only, so allegiance and loyalty were assured.

Dorcasia, left Barry Dock and carried out a routine operation that always happens when a ship leaves a repair yard. Compass adjustment. This was particularly important in the case of this ship as she only had magnetic compasses, whereas my previous ships had gyro compasses in addition. Compass adjustment consists of swinging the ship's heading and adjusting the compensating magnets, attached to each binnacle (the structure that encloses the compass) to achieve minimum error for each heading, thereafter to compile a 'deviation card' which, theoretically, aids the navigator to calculate the compass 'error' wherever he may be. We quit the Bristol Channel on 12th June 1948, bound for Port Said.

As far as the Half Deck was concerned it was still just James Cormack and myself, a continuation of Alexia, with the same boss. The Mate kept me on watch with him, ostensibly as his understudy, however I knew differently! We had a single public toilet on our deck, when I followed my boss, prior to going to the Bridge at 0400 to take the morning watch, the w.c. smelled of pure Gordon's! As soon as the Second Mate disappeared down the ladder, he lay down on the Chartroom settee and fell fast asleep! Scary moments and a rapid learning curve for this boy! The Captain, at some point, discovered some of what was going on. Both he and the Mate detested one another! Apparently it stemmed from the War. Each claimed to have been in command of the first ship to enter Tokyo Bay at war's end when the Japanese surrendered to General MacArthur. As I indicated earlier, the Mate had been in command with the RFA. Who was correct was never ascertained, however it certainly soured the already charged atmosphere that pervaded the ship on our outward bound voyage. The Master was also a drunk, but not as hopelessly affected as the Mate. The latter floated in a perpetually alcoholic mist complete with a beneficent smile. The former became tanked-up and did a creditable imitation of a raging bull, complete with broken china!

From the Suez Canal we went to Abadan, the big British Petroleum refinery in Iran. Abadan is situated on the eastern bank of the Shatt-al-Arab, the seaward end of the confluence of the mighty Euphrates and Tigris. The east bank of the river marks the border between Iraq and Iran, consequently the river belongs to Iraq and the pilots (men who guide ships through harbours and rivers) are Iraqi Prior to picking up the pilot, we went aground in the river delta, a quite common occurrence in those days with visibility reduced by suspended sand in the atmosphere, and, of course, not having the benefit of radar or a gyro compass. The shelf was gradual so no damage was sustained. We eventually located the pilot station at Fao by homing-in with DF bearings. We berthed at Abadan on 7th July in appalling heat! The area is, without doubt, the hottest part of the world at that time of the year. The ship was like an oven, with temperatures 120 degrees (plus)Fahrenheit, in the shade! No air-conditioning, no cool water, four flies, of the most persistent tenacity, to every square inch - hell on earth, believe me! Yet in this cauldron, my situation changed dramatically. The Chief Officer left the ship on medical grounds (!) immediately upon arrival - undoubtedly aided by a fervent desire on the Captain's part! The second and third officers moved up a rank and I was promoted Acting Third Officer. Coping with the heat and the sudden responsibility became a piece of cake, I felt ten feet tall! I was about to receive something like twenty pounds a month, have my own cabin with a steward to do my bidding - what more could I ask?

Despite the unsettling knowledge that I would never be able to please my Welsh boss, the next seven and a half months were very happy if physically uncomfortable. For most of the period we loaded various gasolines, kerosene and gas oil at Abadan for ports in India and Pakistan. This was a very interesting period. Our first discharge port was Rangoon in Burma however, in the Irrawaddy delta, where we had to moor to the jetty with anchor chains, such was the strength of the river current! I well remember the sight of the gold leaf dome (reputed to be the largest single gold leaf roof in the world) of the Buddhist temple Shwe Dagon, readily visible from our berth. I had a run ashore and found the place quite enchanting. On our way to Rangoon we passed quite close to the Andaman Islands, where, the Admiralty Pilot warned head hunters were still active! No navigational errors there! We returned to Abadan. The next few months we suffered from the steaming heat of the South West Monsoon whilst in the Arabian Sea and Bay of Bengal, and the livid heat of the Persian Gulf. The consequence was that we all developed heat rash which is one of the most irritating complaints.

Our next discharge port was Bombay. This was the period of post Independence in India and Pakistan and whereas we didn't witness any of the ethnic violence that was prevalent at this time, we beheld the practical consequences of the partition in Bombay. Thousands of refugees thronged the wharves where we berthed, living in the open with the flimsiest of shelter and no sanitary facilities. However, incongruously, we received an invitation from a local cricket club to play them at, of all places, the Bombay Test Ground! This we did, with your writer furnishing a modest contribution to our abject defeat! From Bombay we went down the coast to Goa. This was an anachronism if ever there was! Goa was, at the time, a Portuguese colony. Later ceded to India, it had all the trappings of the colonial power with the poverty of India. The port was Mormugao, a strikingly pretty place, as I remember, if somewhat smelly.

There followed two consecutive voyages from Abadan to Madras and Calcutta. The most noteworthy memory I have of Madras was that of the Anglo-Indian community. A pathetic body of people at that time of traumatic change in the sub continent. A measure of protection had been afforded by the British, from whom they had descended, during colonial times. They were in a state of flux now that the British had departed. We met them at the Seaman's Club in Madras the girls (and their mothers) were most keen to cultivate any Britisher who might eventually marry them and take them 'home' (their term, not mine). Calcutta was a colourful city, wealth and poverty in juxtaposition, the din and variety of Chowringee with its miscellany of small shops selling everything imaginable! Calcutta lies on the River Hoogly, a distributary of the River Ganges. Dorcasia, moored to the berth at Garden Reach using anchor chains, in a similar manner to that of Rangoon, because of the fearful flow of the river in full spate. It was here that I discovered the Britisher abroad at his least attractive. The pilotage service, at that time, was exclusively staffed by Brits, and they had created a hegemony that was unassailable! They boarded in full uniform, had a servant to carry their bag and spoke only to the senior officers! As we lay alongside the oil jetty, bodies of dead cattle looking like huge balloons floated past the ship, and, it was said, if one looked hard and long enough, humans as well.

Our final discharge on the sub-continent was Karachi in Pakistan, then a peaceful city. We stayed alongside after discharge, undergoing repairs, which enabled everyone to get ashore. After our penultimate visit to Abadan we went to Singapore to discharge at Pulau Sambu and Pulau Bukom, two islands off Singapore with Shell installations, one Indonesian and one Singaporean. On finishing discharge we gas freed and dry-docked for emergency repairs in Keppel Harbour.

Singapore was the centre of Shell's marine activities in the Far East, with a satellite company office at Shell House on Connor's Quay, complete with marine and engineer superintendents and a staff to deal with ships' personnel. People often ask me which, of all the ports, I have visited, I like best. I invariably say Montevideo because of the grand impression it created in my mind. However, if I'm asked which is the most interesting place, it has to be Singapore. These were pre-independence days when I first visited with Dorcasia, long before it became the jewel of industrial states with its puritanical efficiency. Four ethnic groups lived on the island; predominating were the Chinese followed by the Malays with substantial minorities of

Indians and Europeans. It was a marvellous city for seafarers with great facilities and entertainment. Anglo-Saxon personnel, joining and leaving ships, stayed at Connell House, a guest house run by a non-profit trust, where one lived comfortably in airy rooms and enjoyed good food. Of course we lived on board during our repair period but were able to meet up with the chaps staying in Connell House and hear the gossip! Naturally the crew were delighted at the turn of events, despite having their homes in China their second home was Singapore. For me, it was a great experience! Change Alley (next to the Shell Building) was a narrow lane packed with shops selling everything imaginable at bargain prices - a great place to explore. At night we went to Bugis Street and Albert Street to eat from stalls that produced the most delicious Chinese and Malay food. I first met a transvestite in Bugis Street - it was renowned, world-wide for these people. At the time I really didn't know of their existence and was quite shocked to realize that the gorgeous girl I was looking at, was a man! I realized this was so when he asked, in the deepest bass voice, for a packet of Luck Strike cigarettes from an adjacent stall. I found it quite confounding!

We sailed from Singapore on 14th January 1949, once again, for Abadan. We had a glorious voyage back to the Persian Gulf, as it was the height of the North East Monsoon, the good weather season. It was devilishly cold in Abadan, with frosty nights and clear days . I thought that, at this point, I would write some more about our life aboard a 'Chinese' ship. As far as we officers were concerned, we lived like fighting cocks! The food was excellent and plentiful. We were served with regular Chinese meals, by popular demand. The breakfasts were meals to die for (for young, hungry men anyway)! We always had a fresh fruit juice, papaya or grapefruit, a kedgeree or curry followed by the main dish consisting of two eggs, bacon etc. etc. plus sauté potatoes! As Third Mate, one of my duties was the supervision of vict-ualling and compilation of records, together with the ordering of provi-sions (naturally assisted by the Chief Steward) so I made sure we had plenty. Of course I was very inexperienced and fell foul of some unscrupulous ship chandlers. I well remember ordering two dozen boxes of dried mint (for sauce), thinking that they would be small 2 oz packs, only to find on leaving port that we had been supplied with 24 boxes, each containing 24 small boxes! I was mortified and had to answer innumerable letters from Wacca Wilson (the Victualling

Superintendent) explaining my misdeeds! As already described, the crew members came from different parts of China and consequently ate different types of food. The deck ratings were quite apart from the others in this respect. Accordingly there were two crew cooks. Aboard Dorcasia, the crew were accommodated in the Fo'cas'le Space (at the bow) and they ate their meals on deck in two large circles, surrounding each of their array of dishes, The Bridge officers used to watch them, surreptitiously of course, through binoculars and marvel at the delicious looking display of food! In one of the ports I was approached by the Bosun and asked to secrete a mysterious package in my cabin for which he offered me a huge wad of U.S. dollars! Naive I may have been, stupid I was not! I realized, immediately, that he thought because of my immaturity he would inveigle me to smuggle opium on the crew's behalf. Fortunately, I courteously declined, and no 'loss of face' was inflicted. I learned rapidly to avoid this oriental phenomenon, loss of face, it could cause untold difficulty. There was a tolerance among officers of a need in some crew members, usually the older men, to use opium. In fact, there was usually a room set aside for the smoking of opium, one of those practices when eyes were shut for the greater good! The heads of department lived in almost feudal splendour! Each with his servant to look after him. Discipline was meted out by these petty officers, and rarely did the master have to resort to the practice of 'logging' a rating (universally used aboard British crew ships, this was the means of wielding discipline by log entry and fine). On Chinese crew ships, a conversation with the Bosun, No.1 Fireman or Chief Steward sufficed

We went to Stanlow and Ardrossan, via the Suez Canal, where at the latter port I 'paid-off'. I have indicated that I did not see eye-to-eye with the Captain, in fact we had had quite serious confrontations in the time I had sailed as Third Mate. It was the practice at that time to issue confidential reports upon an officer's ability and conduct, without the officer sighting the report. However the subject of the report should have been informed had anything detrimental been written. I left Dorcasia quite satisfied that I had done a creditable job, returning home to Merthyr Tydfil on March 1st 1949, St. David's Day, with a light heart and just dying to see my girl!

I had a wonderful furlough. I was due two months leave, as it tran-spired I was home for three. During this time I was able to spend the whole of the Easter vacation, a month at least, with Joan. The time we had together, further strengthened our bond and established the bedrock of a lifetime's relationship, one based on love and trust. To this day I thank all that I hold dear for my great, good fortune in meeting this lady. I became friendly with her mother and father, and that too, over the years, was a joy and a strength in difficult times. When Joan returned to Aberystwyth, I was at a loose end and practically broke! I tried all ways to visit her - even to the extent of attempting to organize a charabanc for a day's excursion to Aberystwyth, so that I could have a free seat! No luck, I'm afraid. I contented myself with long walks, chiefly with my younger brother, Tom. He was awaiting call-up to the Army, having passed the Civil Service examination for entry to the Royal Military College, Sandhurst.

I only had a few months qualifying sea service to complete to enable me to sit for my Second Mate's Certificate (ticket, as it was called). I fully anticipated an appointment as Third Mate, but such was not to be the case. One of life's bitter pills awaited me! Perhaps, because of the short time left to complete my sea-time or possibly the reason lay in my previous report from Dorcasia, I never knew. I was appointed to Hyalina, the Commodore ship, as senior apprentice. Back to the chipping, scraping and red-leading! I was determined to acquit myself favourably despite having to swallow my pride. In fact, the ship was very interesting. She was nicknamed the 'greyhound' and was one of two of the fastest tankers afloat. The Commodore, Captain Shaw (aka Butcher Shaw) was a 'character' who had the most disconcerting habit of removing his dentures whilst talking or eating, continuing conversation with rubbery lips and a full set of gums! However, he was a fine man and despite his fearsome reputation, a kindly soul. Both Hyalina and her sister Helicina were committed to a liner trade between Curaçao and Thameshaven, the Shell refinery on the north bank of the Thames, near Stanford-le-Hope (or Stanford-no-Hope, as it was referred to in the Fleet). Whilst serving I completed five Atlantic round voyages. My fellow apprentices were a great bunch of lads, we had dedicated training and were treated well. The ship had radar, which marked an advance in navigational safety and performance. At that time, commercial radar installations were rare and the equipment cumbersome. The gubbins was housed in an air cooled cabin on the Monkey Island, the display in the Wheelhouse. The standards, in all respects, aboard Hyalina, were high - due I suspect to the calibre of the men manning the ship, so my early mortification was soon forgotten.

Towards the end of my sojourn aboard Hyalina, I had the entirely unexpected news that I had won the Royal Society of Arts, Thomas Grey Memorial Trust sextant, for my examination results in 1948. In addition, I was to be presented with a set of drawing instruments by the Anglo-Saxon Petroleum Company Limited. I had a congratulatory letter from the Managing Director which I was obliged to reply to - my first typewritten letter, ever!

I left Hyalina on 18th October 1949, thus completing my apprenticeship. My parents now lived in Ebbw Vale in Monmouthshire because my father had been promoted to bank manager. Within a week of my arrival home I went to St.Helen's Court, in the City of London, Anglo-Saxon's H.Q. to receive the sextant and drawing instruments - even had a write-up in the local press! I was granted study-leave by the Company in order to work for my Second Mate's Certificate. I secured digs in Cardiff with a Mrs Hughes and enrolled at the Nautical Department in the Technical College to prepare for the examination. So far as I am aware, no public examination, other than the then Board of Trade, demanded a pass mark of 70%! So there was no slacking, one worked hard at the various subjects: navigation, ship construction, ship stability, electronics, cargo work, meteorology and engineering. The killer was the oral examination! There were some fearsome examiners around the country, none worse than the one I had for Second Mate's! I forget his name, but it was said that if his hair was ruffled, you stood a good chance, if it was slicked down - tough! The oral exam took about an hour, covering seamanship and knowledge of the collision regulations. These examinations were ordeals that had no equal in a seafarer's experience! A word about my digs. We were three students at Mrs Hughes' house, I was one of two in the front bedroom in freezing conditions! We were sent off each morning with a fine breakfast under our belts. However this was subject to one being able to tolerate the sight of our landlady with a fearful red gash of vivid lipstick, roughly in the area of her mouth, a fag hanging therefrom, with the ash about to drop into the frying pan, plus the sight of elasticised knicker bottoms around her knees over wrinkled lisle stockings surmounting the biggest slippers you ever saw! It took the most hardened of men to survive the sight of that vision! I received my 'ticket' on the 13th February 1950.

So ended my apprenticeship, and the commencement of my chosen career.

CHAPTER FOUR

JUNIOR OFFICER

I was now a certificated deck officer, qualified to sail as Second Mate. The practice was that, in most cases, you sailed in a rank below your certificate. This would be changed if there was a shortage of officers, in which case you would sail in your certificated rank. One of the requirements of a deck officer was that he carry his sextant to whichever ship he was appointed. The purchase of a sextant was an expensive outlay, particularly if one had just been ashore for three months studying for one's certificate. In this respect, I was fortunate to have acquired mine through the benevolence of the Thomas Grey Trust. Of course a new uniform had been bought together with new sets of 'whites' and accessories.

My first appointment as a fully blown Third Mate was m.v. Dromus, a sister ship to Dorcasia, also manned by a Chinese crew. I reported to London initially, on 23rd March 1950, then travelled to Hamburg via the Harwich/Hook of Holland ferry thence by rail to Hamburg. Britain was an austere country at this time, labouring under strict rationing of food with shortages of most of what we would now consider essentials. I was taken aback by the contrast in Germany! The Brits had been on the winning side, the Germans, the losers! There was plenty of everything in Hamburg, particularly food of all types. I was met by the Agent, an ex U-Boat commander, a jovial character full of bonhomie and boundless Teutonic confidence. The ship was discharging crude oil at the Shell installation in Hamburg's Oil Harbour. We sailed on my twenty second birthday, March 27th, for the Persian Gulf via the Suez Canal. I thoroughly enjoyed my brief stay aboard this ship, the staff were very agreeable, the Master benign and the food excellent! We loaded crude oil at Mina al Ahmadi in Kuwait for Stanlow, thereafter dry docking in Liverpool after tank cleaning in the Irish Sea. We docked at the beginning of June at the Harland and Wolff yard in Liverpool. Three weeks later, at the end of June, I was transferred to t.e.s Thallepus, also in dry-dock across the river at Birkenhead. In between times I had wangled some unofficial leave and went to Aberystwyth to spend time with my girl, who had finished her year-end exams and was free to spend time with me. We had a wonderful few days together, lovely weather and great beaches at Borth. We were so happy. Joan and I were determined, from the start of our relationship that whatever time we had, we would live it to the full, a philosophy that served us well in the following years, we never stinted in the pursuit of enjoyment during our precious days together.

Each ship, in its own particular way, was interesting. A truism perhaps, but it was particularly so in the case of Thallepus. She was a T2, American built during the war years, one of the most successful ship classes ever created. The T2 was on a par with the Liberty ship, a dry cargo workhorse (also constructed in the U.S.A.) which solved many a wartime transport predicament. Anglo-Saxon, in concert with most large tanker operators, purchased a number of these ships (twenty-odd, I recollect). Radically different from European designs, the T2 was a bigger ship of some 16,000 tons deadweight, more powerful in both propulsion and cargo delivery performance, yet, as indicated earlier, it lacked the flexibility of the design evolved across the Pond. A welcome experience for this budding tankerman! I had, for many years, cast envious eyes upon our fleet of T2's. As with all things, the grass is not necessarily greener...! The class names, beginning with the letter 'T', were not attractive. Often enough, they were difficult to pronounce. One name, Tomocyclis, was the cause of a mini uproar! At an unspecified discharge port, the crew were over the side painting the bow names, concluding the work as darkness fell. The ship sailed that night and arrived at Curaçao to load the next cargo, where indignation was aroused by a Shell ship entering Santa Anna Baai with the name 'Tomosyphilis ' emblazoned upon its bows! Red faces, angry exchanges were the order of the day! British fitted accommodation aboard ship, at least with Shell, was always of a high, comfortable standard with carpets, curtains and fabric covered settees. The T2, was spartan in this regard, with tubular steel furniture, plastic covered settees, no curtains and bare decks in the cabins. However each cabin had a toilet and shower. Each alleyway had a cool water dispenser and the pantries had magnificent American fridges! Anglo-Saxon furnished the cabins, a la European style, so we had the best of both worlds. Mark you, because of the 100% welded construction, T2's had been known to split in two (!), so Lloyds, the classification society insisted on their having longitudinal straps riveted on the hull, above the waterline and on the main deck. The plating under the straps was cut for the entire length of the strap, so that any cracks that might occur would be arrested at the strap. The main propulsion unit was turbo-electric, i.e. steam driven turbines powering electric motors which drove the propeller shaft. The cargo pumps were also turbine driven, as opposed to the then universal practice in European ships of steam reciprocating ram pumps. So given a straight cargo, the T2 would out - perform any comparable tanker with its much faster speed at sea, and its more powerful pumping system.

So much for the few technicalities! We had a real 'character' as master! Captain Robson by name. He exemplified the huge sacrifices that men and their families had endured in their younger days. I cannot remember with whom he had served in his training years, but on obtaining his master's certificate in the mid-thirties, because of the depression, he was only able to secure a berth as quartermaster with the Blue Funnel Line. He married at that time, going on to serve for a year as quartermaster, running between the Far East and Australia, then was fortunate to land a post with Straits Steamship Company, a subsidiary of Blue Funnel, which traded exclusively around Malaya and the East Indies. He joined Straits as Fourth Officer, served for three years and transferred to Anglo-Saxon Petroleum's Eastern Fleet, which was based at Singapore, and served another three years as Third and Second Mate before being repatriated to Britain. Just married, and away for seven years without seeing one another! What an impossible ordeal for them both, but when I sailed with him and met his family, I was so impressed by their devotion to each other. Such is the courage and steadfastness in certain human beings! He was an excellent man to work for, a competent ship handler, a firm disciplinarian, fair minded and just. Not without a peccadillo, however! He had an irresistible penchant for smuggling! Had I been a student of the clandestine art, I'm sure I wouldn't have found a more expert teacher! I believe his pastime caused him some grief in later years! Additionally, he suffered from a speech peculiarity caused by loose dentures! Why he failed to have them corrected, I don't know! His delivery was often comic and we had difficulty in keeping straight faces!

We sailed from Birkenhead on the 4th July 1950. We made our way, once more via the Suez Canal, to Mina al Ahmadi and returned to one of Shell's lesser refineries at Heysham in Lancashire. As far as I was concerned, the highlight of this visit was that Joan was able to visit the ship, so we had five idyllic days together (although, in those days, ship visits by girlfriends were officially forbidden, certain masters were more than understanding!)

I thought that at this point I would briefly describe the Shell marine organization as it was in my early days, in fact as it continued to be during my career, with possible semantic exceptions. Perhaps an even briefer look at the major tanker operators. Each of the main oil companies supported a 'house' fleet, consisting of a number of types of ship each type fulfilling a particular function, viz., crude carriers, black oil (refined products), lubricating oil, white oil (gasolines, kerosenes etc.) ships. Probably, the British Tanker Company, the marine arm of British Petroleum, supported the largest fleet of 'company' ships under the British flag. Shell's main rival, Esso, espoused a somewhat different marine philosophy, tending to own less 'company' ships, chartering independently owned tankers for their larger requirements.

Shell operated the largest maritime organization in the world. The company controlled a number of national fleets, all wearing the same livery, managed by national personnel with the overall view and policy decisions being made by a gubernatorial organization called Shell International Marine. The name of the game was comparison. Comparisons between national fleets, between 'company' and chartered ships, between ships of different 'outside' companies and Shell's ships. The policy, in those times, was to operate a good company organization so that Shell would never be held to ransom by independent shipowners. There was a balance of course, but the ownership of company ships was akin, in commercial terms, to a national asset. So within the Shell 'family' we, the British, operated internationally alongside Dutch, French, German, Canadian, Japanese and Argentine fleets. There can be little doubt that in terms of a comprehensive ability to transport the widest variety of oils, Shell were pre-eminent. In addition to the normal hydrocarbon oils (with a particularly respected capability in the safe transport of the industry's most expensive product - lubricating oils) such disparate cargoes as whale oil and linseed oil were carried. The former was loaded in South Georgia by ship-to-ship transfer whilst the latter was taken aboard from road tankers in Uruguay. Later, of course, the organization was the leader in the carriage of chemicals and liquid gases. Eventually, Shell, had a meaningful presence in the world of ore and coal cargoes! No other oil company could match this comprehensive expertise.

The purpose of the preceding paragraph is to explain the international nature of the fleets and to give background to the next experience we had aboard Thallepus. We sailed from Heysham in late August, bound once more for Mina al Ahmadi via the Suez Canal. Once clear of the Red Sea we were instructed to go to the aid of a French Shell tanker, another T2, named "Junon" with the possibility of our having to tow her to Bombay. She had suffered a major engine failure but was able to move slowly under her own power. We had the experience of moving an anchor cable from the bow to the stern area, no mean physical feat, in order to provide a substantial connection for Junon's cable, should the need have arisen to tow. In the event we were not called upon to do so, however we escorted her to Bombay at a snail's pace. We witnessed a funeral service of an engineer killed in the engine breakdown incident, as we circled Junon, in a measure of respect. Once Junon was safely anchored, we resumed passage to Mina al Ahmadi, loading for Rotterdam. We arrived in Rotterdam on the 15th October, sailing the next day for Venezuela.

There was flurry of cables between London Office and Thallepus when we left Rotterdam, because the cargo out-turn (amount we discharged) did not match the bill of lading (quantity of oil said to have been loaded and agreed upon by ship at the loading port). A certain percentage difference was allowable, however our difference exceeded this figure. Naturally there was consternation on board. Investigation revealed huge quantities of sludge covering all the tank bottoms. The cargo suppliers at Mina al Ahmadi had probably drained a few shore storage tank bottoms into our ship during the loading operation, the sand and gunge settled during the loaded trip and remained, unpumpable, across the cargo range. I was relieved of my navigational duties and put in charge of the tank cleaning operation. What a job! Firstly, all tanks had to be machine cleaned with hot water (in those days, Shell used portable Butterworth machines - cast bronze casing enclosing a water turbine with a revolving triple jet outlet, revolving in azimuth and in the vertical plane, which were suspended at various levels on a rubber hose). In 1950, the tank drainings were pumped into the ocean, outside territorial limits, so we left a trail of black across the Atlantic! Secondly, we had to tank dive and remove anything that was left after the washing - and there was plenty. The sludge that the hot washing had failed to dislodge lay on the stringers and tank bottoms which was swept and shovelled into heaps, put into heavy rubber buckets and lifted by line and pulley to the tank hatch, thereafter to be dumped overboard. Undoubtedly hundreds of tons of the stuff were removed, because to allow it to remain would contaminate a future cargo. I would challenge anybody to dispute the statement that Middle East crude oil sludge is the vilest, stickiest and most obnoxious substance known to man! I, together with the crew, worked from sunrise to sunset removing this glutinous, evil maleficence - I have to confess, it was worse than PF4!! We managed to complete the task before presenting the ship at Punta Cardon, by which time I was totally exhausted and almost black - such was the difficulty of removing the stuff from one's body after so many days almost immersed in the muck, not to mention the cumulative effect of hydrocarbon vapour!

Punta Cardon was then one of Shell's newer refineries, situated on the south side of the Paraguana Peninsular in the Gulf of Venezuela. This was to herald the beginning of a trade pattern that lasted for some five months. North American demand for fuel oil was now beginning to increase with the advent of winter, so Thallepus loaded a full cargo at Punta Cardon. Six days later we arrived at Perth Amboy in New Jersey, the next day on 5th November 1950 we sailed for Mamonal in Colombia, at the western end of the Caribbean, near Cartagena. At Mamonal we loaded a full cargo of crude for Curaçao, a journey of about one and a half days, after discharge we back loaded a cargo of fuel oil for the Bronx in New York. This program embraced the handling of some fifteen cargoes in what was an exhausting schedule, one week in tropical temperatures, the next in North American sub-zero conditions. The discharge ports in the USA were mainly in the New York area, however we also went to Savannah, Baltimore and Searsport for a change of scene. The wear and tear on a ship on this trade was palpable, weather on the north east American coast was punishing and so much time had to be devoted to cargo tank preparation there was little left for maintenance on deck. The consequence did little for the corporate image (PF4, notwithstanding!), one was reminded of Masefield's 'dirty British coaster, butting up the Channel'! We quit this trade at the end of March 1951. Listening to American radio programmes, almost exclusively, we were alarmed that we were about to be involved in another world conflict with the war on the Korean peninsular in full spate. Fortunately that was not the case. We loaded our final cargo of fuel oil in this period at Curaçao for Hull (Saltend), which we completed discharging on 13th April prior to tank cleaning in preparation for drydocking at Cardiff.

I have described the structure and origins of the 'Chinese' crewing system as it was in those early days of my seafaring career. In contrast, I should also describe the background and ethos of a 'White' (British) crew in the early fifties. Only some of the petty officers (foremen and senior ratings) were under contract to Anglo-Saxon Petroleum, the remainder of crew members in any ship's complement were recruited from local port 'pools' (somewhat similar to the American convention of hiring halls). These local crews were diluted by personnel from other ports whenever sickness or desertion made replacements necessary as the voyage progressed. However, basically, they were mostly from one part of the country. In seafaring parlance they were referred to as 'crowds'. Therefore a Liverpool crew was referred to as a Liverpool crowd, or even more deeply into the vernacular as a 'Scouse crowd', London: Cockney crowd; Tyne: Geordie crowd; Cardiff/Swansea: Taff crowd and so on. As deck officers we had our preferences! For instance a Falmouth or Plymouth crowd was considered a good choice, whereas a Byker crowd from the Tyne presaged problems! A Glasgow crowd could make life very difficult, a mixed crowd from Belfast and Dublin nigh impossible! These are, of course, very broad generalizations. Because of Anglo-Saxon's limited history in the employment of

British crews, having been employers exclusively of Chinese crews until the outbreak of World War 2, there was little identification among British seamen with Anglo-Sax (as it was known, colloquially). The cream of the crop went to the better cargo and liner companies, the remainder of the best, to established British crewed tramp companies. We in tankers often had to 'do' with the less desirable characters that abounded in the ports around the UK. The National Union of Seamen was a strong influence upon our work forces, sometimes for the good, sometimes not. The concept of a good day's work for a good day's pay, was not one that many ratings espoused! Furthermore, work in port, such as taking stores or painting the hull, was for the birds! One did not have the King's or Queen's Regulations to back up discipline - as the armed forces enjoyed. The source of discipline was the 'logbook'. A miscreant was logged for misdemeanours, and, if appropriate, fined. Most considered the penalty to be worth the crime, like taking a day off in port and getting legless or having a fight with another 'crowd' (a huge source of enjoyment in foreign parts!). A ship often sailed in a state of jeopardy, with half the crowd stoned out of their minds! Nothing could be done about it until the queue outside the Master's cabin, the day after leaving port, indicated the level of revelry that they had been enjoyed! Mind you, the disciplinary system was not entirely toothless. A second offence in any one of the categories occasioned a double fine. Some of the captains were literally masters at the art of interpretation of regulations, weaving elaborate webs of fines and forfeitures! Then there was the ineffectual master who was unable to exercise discipline through indifference, fear or serious character defect! So much depended upon this man. Captain Robson was a pleasure to behold, often reducing offenders to abject misery! The final sanction was the 'DR'! This instrument of punishment simply meant that should a seaman's behaviour warrant it, the master entered these two dreaded letters in the line at the end of a seaman's engagement entry in his discharge book (his record of employment). Once entered, and particularly if it was a double DR (for ability and conduct), the guy was doomed to uncertain future employment aboard any ship. What did these letters mean, you ask? Just " Decline to Report"! White crews were hell-bent on getting as much overtime as possible, and the success of a maintenance programme often depended upon the level of overtime they received. No overtime, no bloody work. They were experts at moving a paint brush within a limited area, or chipping a single square of rusted steel with remarkable diligence - getting nowhere! Boy! Did I become an authority on the subject of 'swinging the lead'! But, Hey! In an emergency, they were the tops! The Brits always rose to the challenge! They had a marvellous sense of humour, which was conspicuously absent with Chinese crews. There were swings and roundabouts, and whatever you had been sent, you had to put up with, often for a year or more! Matters improved out of all recognition when Shell established their own reservoir of men, but at the time I'm describing, one had difficulties!

Ah! Drydock in Cardiff! Joan stayed with an aunt in the city so I was able to see her every day for the best part of a month in April/May 1951! I was even able to have my parents down to the ship for a meal. After a winter on the American eastern seaboard, the ship looked more than a little grotty, so the image I would have wished my parents to witness wasn't what I would have hoped for! Nevertheless, they were, surprisingly, quite impressed. Joan was able to spend the days on board. In the evenings we would go out 'on the town', so we had a great time. Joan had graduated in 1950 but was still attending Aberystwyth University as a teacher training student and was due to finish her education at the end of the academic year in June.

I had formed a firm, lifelong friendship with the Second Mate, one John Jordan. He is the second of the 'special' people with whom I sailed. He had served his time (another term for apprenticeship) with Clan Line - a prestigious company that sailed to South Africa and India, then as part of his career development, transferred to Anglo-Saxon. He was a dogged little fellow which had earned him the sobriquet of 'Perseverance' Jordan, in turn this had been shortened to 'Percy'! Just a year older than myself, we got along famously. I think he envied my relationship with Joan, the stability it gave me, to the extent that when he next went home on leave he started dating her best friend, June! Although, this friendship didn't last long, it was an indication of our regard for one another. He stayed with Anglo-Saxon a little while longer, serving as Chief Officer and then moved to General Steam Navigation, the prime coastal company. Of course there was method in this madness! His aim was to become a River Thames pilot and he needed the coastal experience to qualify, which was fulfilled by this last career move. We met on numerous occasions in later life, he married a teacher named Pauline and produced a fine brood of sons. Sad to say, he died recently.

We sailed from Cardiff in the second week of May with a Taff crowd. As far as I can remember there were no interesting events to record on the ensuing voyage to Punta Cardon, nor on the loaded trip to Rotterdam. I 'paid-off' there, on the 7th June 1951, having completed fourteen and a half months' service between the two ships, Dromus and Thallepus.

I went home for a seventy three day furlough, during which time I attended a Merchant Navy Defence Course in London in mid July. I was fortunate to visit the Festival of Britain whilst there. In those dreary post -war days, the Festival was an expression of national hope - sorely needed at this weary time in the country's history. Another odd fact! One of my fellow students at the MNDC course was a chap called Warwick, who later became a famous master of the QE II. Again, Joan and I had a wonderful summer together, she had secured a teaching post in Liverpool and I learned that I was to be promoted to Second Mate! We were brimming with confidence and the sheer happiness of two young people in love! At about this time Joan and I made a pact that if our relationship was to prosper we had to be true to one another. During the following thirty three years of seafaring, through thick and thin, we kept our promise to each other, thus forging a bond that sustained us in what was, in difficult seafaring constraints, a firm, happy courtship and marriage. A great source of family pride during that summer was that Tom, my brother, obtained his Army commission following the passing out ceremony at the Royal Military Academy at Sandhurst to which Joan, my parents and I were privileged to attend. He was appointed to The East Yorkshire Regiment, an infantry regiment whose HQ was at Beverley.

My first ship as navigator, for that is the prime function of a Second Mate, was my second 'N' class ship, Nassarius, Captain John Carmichael in command. I joined her in Falmouth at the end of August 1951, at the same time as Joan went to Liverpool to start her first teaching job. It's worthy of note at this point to mention that Joan shared digs with one of her university friends, one Gill Thomas, who was romantically involved with George Holeyman a second mate serving with PSNC (Pacific Steam Navigation Company) trading to the west coast of South America . Both girls subsequently rented a flat jointly in Penny Lane (before it became famous!) which was to be so important to both George and myself in the following years. More of that, later.

A few words about the allotted duties a junior officer was responsible for in Anglo-Saxon. As Third Mate you cared for the maintenance of lifeboat equipment, pyrotechnics, the signalling outfit together with the upkeep of all flags. A second mate, as navigator, was responsible for the correction of all charts, the maintenance of navigational equipment, the daily winding of chronometers and the weekly winding of all the ship's clocks. Additionally he was responsible for all fire-fighting equipment outside the Engine Room. These were extra mural activities. Both officers' prime function was watch keeping, at sea and in port, traditionally the third mate kept the eight to twelve watch, the second mate the twelve to four. The remaining watch, the four to eight, was the mate's responsibility. Most enthusiastic officers put in daily periods of extra hours called 'field days' during which they tended their various responsibilities.

We sailed from Falmouth on 27th August 1951 manned with a British crew, a West Country crowd, who were quite amenable and set the scene for what proved an enjoyable ten months away from the United Kingdom. Although the normal practice was that one sailed in a rank below one's certificate (as indicated earlier), I was quite ready and able to take on the new work. In fact I relished the job! Navigation is an inexact science, or, as some would have it - a precise art. There are two distinct areas to navigation: coastal and deep-sea. Whilst coasting one can normally obtain accurate positions every twenty minutes and make the necessary adjustments to ensure safe passage. Out of sight of land, the sextant was the only instrument that one used (occasionally in conjunction with the sounding machine) but so much depended upon variables: visibility, cloud cover, horizon clarity, ship movement, correct time and above all the skill of the navigator himself. Given good conditions, the master would be assured of a minimum of three accurate positions each day: morning and evening observations at twilight, using the stars, and a noon position using the sun. Later, satellite navigation, Loran and Decca, became the modern navigational systems. At the time I'm relating, however, the only modern item of navigation equipment Nassarius possessed was a gyro compass, and very much appreciated at that.

We had orders to proceed to San Lorenzo in Lake Maracaibo, to load crude oil for Curaçao. Recently, the approach channel to the lake had been dredged to take bigger ships (if you recall, this trade had been operated by mosquito tankers in earlier years). It wasn't an easy approach, and, until we had experience it was a difficult task to reach the pilot station at the entrance to the lake. Anyway, we made three trips, San Lorenzo to Curaçao, before beginning the next phase of our trading.

After the discharge of our final San Lorenzo cargo of crude oil at Curaçao, we back loaded a full cargo of black oils (fuel oil and diesel oil) for Sydney, Australia. This was new territory for me and the immediate future was very exciting indeed! To begin with we were to transit the Panama Canal which was one of life's more impressive experiences, if for no other reason than it exemplified man's huge achievement in conquering massive natural barriers! Truly, one of the wonders of modern times. However, I'm jumping ahead. We sailed from Curaçao on the last day of September 1951, arriving at the Caribbean end of the Panama Canal at Cristobal on 3rd October, clearing the Canal at Balboa on the Pacific side, a day later.

Undoubtedly, the Panama Canal is the Queen of all canals! I have passed through a number of canals in my lifetime (Suez, Manchester and Kiel come to mind) but none of them compare with this one. Its history and governance are well recorded, so I'll content myself with a brief description of the physical nature of the enterprise. The sea level part of the canal on the Caribbean side runs for six and a half miles from the Cristobal breakwater head to the Gatun Locks. This set of three locks raises the ship eighty five feet to the level of Gatun Lake (artificially created by damming the River Chagres and forming one of the largest man-made bodies of water in the world, spanning more than 163 square miles). The canal construction was finished in 1914 and substantially nothing new has been added since that year, in fact, when Nassarius transited in 1951, the 'mules' (electric tow trams which control the movement of ships through the lock system, by dint of self reeling towing wires on each mule) were original units built in 1913! They were subsequently replaced with new mules of Japanese manufacture. The ship then navigates the lake via a buoyed channel for some twenty three miles to Gaillard Cut - a passage blasted out of solid rock, eight miles long (as the reader will appreciate, this section of the canal comprised the principal excavation task encountered in the project's construction). At the south end of the Cut, the ship enters a series of three locks, the first, at Pedro Miguel Locks, thence after a short move through Miraflores Lake she is lowered to sea level by two locks at Miraflores Locks (these locks have the highest lock gates in the system, because of the tidal variations on the Pacific side), thereafter out to the Pacific via a buoyed channel through Balboa.

The Pacific Ocean lived up to its name! We had a peerless passage to Sydney, seas calm, weather beautiful - a mate's dream voyage with ideal conditions for deck maintenance. We had a happy crowd and the officers got along well so it was a contented thirty three days. According to date, we took thirty four days but we 'lost' a day crossing the International Date Line. This 'loss' or 'gain' of a day (depending on whether the ship was voyaging westwards or eastwards) attained major significance to the crowd. They wanted the crossing to take place on a weekday going west and on the week-end going east and I'll leave you to work that one out! We had one quite exciting event en route, we called off Pitcairn Island! Populated by descendants of the mutinous crew of HMS Bounty and their Polynesian womenfolk, the island had become an outpost for the Seventh Day Adventists. No ship can berth at Pitcairn because of the sheer sides to the island so any meeting with the inhabitants has to be at sea. I well remember the sight of the long boats pulling away from the coast, all by oar power, and skilfully making the short but rough journey to Nassarius. Now all this was against company policy, the call at Pitcairn was very much off the record, so the stoppage was recorded as one for ERP (Engine Room Purposes!). However, it afforded one of those rare delights that occasionally come the way of seafarers! To this day I have a box (ostensibly made from the timbers of Bounty - that's what I tell folk!) in the shape of a book, inscribed by one Vernon Young a descendant of Edward Young of HMS Bounty. Others had artifacts from people with names like Christian et al. We took their mail for posting at Sydney and supplied them with food and paint items that the islanders had difficulty in obtaining. The greatest delight was to hear the oarsmen singing hymns, beautifully, in thanks, as they pulled away from the ship to go back home - a very moving few moments.

There was something very satisfying for this young navigator to see the lights of Sydney right ahead, on schedule, on the morning of the 7th November 1951! Whenever a ship leaves port bound for wherever the destination may be, an ETA (estimated time of arrival) is sent by radio to charterers, owners and the agent at the destination port. Should this estimate change radically, a new ETA would be sent to the same recipients. In the last few days of the voyage, more precise estimates are transmitted on a daily basis until the ship reaches the range of harbour radio when control would be assumed by the harbour authority. Pilots and tugs are retained by the agent in timely manner for the ship's arrival so that the operation of entering harbour and berthing is carried out smoothly and efficiently. Traversing the Pacific (or any large ocean), a master will seek the most economic voyage plan. The shortest distance between any two points is not a straight line! Rather it is a great circle - a track that would be a straight line on a globe, but not on a flat chart. The route from Panama to Sydney embraced two great circles (a composite course) to avoid island groups. Estimating passage time on such a long voyage is not the easiest task demanded of an embryo Magellan, so it was particularly pleasurable for me to have calculated our ETA, leaving Panama, to within a few hours of our actual arrival. One of those happy flukes!

On a personal note. A trans-Pacific voyage gives one plenty of time for reflection. As Second Mate I kept the twelve to four watch, known as the afternoon watch during daylight and the middle watch during the early morning hours (also referred to as the graveyard watch!). One was left, very much, to one's own devices as the Old Man (the universal term for the Captain or Master) was asleep during both watches. As already indicated, the weather was beautiful with crystal clear tropical night skies, which made a young man's mind turn to romance and courtship. Joan and I wrote to each other every possible day and I developed the notion that she and I should marry when I was due to arrive back in the UK, sometime in 1952. So it was, I proposed to her on that long haul across the world's biggest ocean. She accepted. I arranged for my mother to accompany her in the purchase of an engagement ring - I quoted a limit on what I thought I could afford, but my mother arbitrarily upped the amount!! The major and most successful decision I ever made! She was forever my tower of strength and my dearest friend, a lady who deserved and received my lifelong devotion.

I loved Sydney! I went there on many occasions during my career and always enjoyed my visits. A lot had to do with the nature of the Australian. A spade (pronounced 'spide'!) was a spade and that was that! Great people to work with, I thought then and throughout my later life. The passage through Sydney harbour was always an experience, boarding the pilot outside the Port Jackson heads, usually in a heavy swell, then the passage into harbour when, particularly at week-ends, one had to contend with myriads of small craft. Before the construction of the Opera House, the outstanding sight was Sydney Bridge, which all Shell ships passed under en route to Gore Bay, the Shell installation. The ship also passed close to the Governor General's residence, I remember seeing General Slim and his lady waving to us as we proceeded past on one occasion. The discharge operation at Sydney passed off without incident, we were alongside for three days, which afforded the opportunity for everyone to have a run ashore, so we sailed a happy ship on the 10th November for Miri in Sarawak.

During my time aboard Nassarius we made a round-the-world voyage. I will be describing ports in some detail, because for some, the particulars will be of interest. However, should the reader find the minutia wearying reading, my later accounts will not be as elaborate!

The passage to Sarawak took us up Australia's eastern seaboard. We boarded a pilot at Sydney to take us through the Great Barrier Reef - this was an optional but wise choice, in our case it was company policy to do so, safety being the watchword. The section of the coastal passage from Sydney north to the Barrier Reef's southern approach was conducted by the ship's navigators as a normal passage, thereafter from Cape Manifold the routing through the reefs was under the guidance of the Reef pilot. A really spectacular experience! Wonderful sandy beached islands and colourful reefs unmistakable in the crystal clear water inside the barrier. We disembarked the pilot at Thursday Island in the Torres Strait, north of Australia's northernmost point, Cape York.

To reach Sarawak we had to set courses through the Arafura and Flores seas, passing Timor, Java and the south coast of Borneo, thence into the South China Sea to our destination. This was the beginning of a period of trading 'out east' at it was referred to within the Fleet. Basically this meant that we loaded and discharged in an area controlled by Singapore (the Shell organization's eastern HQ). For we officers, or 'staff' as the company preferred to call us, this meant an addition to our pay, known as the Eastern Bonus. It actually applied in the area east of Suez and west of Panama, so we had been paid the bonus since the 4th October - which made for even happier spirits! In total we were to be 'out east' for seven months. Sarawak, together with Sabah to the north, comprised the area known as Eastern Malaysia (with the independent Sultanate of Brunei taking up a small chunk of land in the middle) situated on the western side of Borneo is encompassed by the Indonesian province of Kalimantan. Miri, with its surrounding oil fields, was the main Shell crude oil source in the Far East. Ships were berthed at sea moorings, using a combination of anchors and mooring buoys (large flat cylindrical buoys with big hooks to take the ships' hawsers). They were uncomfortable berths in that weather could become so bad that it was occasionally necessary to quit a berth to await moderation in conditions. Berthing in an open roadstead is one of the more dangerous operations carried out in tankers, sea movement often causing ships' hawsers to part during the operation, occasionally causing injury to the seamen, decapitation and loss of limbs among some of the perils. We loaded our first cargo of Miri crude for Pulo Sambu, an island off Singapore but under Indonesian jurisdiction. In those days, crewmen could go to Singapore by liberty launch, so we continued to have a happy ship! We shifted ship (a term to describe the movement of a ship, within port limits, from 'A' to 'B') to Tanjong Uban, a Caltex installation in the same area, to load a cargo of fuels for Auckland in North Island, New Zealand. My memory fails me as I try to recall the route we took, suffice to say we arrived safely at Auckland on Boxing Day 1951 and that we sailed on New Year's Eve! A Christmas/New Year really messed up you might think? Not so, in fact. It was always far better to celebrate this particular week of joyous festivities at sea! British crews would probably, collectively, become so inebriated that it would be almost impossible to efficiently operate a ship during these merry days in port! One had to be realistic in these matters!

Our next loading port was an obscure crude oil installation at a place called Sorong (aka Serong) in what is now West Irian, then Dutch New Guinea. This really was a primitive outpost with just the bare essentials to enable a tanker to load a cargo. Tropical forest of the densest type fringed the jetty area. The locals were very ethnic in appearance - Melanesians, dark skinned with negroid features presenting one of world's most fearsome looking people! However, they were of a gentle disposition with huge, infectious smiles. We loaded in pretty good time for those days, less than a day alongside, then off to Yokohama - port of every sailor's dreams! It was rumoured that the ladies of Yokohama certainly knew how to entertain gentlemen of a seafaring persuasion! In the event, Nassarius spent five days at Yokohama, I seem to recall that there was difficulty in discharging the cargo because of its high viscosity and the ambient below- zero temperature in Japan in late January. The staff and crew had a marvellous time! These were days prior to the Japanese economic 'miracle', so one bought souvenirs or china. I purchased a wooden crate containing an 80 piece dinner service to start one side of our forthcoming married life in suitable manner! (it actually lasted us for yonks - seafaring slang for an awfully long time!). There will be another story associated with this crate a little later. I stowed the box in the Master Gyro Room well lashed and tommed-off (another sea expression for wedging something to prevent movement in a seaway) as the gyro room was my domain, and kept locked by me. Inevitably, a host of our jolly-jacks left with unwanted souvenirs which appeared within the next week!

Our next loading port was Miri where we loaded for Balik Papan, located in East Kalimantan, on the eastern Borneo seaboard. This was Indonesia's second largest Shell refinery where mostly 'local' crudes were processed. The name Balik Papan became something of a by-word during wartime in the UK, because one of Britain's comedians, possibly Kenneth Horne, used to refer to the place as 'Belik Peparn' in a fruity English voice! At B.P. we back-loaded for Surabaya on the northern coast of Java, a mere two day voyage. Surabaya was one of Indonesia's more sophisticated cities. Very influenced in style by the former colonial masters, the Dutch, who seemed to have a genius for impacting the local architecture with the best of Holland's design charm. The Dutch influence upon these parts was not confined to architecture alone! The legacy of colonialism was very evident in this part of Java, in the union of the Dutch man and the Malay woman, producing some striking looking people, particularly women!

Whilst serving aboard Nassarius, I became very friendly with another man of my age. His name was Matthew Brown Gillespie, as you would expect, a Scot! (locally known, in Greenock as Matther Brune). Although my age, he was sailing as Junior Engineer, later becoming Second Engineer before leaving Shell some years later. Anyway, Matthew was the finest of men. He had 'served his time' at Kincaid's an engine building works at Greenock and had been called-up for national service at the end of his apprenticeship. He served with the Palestine Police Force for two years or more in the mounted division. Matthew had very definite views as to the rights and wrongs in the conflict between Arab and Jew, during the pre-independence struggle. This young man had been taught survival techniques and crowd control methods which served him well during the many fracas he became involved in during his term in Palestine, and his experience was shortly to prove crucial to a number of us. One of the saddest things he was obliged to do was to shoot his horse before he left the service in Palestine. There were even sadder things for him to face when he returned to Britain. Matthew was a good looking man, and, as is usually the case, married an outstandingly beautiful girl. Anyway, to shorten the story, she developed a fatal disease soon after his return from Palestine. Apparently he nursed her for many months, such was his love for her, he wouldn't allow anyone else to care for her in her extremity. She died of uraemia in the end. Matthew locked himself in the house with her body for days, not allowing anyone near, such was his distraction. Eventually, exhaustion came to his rescue and the poor girl was interred. Some time later, in an effort to assuage his grief, he joined Nassarius and I became his best friend during that time we sailed with one another. Life is stranger than fiction! Eighteen years later we met again. I was master of a ship docking at Greenock and Matthew was the engine room repair foreman at Scott Lithgow's Yard. Well, for all that I have written about our friendship, and the fact that he saved my life, we were virtual strangers, unable to revive our relationship - which saddened me enormously. The reasons were quite apparent: he had re-married which made reference to his life prior to having met this lady, difficult; secondly, and probably more importantly, he had taken up Free Masonry with great zeal and was at a complete loss to understand my disinterest in that organization, so much so that he found a common ground too difficult to establish. For a short time he was one of my greatest friends, we'll just have to leave it like that. Should he ever read this, he'll learn of my deep regret.

We returned to B.P. having loaded some stock at Surabaya for processing. On completion of discharging we went up the east coast of Borneo into the Celebes Sea to Tarakan, another of those jungly remote outposts to load a cargo of heavy crude for processing at B.P. This area was full of interesting fauna. Chief among them were the orangutans (Malay for 'wild man of the woods'). At about this time, legend had it that an Anglo-Saxon ship had transported one of these lovable apes from Borneo to Sydney, at the request of the Sydney Zoo . Apparently, the young fellow was in an airy cage on the Old Man's deck and was cared for by him during the voyage south. The cage was lifted off at Sydney with a distraught ape, quite beside himself with grief at losing his friend the Captain. The legend continues, the ship made a return visit to Sydney, whereupon an urgent plea was made by the Zoo for the captain to visit his hairy friend, apparently the reunion was so touching, hardened men wept! The orangutan prospered thereafter. Other creatures were huge pythons whose favoured menu included orangutans and any person who might stray into their territory. Perhaps the worst were the kraits, small deadly snakes whose bite presaged an early demise unless attended to immediately. Don't mention insects!

We returned to B.P. to discharge our Tarakan crude and loaded light fuels for Ilo Ilo on the Philippine island of Panay. In this port I nearly met my nemesis. Nassarius discharged her cargo into barges whilst lying at anchor, a relatively small quantity had to be dropped off, prior to proceeding to Manila. A few of us went ashore by liberty boat to the local cinema on the day we arrived. I went with Matthew and after the film met up with the Chief Engineer and his wife. We were strolling back to the liberty boat departure berth when we were set upon by a bunch of men armed with wicked looking knives and brandished pistols! I was almost petrified with fear, but survival is man's prime instinct and I had to fight the fight of my life! We were, at least Matthew and I were, bigger than our assailants - the Chief was diminutive! His wife, a Scot of enormous courage, joined in the fray with passionate Border Reiver zeal! However it was Matthew with his training and bravery who saved us all. He became a fighting machine, a one man squad in fact, with my somewhat inept imitation of Sugar Ray Robinson, we managed to scramble aboard our launch, having thrown three of the wharf rats into the drink, and get away with no more than a few cuts and bruises and severely damaged egos!!

From Ilo Ilo we went to Manila to complete discharge. I didn't go ashore after my traumatic experience and was quite content to reflect upon my good fortune and to lick my psychological wounds! We were two days at Manila before leaving, once more, for Miri. We arrived at Miri on the March 18th 1952, sailing four days later, I suspect we had some berth delay prior to loading. We left Miri bound for Japan once again with great expectation amongst the crowd! This time we went to Shimotsu near Wakayama, a delightful little town in the orthodox Japanese style of picture book buildings with small archetypal foot bridges over streams. The place seemed to be so quiet and tranquil until it was realized that a ship was in port! The town opened up like a blossom - bars were lit, restaurants opened and the ladies appeared in traditional costume, ready to entertain as only the Japanese girls know how. Everyone enjoyed themselves enormously!

We returned to Miri to load for Singapore - Pulo Sambu. On completion of discharge we went to Pladju, the location of Shell's major oil port in the Far East, situated up the Palembang River, near Palembang itself. This was the first, of what were to be, 92 visits to Pladju in my career! I don't know if this is a record, but my word, it was almost my home port in the following decade! Nassarius could only load a part cargo because of draft restrictions at the river bar, so we completed loading at Balik Papan. We loaded the strangest of cargoes: slack wax and waxy residue, both of which had to be heated to prevent solidification! Our destination was Stanlow and Rotterdam.

We left Balik Papan on 29th April 1952 on what was to be my last voyage as a single man! It took us until mid June to complete the delivery of this cargo at Rotterdam. As already written we went to

Stanlow first, thus completing our voyage around the world. However my thoughts were with a young teacher in Liverpool and not with my first global feat of navigation. Joan came aboard at Stanlow and we went to her flat in Penny Lane. We hadn't seen one another for ten months, so there was a lot to catch up on. Fortunately we had kept up a regular and full correspondence, so we knew most of what had happened in that time. Of course, it was the face to face meeting and the inevitable shyness that had to be experienced and absorbed. Luckily, we had the knack of picking up where we had left off, so we were soon laughing and giggling and I had my first look at her engagement ring just weeks before we were married!

This may seem almost an aberration when I write about cockroaches! In the seven years that I had been seafaring, these creatures had been my shipmates on every ship except the T2, Thallepus. Every other ship had been infested with the little beggars, effective control was a little way off in 1952, so one lived alongside them - never in harmony! The purpose of this reference is that I mentioned earlier that I had stowed my crate of china in the Gyro Room some months earlier, during which time our little friends had taken up residence within the straw packing in the crate! Joan and I, plus china, travelled from the ship to her flat by taxi arriving there in the evening. We had a few drinks with friends then had an early night, because both Joan and her flatmate had to teach the following morning. I said I would unpack the china whilst they were working! I guess you know what comes next! Hundreds of cockroaches scurried out of the crate in all directions, to my impotent horror! Coward that I was I didn't leave a note explaining the appalling truth! I went back to Stanlow before the girls returned, I had left the china in washed and dried piles with the packing neatly in the crate and done a bunk. Later Joan told me of her mystification whilst bathing that night at seeing a few 'beetles' running along the edge of the bath! They didn't survive, thankfully for me, as it was to be our first married home in the autumn!

I wrote earlier, in Chapter One, of the defining point in my life when I met Joan. Our marriage in the July of 1952, was undoubtedly another. The whole period, from leaving Nassarius in mid-June until I joined my next ship at the end of January 1953, was one of unparalleled happiness for me - and I suspect for her too! Nearly seven and a half months together, never apart for more than a few hours - it was such a contented time, and one, which I'm convinced established our marriage on a good foundation. As I've written, Joan was teaching, and I arrived a month before she started her summer vacation, so was able to help with the last-minute arrangements for our wedding and honeymoon whilst she completed her term's work. We honeymooned for a week in St.Ives in Cornwall in what was idyllic weather - hot, peerless days and wonderful food (austerity still existed in Britain, food rationing in force). After the end of Joan's school holiday, we commenced our married life proper in her flat in Penny Lane. Gill, Joan's flatmate, soon married George Holeyman (I was 'best man' at their wedding in New Quay) and so we started sharing the flat with the other couple. One might be tempted to think that such an arrangement would be a recipe for disaster! Not so! We all got along famously and managed to share equitably whilst preserving our privacy.

I went to the Liverpool Technical College to study for my First Mate's Certificate almost as soon as we arrived back . Minor logistical difficulties arose in providing myself with adequate studying facilities in the already crowded flat! Compromise was the order of the day! I used the top of the gas stove on top of our bed as a table, which gave me quiet and allowed the others to carry on with their normal activities. George was not about to go back to sea, so he resigned from PSNC and took relieving work in Liverpool Docks with any cargo ship that needed temporary replacements. Sometimes we would both take a day off, go into the City and have a good day's drinking, perhaps take in a movie or a slap-up meal, and return blissfully lighthearted to the flat to be greeted with heavy silence and stony faces from our hard-working spouses, who, for some reason could find little sympathy for our conduct! Still we had marvellous week-ends! Dancing at the Tower Ballroom in Birkenhead, or a night out in Liverpool itself - ever a great city for fun and entertainment. Were we happy, or were we happy? Of course there was the worry of examinations, but fortunately I succeeded in passing and obtaining my ticket in mid-December. That made for a happy Christmas back home in South Wales, shared between our parents' homes in Ebbw Vale and Merthyr Tydfil. Joan helped me enormously when I was studying for exams, she would test me and support me whenever things became difficult - it was so helpful to have a girl who understood the stress of the process,

76

having done so much herself. I have already written of the high standard demanded in all board of Trade examinations, one had to achieve a minimum pass mark of 70% in every subject and not just an overall percentage of seventy. Naturally, for the First Mate's Certificate of Competency (to give it its full name!), one had additional subjects to contend with, cargo work, meteorology and a more substantive paper on ship's construction and stability. Obviously, in the overall picture of the industry, tankermen were in a minority so that the emphasis was always on dry cargo work and dry cargo ship construction and stability. One had to work ever harder to overcome one's inexperience in this field. Practically all the examiners were from cargo ship backgrounds and tended to deal with situations which arose aboard that type of vessel. One had five three hour written papers at the beginning of examination week followed by the dreaded two hour oral grilling during the latter part of that week. Fortunately one had the result at the end of the week. If one failed, one had to wait a minimum of a month before re-sitting. If, in the opinion of the examiner, one failed badly, one was given 'sea-time'- this meant that one had to back to sea, serve the additional time that had been allotted and go through the whole procedure again! It was, frankly, nerve racking and the cause of desperation with the less fortunate, one's career was 'suspended' until success was achieved. We returned to Liverpool in the New Year where we had three more weeks together before I joined Tenagodus at Heysham.

Our first parting was very difficult, it seemed as if the world had ended - we had become so close to one another. However, such was my wife's calibre, we overcame and got on with our lives. I was only aboard Tenagodus for little more than a month, during which time I went to Punta Cardon, Brooklyn, Mamonal and Curaçao and was there transferred to Trigonosemus (now there's a name to conjure with!). Such an event was not unusual, personnel were shuffled about from ship to ship according to need. I wasn't particularly pleased with the transfer, because the reputation of the Master aboard Trigonosemus was legendary! Again I was aboard this new ship for only twelve days! From Curaçao we went to Las Palmas in the Canary Islands where I paid-off with appendicitis. I was a lucky man. There were more shipboard deaths from this medical condition, at this time and historically, than from any other cause - such was the danger this disorder presented to the sailor, particularly young men in their twenties. Before I go further, I should add, that in this very short stay aboard Trigonosemus, I learned so much from Captain Waters (the man whose reputation was so unjustifiably maligned) about the necessity for navigational precision that his influence stayed with me throughout the remainder of my career. He was an absolute stickler for accuracy in every aspect of navigation, it was salutary experience! I found, in fact, previous to this experience and later in my life that those men with 'reputations' often enough gained their renown because they were efficient and competent - which didn't always go down well with some of my brethren!

I was hospitalized in the Queen Victoria Hospital at Las Palmas, a British operated establishment - a small cottage hospital with modest facilities. My condition was acute so the surgeon operated upon me at first light. The operating theatre had one wall constructed with glass bricks, facing east, so that the room was well lit in the morning. I had the surprise of my life to learn that my appendix was to be removed with the aid of a 'local' anaesthetic as there were no means of administering general anaesthesia. I was less than thrilled at the prospect! I had a lumbar injection which paralysed the lower regions of my body so no pain was felt south of the injection! However I saw the whole thing! Because the light was sufficient from the glass wall, the operating table light was switched off. The reflective surface of the light bowl consisted of a mosaic of mirrors, so I concentrated on one of these mirrors and witnessed the whole procedure! The surgeon, a Spaniard, noticed my interest and promptly gave me a close-up of my diseased appendix, a disgusting sight! He murmured something to the effect that I was a lucky man! I was indeed very fortunate, and, until I left the sea, this condition and other abdominal defects in crew members taxed my mind more than any other illnesses I had to contend with as Mate and Master. However, more of that later. My stomach wound healed well but I suffered the most excruciating headaches for many weeks after the operation, the aftermath of the lumbar injection.

I travelled back to the UK aboard 'Llangibby Castle', a Union Castle liner, as a First Class passenger, there being no other accommodation available - junior officers normally travelled as 'tourist class' passengers. This was luxury indeed! Although I had been 'well brought up' I was little match for the array of eating implements and vessels before me when I sat down for my first dinner!

This is the truth, I very nearly drank my finger bowl! I was saved from this ultimate embarrassment by someone, at another table, dipping his fingers into his bowl and rubbing his finger tips together! Callow young man that I was! It was a very restful six days. I left at Tilbury, on my twenty fifth birthday, and went home for three weeks sick leave plus two weeks furlough. In the event, the doctors were somewhat concerned with the residual headaches I was experiencing, they prolonged my stay at home. Naturally, despite the uncomfortable circumstances, Joan and I made the most of this unexpected time together and we lived it to the full!

There's one beautiful ship's name that figured throughout my career - Opalia. I joined the old 'Opalia' at Runcorn on May Day 1953. Joan and I were so lucky, in tanker terms, during these early days of our married life, and our good fortune continued until the end of 1954. Runcorn is a town through which the Manchester Ship Canal passes. After Runcorn, Opalia went up canal to Barton in Manchester to complete discharging her cargo then to Old Trafford to tank clean for dry docking at Birkenhead. The ship was at Birkenhead for three weeks being converted to take over local trading in the Gulf of Suez. I saw Joan each day, we had parties on board and on off-duty nights I was able to go home - it was great!

In the previous paragraph I made reference to local trading in the Gulf of Suez. There were small oilfields situated at Ras Gharib and Hurghada on the western side of the Gulf and the output of crude oil from these fields was processed at a refinery in Suez. Traditionally, Shell had operated this trade and continued to do so when the industry was nationalised by the Egyptian government. The ship, Kellia, which operated the shuttle service between the fields and the refinery had reached the end of her useful life, and was to be replaced by Opalia. On reaching Suez, Opalia had to undergo further conversion, so another three weeks were spent in a dockyard at Suez. At the beginning of July we entered service loading at either Ras Gharib or Hurghada and delivering the cargoes to Suez, this was more of a proving exercise prior to handing over Opalia to the Egyptian staff of Kellia which we did in mid-July. We, in turn, took over Kellia.

Kellia was a really old ship! Not only was she old, she was decrepit and filthy! It was our job to deliver the ship to ship breakers at Barry in South Wales. There was one magnetic compass which was hopelessly incorrect with a madman in command! This guy had been touched by the sun, ably assisted in his efforts to achieve total insanity by huge quantities of scotch whisky, his national beverage. Although the staff of the ship operating the shuttle were Egyptian, the Master was British. So we lost our quiet, efficient and gentlemanly Captain of Opalia for this unpredictable clown. I'll never know, to this day, how we managed to successfully deliver the ship, but, somehow, we did! I was worried sick by having to navigate the old girl to Europe, having to contend with silverfish, bed bugs and millions of the ubiquitous cockroach - including the giant Bombay Charlie, a three inch monster! We had no refrigerators so we ended up eating hard tack and salt pork - a throw back to Nelson's era! Even the galley was coal fired! The main engine was unique - a single acting blast injection Polar Atlas, so there you go! More a bloody nightmare than anything else! Boy! Was I glad when we berthed safely at Barry. Joan came aboard and was well and truly bitten by the bed residents! The madman in charge ordered me to kill the ship's dog, immediately prior to our arrival in Europe. Because of the quarantine regulations in Britain and the fact that carrying a dog was contrary to company regulations, the little mutt had to be put down. I drugged the little guy with laudanum and when he went into a coma I put him in a weighted bag and into the sea - one of the most unpleasant tasks I ever had to perform. I left that ship almost gibbering with relief!

Joan and I left Kellia to travel to Ebbw Vale, where my parents lived. In those days we officers carried huge amounts of luggage in old fashioned trunks and heavy leather suitcases. We went to Newport on the main railway line, transferring to the local 'valley' line to go to Ebbw Vale. It wasn't quite as simple as that, however! Half way up the valley, passengers had to transfer to another platform at a station called Aberbeeg. I had mountains of the stuff so I was assisted by an elderly porter who after having hauled all this baggage across the railway line to the other platform, said in typically South Walian drollery, "Come for the week-end, 'ave you Sir?" I just about collapsed with mirth!

Once more I was home, part of the time in South Wales and the remainder at Liverpool. Gill and Joan resumed teaching in early September, whilst George and I enjoyed ourselves as men of leisure!

We four lived in the upper floor of a semi-detached house in Penny Lane. The owners, Mr and Mrs Sanoff were an elderly Jewish couple of Russian origin who spoke a heavily accented English. Mr Sanoff had served in the Czar's Guards, prior to his emigration to Britain. A dignified and well-meaning pair, who became somewhat exasperated by George's and my occasional boisterous behaviour, in that we would arm-wrestle and sing and generally treat life as something to be enjoyed! Still Mrs Sanoff would produce the most delicious Jewish fish dishes for our enjoyment, so it was a happy relationship, all in all.

My next ship was Nacella. I joined her at Stanlow at the beginning of October 1953 - she was to be my 'home' for the next year. In those days only the Captain and Chief Engineer were allowed to take their wives with them on 'deep sea' voyages, the rest of us were permitted to carry our wives whilst 'coasting' only. We were, in Anglo-Saxon, essentially 'deep sea' sailors. The definition of 'deep sea', in its simplest form, was a ship which traded outside coastal waters and by similar definition, a 'coasting' ship traded exclusively within coastal limits. The difference between the two trades not only affected our conjugal circumstance but also the terms of getting 'our sea-time in'. The latter expression refers to qualifying service for one's next ticket - which in my case was a master's certificate. Nacella spent long periods on the 'coast', so we gained maritally and lost out with 'sea-time'! I, for one, didn't care one whit! I used to see Joan so much - it was a tankerman's dream! From the time I joined we were engaged in carrying feedstocks (partially refined oils) between Stanlow and Thameshaven, occasionally nipping over to Rotterdam to deliver a consignment from one of the British refineries, our first spell was for two months thereafter we went to drydock in Birkenhead until the third week in December. During term time I used to have Joan aboard at week-ends at Stanlow, during half-term she did a round trip to Thameshaven and back, whilst in Birkenhead I lived at home. We were very fortunate indeed! However all good things come to an end, we sailed for the south of France on 20th December - five days before Christmas.

We loaded at Berre and Port de Bouc for Port Sudan on the west side of the Red Sea. What a hell hole that place was! Myriads of highly intelligent flies (who knew how to defy all defensive measures in their quest to torment humans!) and an unusual race of people who covered their hair with camel dung and gloried in the name of fuzzy wuzzies with huge halos of matted hair. Thence to Kuwait to load for the new terminal at the entrance to the Manchester Ship Canal - Eastham Oil Dock. So we were back again! We went back for repairs at Birkenhead and stayed there for another two weeks! What a life! Living at home again, just couldn't believe it! My good luck continued, we left dry dock and traded within the Mersey area for another two weeks (Stanlow/Eastham/Dingle) before loading for Gibraltar. So Joan and I had another two months together, or at least seeing one another frequently. Very little sea time but a wonderfully happy time!

Nacella loaded fuel oil and diesel at Stanlow, leaving during the first week of April 1954 for the bunkering hulks at Gibraltar. These were old ships converted to static hulls anchored permanently, acting as storage tanks for visiting ships requiring bunkers (the term used for fuel for ships). Gibraltar Bay under the edifice of the Rock was one of life's more impressive sights. From Gib to Banias in Syria to load crude oil (pumped from Iraq) for Pauillac, another Shell refinery in western France. Pauillac is situated on the south bank of the River Gironde, adjacent to the Baron de Rothschild's vineyards, where, I understand some of the world's finest vintages are produced. We always said that smoke from the refinery contributed to the wines' excellence! We went across the Atlantic to Puerto de la Cruz in Venezuela and loaded a cargo of crude for Curaçao, back loading for Alexandria in Egypt. A fascinating place Alexandria, with its underwater city within the harbour, its teeming shops and clever traders. Over to Banias once more to load for Hamburg. The jolly ship's agent I referred to earlier, was now reverting to a much more serious person, Germanic traits much to the fore! From Hamburg to Rotterdam to resume Nacella's favoured trade - the inter-transfer of feedstocks between the two British refineries, Thameshaven and Stanlow, loading at Rotterdam first. We arrived back in Thameshaven in mid July and continued this shuttle trade between the Thames and Mersey for the next three months. Dare I say how happy I was? Joan was with me for most of her summer vacation, and when she returned to work, I still used to see her every week-end! I left Nacella on 26th October 1954 at Stanlow, but an hour or so from our home.

Joan and I were so lucky, in tanker terms, during our first two and a half years of marriage - we spent more than half of that time together - that this foundation stood us well in the sterner days ahead.

CHAPTER FIVE

THE WILD BULL AND THE HYACINTH

1955 and part of 1956 encompassed months that were quite different from anything that I had experienced! In fact, the lifestyle was such that I could have been living on another planet altogether! Anyway, I'll begin at the beginning.

In the last chapter I wrote that when I left Nacella, 'home' was but an hour away. I confess my memory failed me, Joan and I were, in fact, homeless! We had decided during 1954 that we would make our future home in Cardiff, Joan consequently resigned from the Liverpool Authority at the end of the summer term and sailed with me until we left the ship in October. During my furlough we found a flat, furnished it and began another phase in our married life. In early January 1955, I was instructed to join the Dutch passenger ship 'Oranje' at Southampton to go to Singapore for my next appointment. This passage took three weeks, via the Suez Canal, Bombay and Colombo. This experience, in itself, was unreal! It was a wonderful way to earn money, travelling in modest luxury (Second Mates were accommodated in Cabin Class, together with any other junior officers, whilst senior officers travelled First Class) but fearfully expensive in that one had to buy one's drinks etc. at top prices. The time aboard Oranje counted as service towards my next furlough, so that was a plus! A tradition had evolved over the years whereby the two Dutch liners that plied the Europe/Singapore trade, Oranje and Willem Ruys, because of scheduling, invariably passed one another in the Red Sea, usually in daylight. The ships passed as close as they safely could, so it was quite a spectacle for passengers aboard both ships! Unfortunately, at some subsequent passage, hydrostatic attraction brought both ships too close and they apparently touched one another - although no major damage was sustained, the practice stopped there and then! This form of travel was standard during the early fifties, until air travel became more universal.

On arrival at Singapore during the late afternoon of 25th January, I was told by the Agent to be ready to join a ship the next morning, as a matter of some urgency. He had no details of the appointment other than that I was to report to the Shell office at 0900 the following morning, complete with baggage. One usually hoped for a few days at Connell House to accustom oneself to the prospect of having to work again and to meet up with friends and fellow officers! One night was all I had this time.

I reported as instructed and entered a world so utterly different from anything I had yet experienced. I was interviewed by the Fleet Manager and was told that I was being promoted to the rank of Chief Officer but would be paid at Second Officer's rate! I was to be seconded to the Shell Company of Singapore to serve on m.s. Seladang one of their 'local' craft. I was told that as I was to be directly employed by a foreign company, I would only be liable for income tax on whatever money I sent home, so this was a consider-able financial inducement - hence the second mate's pay! So began the most colourful period in my entire seagoing career!

Frankly, to use a common expression, I was gob smacked at the promotion and even more so when I saw the 'ship' I was to spend the next fourteen months aboard! Until that day I had been strictly, a 'big ship' man. I write in the context of the 'fifties' when I refer to ship size, when a twelve thousand ton tanker was considered 'big' - even five and eight thousand ton ships were considered so. Later in my career I was to command a ship of three hundred and twenty thousand tons - now that was big! 'Seladang' was a four hundred ton C.H.A.N.T. (Channel, Harbour and Naval Tanker) built expressly for the Normandy invasion in the Second World War. A CHANT's specific function was to carry a composite cargo of petroleum and water to service the invasion fleet (for those who would be interested, petroleum in the centre tanks and water in side saddle tanks). From what I understand these little ships were considered expendable once they had fulfilled their prime function of crossing the English Channel and delivering their cargoes. Many, of course, survived the war and in keeping with the huge surplus of redundant wartime tonnage were sold to commercial interests. Most went to coastal companies such as Everard's and were put into service around the British coast. Shell, in their infinite wisdom, bought two of these craft (plus numerous bigger ships of varying sizes) to trade in the Far East, with another two trading in East Africa, in the Mombasa area.

Seladang is the Malay name for 'a wild bull which will charge at the slightest provocation' (taken from an English/Malay dictionary)! Her sister ship 'Rusa' was also the name of a bull - but one of a less aggressive nature! What misnomers! They looked as though they had been thrown together in a mad naval architect's worst night-mare! Please excuse all these exclamation marks, but I was embarking upon an adventure whose culture shock was one of such a monumental magnitude that the very recollection sends me into a mood of near disbelief!

I joined Seladang at Tanjong Rhu, the small ship harbour situated at the eastern end of Singapore Harbour. There were myriads of junks, coasters and launches bobbing about in the choppy waters like so many sea birds on the surface. There were many strange looking craft, but none so odd as 'my' ship! There she was, flying light, dancing about, twanging her mooring lines in the swell, her gangway moving around like a mad thing. The first thing you noticed was her bow - Meirform, or somesuch spelling - a vertical stem then cut back at a steep angle with strengthening ribs either side. This design was specifically for beaching at Normandy and fortuitously came into its own later! The funnel was a fright, a thin tube at the back of the accommodation block, known as a woodbine. A transom stern, quite unusual in those days plus a trunk deck gave it an almost bizarre appearance - but as with all ugly ducklings, it was love at first sight! After scrambling aboard I made my way to the Mate's cabin ushered by, what I thought was, an eighty year old quartermaster! The cabin was tiny - everything in miniature. None of your polished wood and brass handles, oh no! Painted boxwood bunk, minuscule closet and chest of drawers-cum-desk. The chap I was relieving, George Sutherland by name, with whom I became quite friendly some years later, was palpably delighted to see me - assuring me that serving in the Singapore ships was the way to go to sea. I was somewhat suspicious of his hearty enthusiasm but had all my time cut out in coming to terms with this alien environment. Perhaps the strangest thing, initially, was my introduction to the Master, one Captain Ex (no names, no pack drill!) He was another post war recruit to the company, an ex Royal Navy officer. I found his cabin abaft the wheelhouse and forward of the funnel, a dark gloomy little box singularly lacking in illumination. I knocked on his door, which led directly onto the bridge deck, and was summoned by a fruity voice within which said "Come", fought a battle with a heavy door curtain and gained access to the sanctum. Between trying to accustom my eyes to the dimness and not knowing quite what to expect, I eventually discerned a figure reclining in the far corner, who was obviously the Captain, donned in a beret, sunglasses, sarong and flip-flops and smoking a cheroot! "Welcome aboard, Number One!" said he "Care for a pinkers, Old Chap?", "No thank you, sir", said I. I was totally bewildered by everything! Nearly funked the whole thing, between my complete unpreparedness for the job and these weird characters who manned this ship. George scurried down the gangway as fast as he could, leaving me in a state of near panic, especially as we had to move from our mooring to anchor in the roads and Captain Ex said "O.K. Number One, take her away, will you!". I had never handled a ship before, and here I was expected to manoeuvre this ship through a forest of craft in the approaches to Tanjong Rhu and anchor the thing to boot! Necessity is the mother of invention, it certainly took me along a sharp learning curve that afternoon, I can tell you! Whilst my boss contemplated his navel, supped pinkers (term used aboard ship for the drink, pink gin, which is neat gin slightly coloured by Angostura Bitters) and benignly viewed the world in a soporific daze, I succeeded in doing the job.

We anchored until 31st January, so I had time, after the initial baptism of fire, to take stock. It's wonderful what a couple of good nights' sleep will do! The Shell Company of Singapore fleet was a motley collection of small craft until replacement ships, built in Europe, came on the scene during 1955 and onwards. In addition to the two CHANTS there was a converted wine carrier called 'Guntur', later, two smart jobs arrived: 'Lang' and 'Landak'.

'Meratus' a small cargo ship also appeared. They were manned by Anglo-Saxon personnel, so the staff were all 'family'. Four Brits comprised the complement of officers: Officer-in-Charge (Captain, really a Chief officer), Engineer-in-Charge (uncertificated, older engineers made up this brigade of worthies whose career prospects were zero, but who were excellent practical men), Mate and Second Mate. The ships were crewed in standard Singapore Chinese manner, except that the Deck crew were either geriatric or defective in some way - eyes missing or psychologically unsuited to deep sea work! There were two sailors and two quartermasters under the leadership of an elderly Bosun. The Engine Room was staffed by three very superior beings called ' drivers' - would be engineers in effect, plus one rating. The catering staff was huge for just four officers! A Cook/Steward and two assistant stewards. Subject to our being able to obtain suitable victuals, we lived like fighting cocks!

The accommodation aboard Seladang, was, as already indicated, small and really basic. After all, why should a craft built for one voyage across La Manche be outfitted in a more luxurious way? Our Dining Room was the starboard bridge wing and our Saloon the port bridge wing! We had a large household refrigerator at the rear of the starboard wing, a small dining table and four chairs completed the equipment for our every meal. Across the Wheelhouse, on the port wing, we had a circular rattan table with four easy chairs as our leisure area. The O.I.C.'s cabin was behind the Wheelhouse, between it and the funnel - a dark little box. On the deck below, at main deck level, the E.I.C. had a cabin at the forward end, under the Wheelhouse. The Second Mate's room was on the port side, forward of two galleys, whilst mine was on the starboard side forward of the officers' washroom. The cabins led directly onto the main deck which were constantly awash with either residual rain water or seas charging down the alleyways. If one wore shoes, the soles became detached in a day or so, because one paddled around in inches of water! We therefore wore flip-flops and had 'white foot' instead! The dining area was always open to the elements, so we wore flat caps and plastic macs to afford some protection from the often lashing rain. Company regulations regarding the wearing of uniform were strict and in the deep sea fleet, adhered to. From what I've already written regarding footwear, formal uniform was singularly inappropriate aboard a CHANT. An unofficial 'uniform' was, however, evolved in these small ships and consisted of white 'tee' shirts and blue shorts plus the ubiquitous flip flops as footwear. Casual wear was nothing more than a 'batik' sarong.

It was considered by Management that although in the main fleet, eighteen months' service aboard a deep sea ship was reasonable, such was not the case aboard these little tiddlers. It was thought, rightly, that psychological stress would be too great between four people living, as it were, in each other's pockets, to sustain harmony and efficiency, therefore a limit of six months' service was the accepted norm. Commendably far-sighted! That is until staff shortage threw that theory out of the port hole! I served for fourteen months aboard that little bucket! But I'm jumping ahead.

So much depended upon the personalities of one's fellow officers. I don't think I would have survived long under the command of Captain Ex. He really was the limit! Anyway, fortunately, he was relieved by Captain Why before we quit the Singapore anchorage. A shy, some would say, melancholy man, of great integrity and intellect. He had recently returned to seafaring after some years as a college lecturer and was older than his contemporaries. The Second Mate, Brian Ham was a bright, efficient lad - the first apprentice to win the Company's Sextant Award. Leslie Winwood was the Engineer, very experienced in this particular trade and despite lacking formal qualification, a humorous, interesting chap. So for me it was a pleasant and enjoyable experience to sail with this first team.

Seladang's equipment is worthy of a few words! Firstly, her dimensions: she was 141 feet in length, 27 feet wide with a hull 11 feet deep (excluding the trunk above the main hull) The main engine was a 240 horse power Polar Atlas diesel, the propeller four feet six inches in diameter turning at 450 rpm. There were two winches, only one of which worked. These were driven by 14 horse power single cylinder diesel engines, which in order to start had to have a tube of blotting paper soaked in saltpetre (dried), the end of which was lit by a match, inserted into an ignition port, immediately after which the engine was cranked to start! A shower of sparks, rust and thick black smoke issued from the exhaust whilst the thing coughed into action - not your ideal tanker-safe equipment I suggest! The navigation equipment consisted of a single magnetic compass on the Monkey Island (roof of wheelhouse) with a projector beneath the binnacle for steering. That was it! The steering system was hand-o-matic, i.e. the course the ship steered depended upon the strength of one ancient quartermaster's gnarled old arm to turn the steering wheel, which was behind the helmsman. The steering wheel was a good five feet in diameter so the man steering the ship turned it by means of a single brass handle attached to the wheel rim on the front of the wheel. The reason for the large sized wheel was to improve the power needed to operate the rod and chain system that went from the bridge to the tiller on the poop - there was no powered assistance whatsoever! You could grasp the tiller and stop rudder movement, which I did occasionally to tease the quartermasters! When a ship's deadweight tonnage is quoted it means the tonnage a ship can carry (cargo, water, bunkers and stores). The official dwt for Seladang was 480, however this had to be reduced to 400 because there was a layer of 80 tons of cement on the tank bottoms, to improve the ship's stability. The biggest incongruity of all was the size of the lifeboats! They were the same size as those carried aboard a 12000 ton tanker! During lifeboat drill if one side's boat was swung out before the other, Seladang listed alarmingly! Whereas we had two washrooms on board - officers' and crew's, we also had that seagoing delight known as a thunderbox! This was a small railed and canvas covered platform over the stern with a pear shaped hole cut in the plate and a canvas door, for modesty's sake, at the front of the structure. Although I didn't use the facility myself, they told me there was little in this world to compare with the exquisite pleasure of having a bowel movement therein at sunrise with gentle zephyrs cooling all things! Whenever we had visitors to the ship we swiftly quenched their contemptuous hilarity at our little seagoing oddity when they asked where the toilet was! We directed them to the thunderbox and revelled in their embarrassment! Although we were the laughing stock of the fleet, we occasionally had our own back!

You may have wondered why the title of this chapter includes the word 'hyacinth'. It refers to the water hyacinth - Seladang's bitterest enemy! As I will describe later, the trade was mostly in and out of rivers where the water hyacinth held sway. Apart from clogging cooling water intakes, great rafts of this weed used to cover the river surfaces from bank to bank and as the wild bull entered a raft, the propeller shaft would often grind to a complete stop causing all kinds of mayhem in the Engine Room plus the ship would go out of control to everyone's consternation! One immediately had to put the engine astern (reverse) to unwind the vines off the shaft - which wasn't always accomplished quickly enough - whilst urging the senile quartermaster to ever greater effort to keep the ship on track, mostly with little success! The consequence usually was that of the bull charging broadside down river in a most undignified manner.

Little did I know that when we left Singapore on the last day of January 1955 that I would load 57 cargoes before being relieved of my post at the end of March 1956. Trading was interrupted three times by welcome visits to Singapore, where one's sanity was refreshed and the body rejuvenated by decent meals in civilized restaurants, visits to air conditioned cinemas and hotels where one could forget, temporarily at least, the genuine hardship of service aboard the wild bull!

The Shell Company of Singapore fleet serviced, almost entirely, ports within the Indonesian archipelago. Cargoes were loaded at Pladju in the main, with odd loadings at Surabaya and Pulo Sambu, in my case of the 57 cargoes carried, 55 were taken on board at Pladju. These cargoes, always one of three products, viz., gasoline, kerosene or gasoil, were delivered to either Djambi or Pontianak with the odd visit to Cheribon. As I mentioned earlier, I made 92 visits to Pladju during my career, of which more than half were aboard Seladang. Pladju is situated some forty miles up the River Musi in central Sumatra, near the administrative centre of Palembang. Djambi (or Telanaipura, as it's now called) lies eighty five miles up the River Djambi (or Batang Hari) which is the largest river in Sumatra. Both rivers are relatively close to one another, each running in roughly the same direction from rising in the Padang highlands in the west thence to the sea on the eastern side of the island. The river mouths are a distance of some one hundred miles apart, so whilst on this particular trade Seladang travelled a greater distance within rivers than at sea! Pontianak is smack bang on the Equator on the western edge of Borneo in the province of Kalimantan, about four hundred miles from Pladju. Cheribon is on the northern coast of Java, one hundred miles east of the capital, Djakarta, about four hundred and fifty miles from Pladju. Pretty close quarters stuff for a deep sea man.

90

Truth be known, these CHANTS (Seladang & Rusa) were ill equipped to conduct the trade they were elected to. They were very under powered and consequently often struggled against currents and strong river flows with the greatest difficulty - frankly one had to be thankful for the reliability of the Polar-Atlas main engine in the avoidance of occasional, certain calamity - water hyacinths notwithstanding, that engine stood up to the unfair demands put upon it. The navigational equipment was absolutely basic. There was no communications equipment, other than a domestic radio receiver to listen to weather forecasts - this was the biggest laugh of all, the only credible meteorology service was provided by Singapore Radio, and we were well outside its scope. We sent our ETA's by letter! It was said, that should we be overdue at the port of destination by whatever margin caused alarm, a 'plane would be sent to search for us! Little comfort, I can tell you! Quite seriously, we were occasionally in mortal danger. The ship's structure was a cause for constant concern, the steelwork was paper thin in parts and the recommended repair kit for trunk deck leaks was a saucepan repair outfit! If we were carrying gasoline, at around midday (when the tanks heated up and increased the internal tank pressure) we would inspect the trunk for jets of gasoline cascading like a fountain through pinpoint holes in the trunking, mark them and repair them with the saucepan repair kit on the ballast voyage!

Our environment was quite foreign! Discomfort was the norm. The climate was tropical, our means of countering the heat and humidity, minimal. To illustrate this, whenever we anchored, the main engine was shut down and services were provided by a 'harbour generator'. This was a low powered, single cylinder diesel driven generator which provided about half the voltage that we normally enjoyed - the lights dimmed, fans rotated at half speed and radios faded! So we lay in pools of sweat, barely able to even read because of the lighting - we just waited for the dawn. Everything that moved, bit! Mosquitoes abounded at night, elephant flies plagued us by day. We had a resident rat colony which defied every effort to eliminate them. Worst of all we had the most voracious cockroach population that ever sailed the seven seas! A particular variety, known as Bombay Charlies or Six Wheelers, each about three or four inches in length would eat the hard skin on the soles of our feet, which made them quite sore, particularly if we had 'white foot' during the rainy season.

Other factors affected our peace of mind. In Pontianak, one went ashore at one's risk - the environs of the jetty were infested with kraits, a very venomous small snake. Estuarial crocodiles, the world's biggest saurians ruled the river, Sungai Kapuas, in and around Pontianak together with pythons which consumed the local pet orangutans. Just above the Shell jetty, there was an Indonesian Army camp where one of the soldiers' wives had her arm removed by a crocodile whilst we were berthed there. In total, a hostile environment for Seladang's crew.

Perhaps the most serious problems we encountered were thievery and piracy. Although, fortunately, we did not experience the latter we contended with many incidents of the former. That's not to say that we ignored the prospect of piracy - I suspect if we were ever in the sights of these evil men, the unprepossessing image of Seladang left them totally cold! Armed bands of thieves were a particular hazard at Pladju, where there was a thriving industry in stealing from visiting ships. We were particularly vulnerable because of our small size and, when one considers the examples of senility that manned the watch - enough said! Constant vigilance was the only answer - and whatever happened you never allowed the would be intruders to board the ship. We armed ourselves with axe handles and staves (made from broom sticks and sharpened mast knives) and we patrolled continuously at night. Although we were occasionally boarded we managed to eject the visitors before they could draw their knives. We were fortunate in that none of us was injured during the whole time that I served aboard Seladang. Others were not so fortunate, crew members were occasionally killed by intruders. In passing, I should add that the man who relieved me in March 1956 was later transferred to Landak (a purpose built ship for the trade) and that magnificent little ship was lost with all hands, without trace - possibly taken by pirates.

Seladang could muster a top speed of six knots, our average time between Pladju and the ports I have mentioned was three days. Loading a cargo took only two hours or so after the discharge of ballast, whilst unloading took maybe eight hours plus ballasting time. Whereas we would move the ship in the River Musi at night (because there were illuminated navigational beacons) we anchored for the night in the River Djambi - the Admiralty Sailing Directions describes the navigation of the river as tortuous.

I'm quite sure that with all the negatives I've recounted, the reader would be surprised to learn that I loved the life! Sure I was there too long, and that was the big moan but otherwise, despite all the discomforts, it was an interesting, testing and rewarding time. It was certainly character building and made one know one's strengths and weaknesses. The period of service aboard this little oddity provided me with a wealth of experience which otherwise would have been lost to me. I had to deal with so many personality problems, living as we were, cheek by jowl in the closest proximity. Invaluable understanding, which served me well in the years to come. Innovation, ingenuity, adaptability and a confidence in one's ability to overcome often intractable problems - these were the pay-offs from that ugly little bull!

Seladang was too small for pilotage (a pilot being one who guides a ship in harbour, in river transits or wherever local knowledge is required to safely navigate) therefore the deck officers carried out their own river navigation, berthing and unberthing at the jetties in Djambi and Pontianak (pilots were used to berth at Pladju and at Javanese ports). This was wonderful! We undertook river pilotage and shiphandling that we would not have otherwise had, the experience widened our acquaintance with this particular aspect of our craft. So for we band of navigators, this was heady stuff! It was so enjoyable learning the quirks and pitfalls of river navigation, particularly the Djambi, the ever changing scenery with many interesting sights on the river banks. However the great joy was the sense of responsibility - to which most young men respond readily. As I've already mentioned, the Djambi was described as tortuous in the Admiralty Pilot, so the work was absorbing and occasionally, intense.

Our 'sea' voyages to and from Pladju to Djambi and Cheribon were relatively simple and coastal in nature and warrant no comment. The voyage to Pontianak was, however, quite a different kettle of fish. As I've already indicated Seladang was very low powered and not really suited to rough sea passages. During the wet and windswept North West Monsoon from November to March we encountered the most uncomfortable sea passages across the southern part of the South China Sea between Sumatra and Borneo, that I, at least, ever experienced in my whole seafaring lifetime. The weather was right on the beam, both ways, and to a man we suffered violent seasickness with the abrupt, jerky motion the short violent swell created. We just went to bed when not on watch, work was out of the question. How the drivers managed to keep the main engine going was something we marvelled at! However, this wasn't the most serious aspect of these sea crossings. Navigation was the problem. Invariably, once we left the coast, no celestial navigation was possible because of lowering clouds and dense rain. Very strong cross currents made setting course to our destination extremely difficult. Firstly, the current strength varied; secondly the little bull had sheer vertical sides and was hugely affected by leeway; thirdly, the seas affected the main engine performance, so that often we were down to about three knots. Take all these factors into account and I defy anyone to estimate accurately where we would make landfall! We used to cruise up and down trying to find a landmark that we recognised so that we could establish a position! Remember we had no navigational equipment, such as D/F or a sounding machine, just our trusty sextants, a somewhat erratic chronometer and a wildly unstable magnetic compass. This was really the cutting edge! We always did find our destination, or otherwise I wouldn't be writing this - however there were some very anxious times. Of course we arrived physically exhausted after two days of nausea. I made eighteen such voyages - not all, I hasten to add, during the wet monsoon, but many of them were,

Crossing the 'bar' at Pontianak was an exercise in patience. The silting in the approaches to Klein Kapuas (the river's name) and particularly at the 'bar' was the problem. We would calculate our arrival draft and find on arrival that could barely move across the mud! We would stick poles in the mud and then carefully watch to see if the pole 'moved' down the ship's side, to indicate that we were winning the battle to cross the 'bar', Sometimes there was such a small clearance, we would only take one hundred tons of cargo in order to reduce our draft in order to cross the 'bar'!

The Djambi River passage comprised a journey of 85 miles. For most of the length, between villages, the banks were covered with dense jungle. After a few transits we would recognize individual trees as our personal navigation marks, each of us developing our own methods of negotiating the stretches of river that we passed during our watch on the Bridge. In the wet season the river was in full spate with plenty of depth over shoals and banks. This presented Seladang with the problem of beating the water flow and one bend, Tanjong Oelak Badar, where the river ran down hill, was almost too much for the little craft when the flow was at its strongest. The secret was to find still water, or water that was relatively slow moving. I have known it taking an hour to beat this obstacle, as soon as the ship strayed into a flow that was more powerful than her main engine we would move astern (backwards), try and try again was the answer and eventually we would succeed. Don't forget the rafts of water hyacinth that I've already referred to! Often, we would career down the river broadside on and temporally out of control! In the dry season, we had to be vigilant to avoid going aground - we did this occasionally but usually managed to float off by using the main engine. On one occasion, we really grounded hard - this is because our new Master wouldn't take advice from me and we actually felt the ship lift physically as she hit the shoal. Now there was one feature that Seladang had which was in our favour (bless her! she needs a compliment or two) - she had a strengthened bow which was intended for grounding, so no damage was sustained in the grounding incident. The aftermath was quite dramatic! As soon as we went aground, the river level fell away leaving the ship almost high and dry. The incident happened in the early evening and we had no means of letting anyone know of our predicament. We hailed Indonesian ships that passed to no avail as we became ever drier and more anxious, then during the night the water level began to rise together with our hopes. At dawn there was probably enough water for us to float off the shoal, but unfortunately we were really stuck. It was decided that I would take a lifeboat and endeavour to attach a mooring rope to a friendly tree in order to pull ourselves off the bank. Great in theory! Imagine, if you will, lowering this huge lifeboat with a crew of oarsmen who were either senile or decrepit or both. No engine of course and I suspect that not one of the boat's crew had ever handled an oar. Talk about Fred Karno or the Keystone Cops - had this little episode of seamanship been recorded it would have registered high in the annals of comedic history! We managed to launch the boat, after that we drifted to the bank, hindered rather than helped by my band of stalwarts. The boat grounded smoothly alongside a nice verdant piece of ground, naturally we had a line from the ship with the dual purpose of either running a mooring rope or preventing the loss of the lifeboat. Anyway, there was a suitable tree near our landing so I decided to jump ashore and secure the line to the tree, as a first measure. As I jumped ashore, to my horror, I realized that I was leaping into a swamp! I sank to my waist and was frightened by a monitor lizard nearby - as was the reptile fortunately. The 'lads' managed to pull me out of the bog but regretfully I was minus my trousers! The suction of the foul smelling mud just drew them off my lower body. To cut a long story short, and embarrassment notwithstanding, we triumphed against insuperable odds. We secured the rope around the tree, recovered the lifeboat successfully, pulled the ship off the shoal and proceeded upriver to Djambi! Although I had lost my pants, I gained hugely in satisfaction and confidence, not to mention in experience!

There were many very satisfying experiences to record of my service aboard Seladang. We used to anchor overnight in the Djambi River and usually made for a particular anchorage that was safe and quiet. I used to love to go up to the bow in the gloaming (covered in mosquito repellent!) take in the delightful scent of mimosa and watch families of monkeys play at the water's edge and just commune with Nature and think of my dear ones. Soon I had to retreat to my hot box and stew until dawn. We used to be invited to the manager's home at Pontianak for a rice table - a superb meal of many courses - another highlight. Food was something we had to go searching for - we had basic supplies brought down by the shipchandler at Pladju (usually in bicycle panniers!). Christmas stock was sent out to each of the small craft, so that was OK. In between times we would cadge whatever we could from other Shell ships at Pladju. The delight of eating lamb chops, for example, or British bacon were pleasures to be savoured. Beer and geneva gin were plentiful and cheap - which proved a danger as I became too fond of the stuff, and had to discipline myself half way through my sojourn - and particularly after a visit to Singapore where we used to go a little mad! The sight of wild pigs swimming in a line across the river, refusing to give way to passing ships, was both amusing and charming! Perhaps the greatest benefit was the weekly batch of mail from home - something that used to sustain us far more than anything else.

Cockroaches, silverfish, rats and ants were our shipmates with whom we waged unrelenting battle. Rentokil had brought out a product which we mixed with water and I had the doubtful weekly satisfaction of spraying the accommodation and literally sweeping up buckets full of cockroaches. The silverfish would eat our clothes and the mildew would put pay to the rest! The rats would run across our feet whilst we ate, throwing a fright into us all. We had no hot water, so we bathed for, in my case, for fourteen months in cold water - when eventually I went home I went to a turkish bath to remove the grime from my pores.

Personalities played a greater part in our lives than aboard bigger ships. The first set of comrades, whom I have already described, made for a very enjoyable period. Subtly, the atmosphere changed as members of the staff were replaced. Now you either tolerated conditions aboard these small ships or you hated every day. Ray Smith relieved Brian Ham and detested the life from day one! This did not enhance the atmosphere! Captain Zed superseded Captain Why as Master. I sailed with Captain Zed a number of times and I suppose I got along with him as well as most. Les Winwood was replaced by a Mr.Nevard (I forget his first name) who lacked the wit of his predecessor. Captain Zed, normally a charming urbane chap, didn't really enjoy the primitive conditions and was given to saturnine moods, which were difficult to deal with. Then Ray was relieved by a character who had recently been sequestered to a mental institution! It was bad enough having to deal with the run-of-the-mill quirks of normal human behaviour, it was quite something else having to contend with someone who was quite unable to concentrate on one task and suffered from the weirdest obsessions. I had to counsel, or try to counsel, this hapless man who was quite incompetent - and therefore a continual hazard. Captain Zed and I had to assume practically all this officer's responsibilities. Indulgence aside, this unfortunate should never have been appointed to any ship and certainly not to one of the small ones! There are many other tales to tell of those months spent mainly in the jungle aboard this woodbine funnelled little aberration - but I must press on. When I left Seladang at the end of March 1956, I had been at sea for a few months in excess of ten years, I've got thirty more years to go!

CHAPTER SIX

THE BYKER BOYS

I left Seladang three days before my twenty eighth birthday, travelled from Pladju to Singapore aboard the Dutch Shell ship "Saidja". The ship was bound for another port, so I was dropped off into a sampan in the Singapore Strait. I landed in the city at Jardine Steps, went through customs and immigration en route to the Cockpit - one of Singapore's better hotels (famous for its Sunday Rijst Taffel - rice table) and began the slow process of re-civilization! The contrast was almost too much. From having 'gone bush' for fourteen months to living in a top rate hotel and flying home first class on a Lockheed Constellation to London (arriving on 30th March 1956), to be met there by Joan, thereafter a few days at the Howard Hotel in Central London, another superior establishment - although wonderful, I had great difficulty in adapting to the transformation. Joan and I went to see some West End shows, during which I fell asleep, then woke up in the middle of the nights in a pool of perspiration. I also found myself nervous in town crowds, so it took some considerable time to acclimatize to society after such a long period in tropical isolation.

I've indicated previously that a goodly part of the 'sea-time' I had accumulated was not considered appropriate, by the Board of Trade, as qualifying time for a 'foreign-going certificate'. The sea time required between a Mate's and a Master's certificate was two years foreign trading. The service aboard Seladang counted, officially, as zero qualifying time! Therefore, although three and a half years had elapsed since I had passed my Mate's ticket, I had nowhere near the necessary time in. Now this could have proved a huge problem in career terms. Shell, fortunately, came to my rescue and made representations to the Board on my behalf and I was granted dispensation. So I went back to college for another three month period, sat and passed the examination. I was then, incidentally, invited by the college to sit for an Extra Master's Certificate. This was equivalent to a degree, and I guess I could have achieved this goal, had I had the wherewithal and had circumstances been favourable for such an endeavour. However, this meant living for about a year without salary, which at that time was untenable, and there were more momentous things afoot! Joan was pregnant and the child was due in the following February. Consequently, our plans centred upon this event and there was no way I could afford to go off-pay - anyway I was more than proud to be considered properly qualified to command a foreign going ship in the British Merchant Navy. The fact that I had obtained a Master's Certificate didn't mean that I would sail as master, this promotion would happen whenever my turn came up - in fact some nine years hence. We continued to occupy the apartment we had rented when we left Liverpool, so it was decided that I should return to sea and make a bob or two

I had been home for six months when I was appointed to Tribulus as Chief Officer, joining her on 1st October at the Dingle jetty in Liverpool. Now this was another of those watersheds in my life! I was always thankful that Joan and I had been together for such a lengthy time in our early days of marriage, we had had a very testing period when I was on Seladang, but now we were to be tested more severely than ever. This period of service lasted seventeen months, during which time our daughter, Rhiannon, was born. It was in this time that my Joan showed her mettle as a seafarer's wife - I could not have wished for a finer lady whose fortitude and strength were an example to all women - she was wonderful in the way she overcame the loneliness and problems that occasionally beset her. Show me a successful seaman and I will look for the woman who sustained him. Joan was three months into her pregnancy when I left her - a heart wrenching farewell.

Tribulus, was at this time, an aging T2. More modern tonnage was slowly making an appearance upon the scene, but as you will be aware I had not been appointed to these new ships. If you regard the Master as the CEO of a ship, then the Mate would be the works manager of the deck department with responsibility for outside upkeep and cargo. Included in his duties was the management of the deck crowd - the organization of watches and planning and control of stores and deck maintenance. Whereas I had learned a great deal about innovation and fighting insects during my service aboard Seladang, I had a baptism of fire in the field of man management aboard Tribulus!

Managing a crew of five (Bosun, 2 quartermasters and 2 sailors) aboard Seladang was an entirely different ball game from running a deck team of thirteen Pool men from Byker! 'Pool' men refers to men employed on a voyage basis, recruited from the 'Pool'. This term has already been explained. (page 53). Byker is a district in Newcastle, on the south side of the River Tyne, an area which used to be renowned for 'hard' men. With the exception of two months, undergoing refit, I had a sizeable percentage of Byker Boys in the deck crowd from the day I joined Tribulus until I left 16 months later. Although I was twenty eight year olds and had been at sea for eleven years - initially, I was no match for these characters. They considered having a green-horn Mate as their boss the finest thing since the discovery of canned beer! The Master, with whom I had sailed previously, was no discipli-narian and consequently this added to their pleasurable anticipation of great times ahead! A little more of this, perhaps later.

By happenstance we were routed to Bandar Mashur in Iraq, this gave us the distinction of being the last Shell tanker to transit the Suez Canal at the height of the international tension prior to the invasion of Egypt by Israeli, French and British forces. We loaded our cargo and were sent around the Cape, calling at Cape Town for bunkers, to discharge at Berre, in the south of France. This gave us the added notability of being the first tanker to deliver a cargo to Europe after the closure of the Suez Canal. TV crews swarmed aboard (yes! even in those far-off days) and I believe my image appeared on French TV, but nowhere else. We back loaded two cargoes at Berre for Genoa and Piraeus before proceeding south, around the Cape (calling at Freetown, Sierra Leone for replenish-ment) to Kuwait to load a cargo for Yokohama, via Singapore. From Yokohama to Sarawak to load for Geelong in Victoria,

Australia. We back loaded for other coastal ports, viz., Adelaide, Port Pirie and Freemantle before returning to the Arabian Gulf to load for Rotterdam, again via the Cape. Here, Joan and I were reunited, after seven challenging months.

During the early, idealistic and often carefree years of our relationship, Joan and I could scarcely have envisaged how problematical a seafaring marriage would be. Sure, everyone would forewarn us but reality stared us in the face during my service aboard Tribulus. At the latter end of my career, an officer's wife expecting a child would assume her husband would be beside her as the birth approached. No such sensitivity existed in our time and therefore Joan had to undergo the ordeal alone - special dispensation was required for even her mother to visit her during the post natal period in hospital! This was a particularly testing time for us both, especially as the confinement had not been trouble free. Of course, the thankfulness everyone felt at the advent of a healthy, lusty little girl (Rhiannon) outweighed the strain we both endured. Rhiannon was born on February 15th and I learned of my fatherhood a day or so later in the South China Sea. I had to wait very impatiently until we reached Australia before reading details of Joan's trial and a description of this lovely baby. Six months were to elapse before I met Rhiannon. Still, as I mentioned at the end of the previous paragraph, Joan came to Rotterdam in early May to visit me for little more than a day so was able to recount the seven months since last we had been together, bringing a lock of Rhiannon's hair and photographs of the lovely little mite. It was a terribly difficult time for us both. She, naturally, needed all my attention after her hardship - but because of operational demands and the antics of the Byker Boys, I was barely able to devote adequate attention to her. It was truly distressing and very difficult to keep a balanced perspective. We were, once again, torn apart. Our morale was at rock bottom and we needed to draw upon our reserves to survive this encounter. She was distraught at the intolerable situation on board, I was equally so at her distress - and I so longed to see my baby daughter. So she left the ship unhappy. Operationally we had discharged our cargo of crude oil and back loaded a cargo of fuel oil for Dakar. My reference to crew members acting up was just another episode in a long history of appalling behaviour on the part of certain men in port.

After Dakar (Senegal), we crossed the Atlantic, loaded a cargo of fuel at Punta Cardon in Venezuela for Haifa in Israel before transiting the Suez Canal - which was once more open to traffic. Having just fought a battle against the Israelis, the Egyptians were a little more than difficult when they discovered we had just delivered a cargo to the enemy! Traditionally, the Suez Canal Company, prior to the crisis, had employed British and French pilots almost exclusively. In typical colonial style these pilots had carved out a cozy, extremely well renumerated niche for themselves. As pilotage goes, the Suez Canal was relatively straight forward - however these pompous characters created a mystique, intended to bamboozle all and sundry, posturing and generally making heavy weather of what was, in essence, a dawdle! So, subsequent to the Suez debacle, the Egyptian government engaged pilots from other sources - mainly from the Eastern Bloc - who conducted the business without fuss or pretence with equal if not more efficiency than their imperious predecessors. The authorities eventually relented and allowed Tribulus to pass south through the Canal. We loaded in Kuwait, discharging the cargo at Eastham before proceeding to the River Tyne for tank cleaning and refit.

The ship underwent a quadrennial survey which meant the refit time extended over a period of nearly two months. We docked at Smith's Yard in North Shields where we signed-off the crew, the staff were reduced and I was left as Officer-in-Charge, so I immediately moved into the Captain's quarters! Before I continue, I should like to explain the difficulties I suffered at the hands of my band of merry men, the Byker Boys, during the preceding ten months.

Pool crews rarely exhibited a pride in a ship - perhaps it would be naive to expect such a commitment, however it was realistic to hope that, at the very least, one could expect an honest day's work for an honest day's money. At sea, it was a constant wrangle with the Byker Boys over overtime - unless they were guaranteed a certain amount, they would 'go slow'. If they figured that I, as Mate, really needed them to turn to in overtime, they would refuse. As I have said, as a novice, they really played me for all their worth! This was really good experience for me, because I had to be as crafty as they, and with time, I did become so - and then some! In port, particularly if it was an attractive place such as Piraeus, Yokohama or an Australian town, they just walked off the ship and stayed ashore until their money was exhausted. They knew, with the lenient Master, that all they would receive, metaphorically, would be a slap across the wrist when I paraded the miscreants for 'logging' the day after we left port. We had serious disorder in Geelong, when the lads returned to the ship, broke, drunk and aggressive. They started fighting among themselves, came on deck and threatened us . The Master was ashore, as was his wont, and didn't return to the ship until the following morning. I deemed the situation sufficiently serious to call in the police. They arrived and marched a few off which subdued the rest. There was blood everywhere and the police commended me for the decision. The Master returned aboard after his carousal ashore and promptly gave me the father of dressings down for daring to call the police to 'his' ship! The offenders returned from a night in the cells without being charged to receive a mild reprimand from my boss. Such was my lot! When the lads were in full rampage, they would scream obscenities at me, the mildest of which would be "You Welsh bastard, wait 'till I get you ashore!!". This made for peaceful nights' sleep! Yet, at the end of the day there grew a mutual understanding, if not a level of affection, between us over the months - as though battle honours were evenly shared! On one occasion I found their behaviour quite unforgivable and that was at Rotterdam when Joan came on board - they pestered me throughout the night, hammering on my cabin door and frightening her. I could cheerfully have committed murder that night. The day of reckoning was the day the crew 'paid-off' before the Shipping Master, a government official who oversaw the release of a ship's crew. On this day the Master (Captain) would recommend an unsatisfactory entry in a seaman's discharge book if his behaviour warranted it - to which the Shipping Master would usually concur. The Byker Boys left with unblemished entries!

There always existed a measure of division between Deck and Engineer departments aboard ship and in shore management. This was usually good natured, but occasionally deeper distrust and even dislike existed in certain people. Shell Tankers, as the company had now become, was very much engineer oriented in the fifties. When a ship was berthed at a refit yard, an engineer superintendent took control of the ship, including the granting of 'local leave'. It was the hope and indeed the expectation that each officer serving on board throughout the refit would be allowed home for a few days. I had the misfortune of having to work with a superintendent who had an almost palpable dislike of deck men! Now I hadn't seen my daughter, Rhiannon, some six months after her arrival into this world and this miserable sod flatly refused to allow me to go home at all! I was almost mutinous - I told him that if he didn't reconsider his decision, I would resign from the company. This had the desired effect and I was granted a few days off to bring my girls back to the ship for the remainder of the refit. I shall never forget the moment I met Rhiannon - although Joan had done her utmost to prepare me and indeed our little girl for the meeting, it was a mixture of poignancy and joy at seeing one's child - one of the more perplexing times in my life. I'm sure the little one was probably frightened by this strange man showing such emotion as he hovered over her carry cot. Anyway, we went pram and all to North Shields and had such a happy period together with our bonny girl making three. All good things come to an end, but I felt so refreshed and happy that we, as a family, had had such a contented spell.

You won't believe this! When we came to sign-on a new crew, guess who were among the crew - none other than the Byker Boys! It was sheer coincidence I imagine, however I was better fitted to take these guys on now, especially as the new Master (with whom I had also sailed before) was a disciplinarian. We sailed from the Tyne during the last week of September 1957. I had another four months aboard Tribulus, spent on the Caribbean/USA eastern seaboard trade, interspersed with the odd cargo lifting from the Lake Maracaibo terminals. In December we took a cargo from Aruba to Buenos Aires and there, as you would expect, the Byker Boys were up to their old tricks! The berth in B.A. lies alongside a street of bars - of which the most famous is Tanker Joe's. Of course, ladies of the night, inhabit these bars and the Byker Boys paid one of these girls to come to the ship's gangway and offer herself to me! I greatly appreciated the generous gesture, but firmly declined the gift! Things betwixt them and me had improved! I left Tribulus at the end of January 1958 and transferred to Diloma - none of your air flight repatriations, oh no! I had to undertake the most difficult of passages to Europe - I had to load a multi grade cargo of lubricating oils at Curaçao and Punta Cardon for Rotterdam. Lube oils are the most sensitive and expensive products a tanker carries, so this was a dramatic change - not to mention a reversion to a Chinese crew. Anyway, it was invaluable experience and the cargo was safely delivered and I went home, exhausted, after having spent part of 1956, the whole of 1957 and a piece of 1958 as a real tankerman.

CHAPTER SEVEN

BORUS AND OTHER THINGS

I left Diloma at the end of February 1958 and stayed home until the end of June. This was a period of 'getting-to-know' Rhiannon. Of course she was too young to comprehend the circumstances under which we, as a family, lived - so I did all I knew how, to endear myself to her. This aspect of a seafarer's life is the most difficult to contend with, it's too difficult for description, at times, one just hopes that the problems between father and children can be worked out over the years with mutual understanding. All I can say is that Joan did her utmost to steer our relationship (Rhiannon's and mine) through the years of separation, with wisdom and love. I could wish for no more.

The appreciation of what a seafaring marriage means, by others, depends upon a number of factors. Firstly, much hinges upon where the family lives. If they live in a coastal town or village there's a general understanding of the lifestyle by everyone, with many families in similar circumstances. In a place like Merthyr Tydfil, there's a zero appreciation! In fact, it's my belief that some of the townsfolk were convinced that I came home between stretches! The compensation, such as it was, was the absence of any professional envy between seafarers and particularly between wives whose husbands' careers were moving at a differing pace. You may not think that this was an important consideration - but believe me, it certainly was! The support of friends was crucial, particularly in the case of a wife, left behind to rear a family. Joan and I were well blessed in this respect, we had a lifelong support from my oldest friend, Lyn Perkins and his wife, Bette. Also, near where we lived we had stalwart support and a positive understanding from other friends, Betty and John Morgan. Both couples' involvement and perception, helped both Joan and me tremendously. Undoubtedly, the buttress in our lives was Joan's parents' constant support throughout the major part of my career - my father-in-law died in 1975, but my mother-in-law continued to sustain us until I finished. I have made reference to this in the preface, but there cannot be any underestimation of their contribution to our stability, from the time I met Joan. I have said to many people that if ever I were called upon to write about the most unforgettable character I had met in my life, I would have to tell you about Ted Morris, my dear father-in-law and one of my best friends. Cultured, kindness itself, fiercely interested in my mode of life and the welfare of his beloved daughter - he together with wise, generous Ethel, his wife, were a huge inspiration in our lives!

At this point in my narrative, the year was 1958. Momentous change was afoot within the tanker industry. Wartime built tonnage was being replaced with modern, efficient ships and Shell, in particular, led the way in tanker design. The old workhorses, the 'N' and 'L' classes, together with the T2 fleet were being superseded by flexible, powerful general purpose ships, the 'H' and 'A' classes - ships which had no equal in comprehensive cargo handling. Specialized tankers were built to carry asphalt while in the field of crude oil transport, bigger and ever bigger ships were constructed until the behemoths of the seventies made their appearance. Shell had no superior in sea transport of all liquids, later, also, to become preeminent in the carriage of liquid natural gas - but I move too far ahead!

Before I moved to this more modern tonnage, I had still to serve aboard one more old banger - but one which gave me plenty of experience in cargo management: loading to exact, even keel drafts and multi product care - albeit, in a small way. My next appointment was Borus, an ex Empire ship (one built by the government during World War Two), of some 5,000 tons deadweight, a very purposeful little ship and an extremely busy 'B'. During eleven months trading I loaded 44 cargoes, an average of one per week. However, once more, I am going too far ahead. During my furlough we had decided to return to Merthyr Tydfil, Joan's parents lived there and my mother and father were about to retire, also to Merthyr. It seemed the sensible thing to do. Apart from our mutual love of the town, it afforded us the comfort of family proximity. We negotiated the purchase of a house in the process of being built. This subsequently proved a problem for Joan because the builder went bankrupt and left her with the shell of a home - another case of a seafarer's wife having to shoulder, what would normally be, a man's responsibility. She managed the whole business magnificently, however there was a cost exacted by the strain she endured. Suffice to say that on my return from service aboard Borus, I went into a lovely home - a credit in every respect to my intrepid wife! By this time, ever mindful of the stress that we both experienced, we developed a philosophy of living life to the full whenever we were together. By that I mean, we enjoyed good holidays in London and elsewhere, travelled around on daily excursions, went to concerts and theatres, ate out whenever we could (ever subject to our financial resources!) - it was, literally, a feast and a famine. To maintain our contact when apart, we wrote to one another practically every day. It was a vocation we tried to make fruitful, and I believe despite an event that shook our foundations a little later, we succeeded.

I left home with Joan to spend a day or so in London, prior to boarding RMS Canton for the voyage to Singapore, at the end of June. A three week cruise, travelling first class, dressing for dinner each evening, wonderful cuisine, cheap drink - what a way to earn one's living! Down to earth with a resounding bump when I reached Singapore. There were four Chief Officers travelling to various appointments, two to a cabin. My companion had a number of mysterious boxes of what sounded like glass objects (by the chinking sound as Canton got under way). He turned out to be an elder in the Plymouth Brethren and the boxes contained bottles, each holding a message from God, which were ritually thrown out of our cabin porthole at noon every day! How many people, between Southampton and Singapore, converted to his sect remained an enigma!

Borus was in Keppel Harbour undergoing refit, so I had some two weeks in Singapore before we commenced trading. Captain Irvine was in command - a man with whom I had sailed previously. A dignified, intellectual man who would read law books as a leisure pursuit, a bachelor whose interests, apart from his obvious love of ships, included flying aircraft and to this end was a qualified pilot. The British race produces some extraordinary people! Borus was run hard and efficiently by Captain Irvine, it was a pleasure to match up to his standards. It was all go, I can tell you! The main loading port was, once more, Pladju! However we occasionally loaded at the Singapore terminals and at Balik Papan. Indonesian ports were, in the main, our delivery destinations: Surabaya, Djakarta, Macassar, Belawan and Padang. The only seaport of any size on the south coast of Java, Tjilitjap (pronounced Jillyjap) was our main discharge terminal, we made about ten deliveries there during my sojourn. There were two notable points to make about a trip to Tjilitjap, one was that the ship passed through the Sunda Strait (between Sumatra and Java) and consequently very close to Krakatua (which despite the film "Krakatua - East of Java", is west of Java!) the location of the cataclysmic explosion at the end of the nineteenth century - the island is, in fact, now two! The other point of interest was that Tjilitjap was the site of Indonesia's largest penal colony, so searches for stowaways prior to departure had to be particularly vigilant. We also discharged at Malaysian ports, viz., Labuan, Kuching, Jesselton, Penang and Port Swettenham - which made for a change of atmosphere and more acceptable provender.

As I've indicated, Borus was a hard running ship and required maintenance on the hoof, as it were. I recall on one occasion we were unable to complete the discharge of a tank of kerosene (paraffin) because the level of liquid in the tank having reached the bottom suction line, could not be pumped below this level due to a defective victrolic joint (a patented device that joined two sections of pipeline together) so I donned a smoke mask (a smoke mask was intended for use in firefighting, it consisted of a manually operated bellows pumping outside air into a leather hood, complete with visor, via a flexible hose thus maintaining a positive internal pressure, excluding the outside atmosphere) entered the gas filled tank, climbed down to the tank bottom lowering the bottom half of my body into the kerosene and repaired the joint. Now this would not have been tolerated officially, and in particular never in the subsequent safety ethos that developed in later years! In 1959, you just did what was necessary to complete the job. As a result of my imprudent immersion in kerosene I paid the price of excruciating agony in my genitalia, which took hours of soaking in the hospital bath to alleviate! During this period of service I became ill with dysentery, lost a substantial amount of weight and succumbed to profound exhaustion. I spent a week in the hospital at Pladju undergoing extensive antibiotic treatment to cure, what was feared to be, amoebic dysentery.

As with Seladang, we carried out an ongoing battle with thieves at Pladju and in the Musi River. A passage from Pladju to sea usually involved staging, i.e., anchoring at Payong, near the river mouth to await sufficient tidal rise to cross the outside bar. Now Payong was famous for huge prawns - the brackish estuarial water favoured these giants and every ship bartered with the locals who would come alongside in their canoes. For those uninitiated, whilst this was going on, friends would be climbing up the anchor chain or heaving themselves up with grappling lines on the opposite side to the trading. They were so accomplished they would clean out anybody's cabin that had thoughtlessly been left unlocked. A physical encounter with these men could be dangerous, and, at odd times, fatal. So the cast iron rule was - never allow the sods to get on board! We therefore evolved quite sophisticated defence squads, armed with staves and axe handles, which together with fire hoses usually deterred a would-be intruder - the old adage was never truer than in these situations - prevention is better than cure!

Living with disparate characters was a sine qua non aboard ship and one becomes tolerant of peoples' foibles, seafaring provides the whole panorama of human behaviour. Aboard Borus, amongst the officers, we had a kleptomaniac! Now this is one weakness that's particularly difficult to condone within the confines of a ship. Everyone knew who the perpetrator was, and the vast majority of the staff lived with this irritation. We soon discovered that all one had to do was go to this guy and request a return of one's property, and this was done immediately! Wilfred Irvine found this too much to bear, upright man that he was, with little patience for such a fundamental flaw. He, together with another officer, would set elaborate traps to catch the man - trip wires, synchronized cameras with flashlamps - the whole paraphernalia. They would hide for hours behind curtains in the hope of catching him red-handed! Our wily thief was also cunning! He never got caught! Most of us, accepted the situation because, outwith his defect, he was a charming fellow! Anyway, it was quite amusing to go to his cabin to survey an almost Aladdin like cave of goodies 'borrowed' from his colleagues!

As Chief Officer I had the responsibility for the training of apprentices and cadets. This was a time when we began to train Singaporeans who together with British boys formed quite a large Half Deck of four boys - for the size of ship, that is. I endeavoured to treat them all in my, perhaps, robust style - so that there was no differentiation on account of background. This philosophy just didn't work, the Chinese boys, particularly, found my approach difficult, and I, in turn, found the 'loss of face' thing equally difficult to comprehend at first. Just another facet of my continuing education!

A change in manning took place whilst I was serving aboard Borus. Sadly we lost our traditional Singapore Chinese crew who were replaced by a Hong Kong Chinese crew. These men were more sophisticated than their predecessors, with all departments Cantonese in origin. All ships, manned by Asian crews, changed to this source of manning in the following year or so.

Earlier, I mentioned my brother, Tom. He, Joan and I had been very close friends throughout. Tom, as I indicated was a Regular Army officer serving with the East Yorks Regiment. He fought for some years in Malaya during the emergency in the mid-fifties and, from all accounts, became a skilled jungle fighter. He lost his platoon in a particular gun fight and this affected him deeply. He resigned his commission in 1956 and just after Rhiannon's birth emigrated to Canada. Whilst serving aboard Tribulus we visited New York where Tom came down from Toronto to see me to spend some time together - we even had a photograph taken at the Empire State Building - of which my mother was inordinately proud! He entered the Canadian Civil Service and eventually held a responsible position in Manpower.

On my ninetieth visit to Pladju, at the end of July 1959, I was relieved of my duties aboard Borus - a sick man. Once more I travelled to Singapore by a Dutch Shell ship, this time it was Sarita. I arrived in Heathrow on August 1st having flown first class with Qantas - my last such experience!

CHAPTER EIGHT

A MOLLUSC FOUND
IN BELGIAN HEDGEROWS

Coming home on this occasion had a great significance for me because I was returning to Merthyr Tydfil and a new house! Joan had managed to find a builder to complete the work that the bankrupt contractor had left to be done. Our excitement at sharing our new home was tempered by the obvious fact that I was unwell; I had lost a substantial amount of weight and I became exhausted by the smallest physical effort. Anyway, to cut a long story short, I was diagnosed as having tachycardia (a condition usually manifested in men who have been under stress - commonly occurring during wartime (!), a fast heartbeat in effect) and was instructed to lie on my back for a month! What a great way to spend a leave in one's new home! Joan and I were seriously concerned about our future, should I be unfit to continue seafaring - I even contemplated purchasing a village post office as an alternative! Rest did the trick, although I was for many years afflicted with a rapid pulse.

Soon after my recovery, Joan and I were at one of the local cinemas when a message was flashed on the screen asking me to 'phone home immediately. We both left the cinema in a bit of a panic thinking that something was wrong at home only to hear that I was to contact London Office as soon as possible. This I did within the hour and was told that at the end of my furlough I was to be appointed to new building (a brand new ship) at Sunderland. I was quite flabbergasted! Having battled with older ships hitherto, this piece of information came as a shock - I was so surprised I even asked if I would be sailing aboard the ship, Arianta! Another strange circumstance was the fact that my employers had notified me at 10 pm! Professionally, this was the most exciting news I had ever had! It did wonders for my self-esteem, I was really determined to strut my stuff with this one!

Arianta (the Latin name for the shell found in Belgian hedgerows!) was the second of two sisters built at Thompson's Yard, Sunderland. The 'A' class were ships intended for general trading, carrying refined products. The feature that Aluco and Arianta possessed that set them apart was that the accommodation block was at the aft end of the ship - the first to be introduced in the Shell fleet. The remainder of the 'A' class were conventionally constructed with accommodation 'midships and aft; in time this type of design was superseded by the 'all aft' layout. She was an absolute cracker! State of the art equipment, epoxy painted cargo tanks, superb accommodation and a finer looking ship would have been hard to find in 1959! Arianta was the first to have submersible hydraulically powered cargo pumps fitted in selected tanks (independent pump with an individual loading/discharging pipeline - for handling special products). Sleek, handsome - at last I was aboard a ship which I could be really proud of!

I reported to the Agent's office on November 4th. Perhaps it would be apposite to explain, precisely, the function of a Shipping Agent. An agency represents the shipowner in the handling of ship's business, caring for joining and leaving personnel, dealing with government departments in matters relating to the ship (customs, health, immigration and police), arranging the supply of stores and victuals, representing the ship in any cargo dispute and perhaps, most importantly, as far as shipboard personnel were concerned, the supply of currency! I joined Arianta as officer-in-charge pending the arrival of the master, so I was the 'boss'(sort of) and dealt with the agents in all matters pertaining to the forthcoming commissioning of ship. My most immediate task was to familiarize myself with this magnificent 'lady'. I searched the ship for every hour God gave me - taking notes and making diagrams and finding shortfalls and defects that had to be remedied prior to the ship sailing. I was determined to 'know my ship'.

I was at the building yard for six weeks prior to sailing. The agents had arranged accommodation at an establishment - digs - known as

Mrs Spence's. Mrs Spence was your archetypical landlady! A number of my fellow officers were also in these digs. We would congregate in the sitting room in the evening after our meat and two veg dinner in front of a small two bar electric fire, shivering in the cold damp November clime when she would sweep in, say "By 'ell, it's boiling in 'ere" and promptly switch off one of the bars! As Joan was able to stay with me we soon moved to more salubrious quarters in Roker where we lived for a few weeks in comfortable surroundings. One's personal life soon had to take second place to operational requirements. The ship underwent successful sea trials and was subsequently handed over to Shell Tankers, whereupon we took over total control.

I have mentioned previously that I would, in the course of this narrative, describe to the reader those men with whom I made firm friendships and those whom I admired, over and above the many others (mostly fine and thoroughly efficient people) with whom I sailed. One such was Captain Alec Howe. I viewed his appointment with some misgiving, because I had listened to the 'galley radio' (shipboard gossip) which painted him as something of a martinet, who would eat mates for breakfast! What a joke! He was very efficient, knowledgeable and professionally the most competent master I had sailed with. How refreshing it was to have a boss who could speak on equal terms as oneself about cargo and maintenance matters instead of my previous experience with masters whose standard response to requests for advice would be "You're the Mate, get on with it!" I consider myself so fortunate to have sailed with two masters, almost consecutively, who knew what they were about (Irvine and Howe). Alec Howe was the person upon whom I modelled myself, we had an excellent rapport, mutual respect and became firm friends, ending only with his untimely death some years ago. He was always warm and kind to both Joan and Rhiannon.

We sailed for Curaçao on December 19th 1959, missing Christmas in the UK, which perhaps was a good thing. We cleared the coast and the bad weather so had a peaceful 'season' at sea, arriving at Curaçao on January 4th 1960. I had spent a lot of time testing cargo valves en route - we had the 'new' butterfly valves, so we had to be sure of integrity before we loaded a complex multi-grade cargo at Curaçao and Punta Cardon for seven Mediterranean ports. A number of valves were found to be leaking, so we had to go along-side a repair wharf at Curaçao to remedy the situation - giving us a spell of nine days in port, enabling us to paint the hull - no longer were we contending with the magic PF4, but high grade epoxy paint. She looked a picture, leaving Curaçao.

I recollect we loaded ten grades of various gasolines plus kerosene, white spirit and dry cleaning fluid, topping off with gasoil. This was a testing cargo for a new ship and the beginning of a series of multi grade deliveries, mainly in Europe and the Mediterranean but with occasional forays to Canada and Africa. In total, Arianta safely discharged nearly 350,000 tons of highly refined petroleum products in her first year's service - a credit, I suggest, to Shell's expertise and to British shipbuilding.

Great change was in the air within Shell Tankers during 1960. To improve the efficiency of the fleet it was decided to acquire the Eagle Oil Shipping Company which included the Eagle Tanker Company. We in Shell watched the process with some foreboding, as I believe did our colleagues in Eagle. The black humour had it that although Shell acquired Eagle, Eagle in fact took over Shell! For sure, the Eagle men gained in the seniority stakes (a colleague in Eagle, who went to sea at the same time as I did, became some eighteen months my senior once he was absorbed into Shell). Inevitably this led to bad feeling with the sense of outrage on our part, and the feeling of discomfort at having to accept new ways on their part. To me, it was easy to understand why the Eagle ships had been taken over, their professional attitudes seemed altogether more relaxed than ours - which may not have been a bad thing! All things considered, it was a happy amalgamation, undoubtedly the Bird men had a lot to contribute and it was pleasant to accede to their more easygoing approach to ship operation. Captain Howe was relieved by an ex(just)-Eagle master later in the year, so it didn't take long for their senior men to take over our crack ships! In fact, another revelation awaited us! The involvement of the master's wife in shipboard matters came as a surprise to we Shell men! Mrs Captain, a well trav-elled lady accompanied her husband to every ship - she was not your average shrinking violet or perhaps even a wife who kept her own counsel (as most ladies, accompanying their men, did). Whether or not she had been fostered in her role as a participant in shipboard matters was something for conjecture - the net result was widespread dismay when she enquired, at the meal table, of our dyed-in-the-wool Shell Chief Engineer, if he had, in fact, remembered to transfer bunkers that morning!! It must be said that our Chief was an absolute gentleman - he finished his meal white knuckled, face suffused, and with bulging eyes, responding with a grimace which represented a smile! She looked after the ship's accounts and was not averse to stopping a crew member and reminding him that either he was having too much overtime or that he would not get a sub at the next port! She was something else, I can tell you!

All that came much later. Our maiden loaded voyage took us to Istanbul, Cyprus, Beirut, Piraeus, Malta, Marseilles and Barcelona. Very interesting and rewarding work and we were particularly encouraged with the ship's performance in handling these cargo grades. At most ports in the Eastern Mediterranean, along the North African coast and in Italy, cargo discharge was carried out by pumping through a pipeline to the stern and ashore by flexible hose therefrom. This added to the complexity because each product had to pass along the same pipe which had to washed through with sea water to avoid contamination one grade with the other. The reason for this method was that tankers in these ports berthed stern onto the jetty. This was necessary for a quick getaway, should one of the local winds, such as the 'mistral', suddenly rise and compel the ship to leave the mooring. Incidentally, the first grade of refined spirit to be discharged by submersible pump from a conventional tanker took place at Beirut - I tried to highlight the significance of this historical event to the jetty operator, but he was singularly unimpressed, merely giving one of those expressive Levantine shoulder shrugs!

From Barcelona we returned to the Caribbean to load at Curaçao and Trinidad, discharging at Rotterdam and Stanlow. Then began a period of intense trading around northern Europe. We made 42 port visits in 4 months, loading at Stanlow, Thameshaven and Rotterdam. We delivered cargo, apart from UK ports, to Scandinavia, Germany and France. It was a pleasure to throw this ship around, she performed so well in every respect and we had a bunch of officers who responded to the exacting professional challenge presented by the trade pattern. Topping it, we were under the command of a superb professional, Alec Howe. Joan was with me for most of the

115

time, so I was exhilarated by the experience, particularly as I was able to share with her the satisfaction I derived from my work. She too, had plenty of interesting jaunts ashore - occasionally accompanied by me but more often by Captain Howe. A place of particular interest was Hammerfest, the world's northernmost port. We were there in May where they had snow still lying on the ground with about 20 hours of daylight each day. It was a delightful little town! All good things come to an end, Joan left me in early July and Arianta left Europe at the end of the month to load at Trinidad.

An unusual event took place whilst we were on the coast. Alec Howe was a bachelor at the time. Senior officers were entitled to have their wives accompanying them on coastal passages, Masters and Chief Engineers could take their wives deep sea. The Company in its infinite wisdom made an exception in Captain Howe's case and allowed his father to do a coastal voyage. Howe senior, a retired Brixham fishing boat skipper, and a deeply religious man, was a delight to know, it was so touching to witness his pleasure at his son's obvious success! It was indeed providential that he made this short trip because within months he died, and Alec Howe had to leave the ship, much to my regret, when we arrived at Curaçao. His relief, as I have already indicated, was an Eagle master and one with whom I also enjoyed sailing.

We now did some more general deep sea trading between the Caribbean and ports in and around the River Congo, Pointe Noire and Douala. Thereafter to Trois Rivieres in Quebec with a cargo of heating oil in preparation for the forthcoming Canadian winter. My brother, Tom, came down to Trois Rivieres to spend time with me whilst we were discharging cargo.

One of the excellent features of Arianta was the fact that the cargo tanks were coated in epoxy paint. This made tank cleaning a much easier task in that there was no rust deposited on the tank bottoms and the ship could be prepared for changes in product more readily. Good tank preparation was crucial for the next cargo of aviation fuels and gasolines for another Mediterranean marathon. We delivered this cargo to Mohammedia (Morocco), Algiers, Bône, Piraeus, Naples, Vado and Marseilles - a fifteen day operation. I left Arianta on November 8th 1960 feeling that I had, at last, become the 'complete' mate!

CHAPTER NINE

THE ANTIPODES AND A COUPLE OF SAINTS

When I left Arianta at Marseilles, I travelled to Paris by the Blue Train. However, I remember so well having a delightful dish of moulles mariniere at the railway station restaurant immediately prior to boarding the train - there's no reason, I suppose, to relate this other than to mention the very high standard of cuisine in French railway restaurants! I was soon home ready to enjoy the first Christmas with my little girl. She was nearly four years old and a delight to us all. As I conveyed in Chapter One, I only had 15 out of 40 Christmases at home in my seagoing career, so this one was really a special one! It's superfluous to mention that I had a wonderful time at Christmas and indeed during the entire time I was at home. Joan and I developed a facility of being able to pick up where we had left off. We had spent more time together than perhaps some of my contemporaries had, she also had a clear insight of my lifestyle aboard ship and with her bright intelligence, appreciated the difficulties that faced us with clarity and resolve. As I've already mentioned, we lived life to the full when I was on furlough. However the strain of the responsibility she shouldered, when I was at sea, was at times almost unsustainable.

This chapter will cover more than two and a half years, from March 1961 until October 1963. During this time I served aboard three ships, viz., Hemiglypta, San Edmundo and San Fernando. The title of the chapter reflects the fact that aboard Hemiglypta I spent the major part of my service trading around Australian and New

Zealand ports and 'San' is Spanish for saint! (All Eagle Oil ships were thus named until a little later when all Eagle names were changed to Shell names). It was to be my last period as Chief Officer of conventional tankers.

I joined Hemiglypta at Stanlow on March 8th 1961. She was one of the replacement 'workhorses' I described previously - very efficient ships, second to none in their ability to carry out their intended general purpose trading. However it came as a bit of a shock to return to PF4 and rust proliferating everywhere, after the experience of Arianta! Still, I think it did me good insofar that I wasn't allowed to become big headed! The Master was one Captain Albert Rylett from the aviary who regarded the amalgamation of Shell and Eagle as a personal affront! He was a benign soul whose passion was 'bods'. He hailed from Hull and that was how he referred to his canaries. Albert MN we called him, after the well known book about a Royal Naval rating, entitled 'Albert RN'. Albert had the unfortunate, and extremely painful, propensity of trapping his genitalia in a locker drawer in his bedroom, as he shut same!! His standard response for anything that went wrong was: " This would never have happened in Eagle!" (which included bruised appendages!) So it became a catch phrase amongst us all!

Hemiglypta was a white oiler (gasolines, aviation fuels etc) with a British crew. Our first cargo was loaded at Rotterdam and discharged at Singapore, after which we re-loaded a part cargo and completed loading at Balik Papan for Australia. The ship was a bit of a rust bucket but she performed superbly. I had the good fortune to have an excellent Second Mate, one Alan Prince, as my number two in cargo matters. I had now developed a cargo philosophy of achieving optimum performance (after my invaluable and varied experience aboard Arianta) at discharge terminals. It was quite simple to achieve this standard. When you pump a liquid ashore you are given a maximum back pressure at which you should deliver the product. Providing a constant surveillance was maintained and this maximum pressure sustained, voila! you turned the ship around in optimum time. This was my function, to make the ship perform at her best regardless of pleas to hang out the discharge time (Albert used to say, "Why don't you circulate, Mate! Give us all a bit more time alongside,"), which, with the enthusiastic support from Alan, we achieved. Shell Australia, with many marine terminals in their dominion, soon became aware of Hemiglypta's performance and after our first visit, wanted her back again!

Our first visit to Australia was relatively short, we arrived at Freemantle at the end of April, discharged part cargo before completing discharge at Melbourne. One arm of my father's family lived in Toorak, an expensive residential area in Melbourne. I sallied ashore to visit them and had a pleasant interlude meeting them all over cucumber sandwiches and Earl Grey. I was able to bring them up to speed on all matters relating to the families at home and, in so doing, thoroughly enjoyed my brief but elegant visit. From Melbourne across Port Philip Bay to Geelong (Shell Australia's main refinery) to load for Sydney and Newcastle, leaving the country in mid May for Abadan. At Abadan we loaded a cocktail of products for Mediterranean ports, beginning with Alexandria, across to Piraeus thence to Tripoli in Libya and Bône in Algeria, up to Naples, finishing at Lavera and Berre in the south of France. I managed to get ashore at Naples on a beautiful Italian summer's day and spent a wonderful day in Pompeii. We loaded at Berre for Rotterdam before proceeding to Immingham for refit. Immingham is on the Lincolnshire bank of the River Humber and quite the favoured repair port for Shell Tankers at that time. 'Time is Money' was ever the axiom with Shell, as with all oil companies of course. Hours spent in port were kept to an absolute minimum, either loading or discharging but especially so at repair ports. Consequently we tank-cleaned, underwent repairs which included a quick wash and brush-up, all in ten days. Ten very happy days. Joan and Rhiannon came to the ship as soon as we arrived and left as the mooring lines were being cast off on our leaving for Rotterdam on 23rd July 1961. A short but magic time for Joan and myself in the pleasant Lincolnshire countryside with the occasional visit to Grimsby for the odd Chinese meal or whatever.

We loaded at Rotterdam for Cape Town, East London, Aden and Colombo. Actually we were making our way out to Australia once more, but Shell in its matchless economic manner made use of every opportunity to make a buck or two en route! From Colombo we went to Pladju to load part cargo, completing at Singapore and Balik Papan. Our first discharge port was, once more, Freemantle -

arriving 29th September. Thus began our Antipodean marathon of three months, until the last day of 1961, in fact. From Freemantle we completed our discharge of 'foreign' cargo at Adelaide and Melbourne. Thereafter, Hemiglypta loaded six cargoes of many different grades at Geelong in this period, delivering small and large quantities to as many as seventeen ports around the Australian and New Zealand coasts. It was wonderfully satisfying work for me, I felt totally professional and on top of the exacting work, aided, in no small measure by Alan Prince. Alan's wife, Doreen, sailed with us from Immingham and was an asset to the ship. They were firm friends of mine but we lost touch with one another in later years, unfortunately. I understand he eventually became Harbour Master at Dubai. We broke every record in both countries by outperforming all other ships that had visited the terminals previously, we created a benchmark in fact.

At the end of the First World War, my mother's younger brother, Eddy, emigrated to New Zealand to seek his fortune. In this he was singularly unsuccessful! However, nobody had seen him since he left Wales' fair shores. On a visit to Wellington I invited him down to the ship as he only lived up the road, so to speak, at Palmerston North. I recognised him immediately! He combined one feature from each of the other six siblings! He so enjoyed his stay aboard Hemiglypta, apparently he never stopped talking about it!

I loved working with the Australians and New Zealanders. They were so refreshingly free of cant and artifice, and, from all accounts the girls were more than generous in the granting of favours! With acknowledgment to one David Pringle who originally recounted this tale: A professor from one of Australia's universities, an expert on the subject of indigenous snakes, was being interviewed on radio in one of Queensland's more remote towns, and the conversation went something like this: " Interviewer: Professor, in your opinion, what is the most dinegerous snike in Australia? Professor: I think the most dinegerous snike in Australia is the brown snike. Interviewer: That surprises me Professor! I thought the coral snike was the most dinegerous! Professor: Naw, it's the brown. Interviewer: Howzat, Professor? Professor: There're more of the bastards that's why!" We were at our final Australian discharge port, Townsville, when we heard of the most appalling tragedy at Mackay, a small port to the south of us, on the day prior to New Year's Eve. Three or four young people in their late teens or early twenties were cavorting in the surf up to their thighs in water when one of them was grabbed by a great white shark, in their efforts to save the victim two more youngsters were savaged and killed, leaving one badly wounded survivor - all within a matter of minutes. A shocking event which had a saddening affect upon everyone in the country. We finally left the coast on New Year's Eve 1961.

We returned to Singapore (Pulo Bukom) to load a cargo of aviation fuel for Woodlands, on the north coast of Singapore Island, for use at Changi International Airport. We went back to the refinery at Bukom and loaded a multi grade cargo for Fiji, New Caledonia and the Solomon Islands. Now this was really interesting stuff! All these islands had an unique character. Fiji, a mélange of indigenous Fijians and imported indentured labour from the sub continent of India. Not a particularly happy mix I gathered. Now I had been at sea for more than sixteen years and reckoned I couldn't be easily shocked! At Suva I was! There was such a liberal attitude to casual sex that bordered upon the amoral! People freely copulated the other side of the jetty in full daylight, within full view of anyone who wished to look! The locals were supremely indifferent! Noumea was next, the main port in the unhappy French colony of New Caledonia. It struck me as the ultimate incongruity having gendarmes in full regalia in the Pacific Ocean - no more ridiculous than bobbies in the Falklands I suppose! Then on to Honiara in Guadalcanal, scene of the famous Pacific War battle. We were the first tanker to visit the island at the new installation. Albert and I planned our berthing strategy in the absence of a pilot, doing a Mediterranean moor and berthing stern-on to the jetty. All went perfectly, which was particularly important as His Excellency, the Governor of the Solomon Islands viewed the operation and stayed for lunch! We only had a small quantity to discharge, more a proving exercise than anything else. The natives were of Melanesian stock, more akin to the Papuans than the lighter skinned Polynesians. So on to Pladju for my final visit to that port - not that I knew that at the time. We took the cargo to Singapore where I paid off at the end of February 1962 and flew home to my girls, satisfied in the knowledge that Hemiglypta had safely transported another 275,360 tons of valuable petroleum cargo to where it had been needed.

I was home at a delightful time of the year, March, April and May. We, as a family, would roam the mountains in the early balmy mornings because we were blessed with outstandingly good weather that year. I painted the house and did the Spring gardening. I went for long walks with my father-in-law, listening to his experiences as a musician, as a miner, tales of his boyhood in Barmouth and his philosophical views on life. He had played in symphony orchestras under the baton of such conductors as Sir Henry Wood and in the first performance of 'The Dream of Gerontius' by Sir Edward Elgar, conducted by the composer. Joan had been born in Nottingham where her father played at the local Kardomah, leader of the trio that played for clients as they sipped their afternoon tea. At nights he played the accompanying music for the silent movies at a city centre cinema. These musical activities disappeared with the advent of talking pictures and the loss of popularity in afternoon tea music . Incidentally, his holiday relief was Cyril Stapleton who became one of Britain's premier dance band leaders. His musical activities were later severely limited by encroaching deafness, until total silence became his burden. Never one to bemoan his lot, he was one of Nature's gentlemen - and a huge support to Joan, Rhiannon and myself. His strength and ours came from his helpmate and wife, Ethel. Two years before he died he suffered the cruelest blow that a man in his predicament could suffer, he lost his sight. For two years he lived in a world of darkness and silence - yet he learned to read a type of Braille and could converse with us, his humour was as acute as ever and never once did he lament his fate! A wonderful, wonderful man.

Almost a revolution had taken place during the 1950's in the training of engineer officers, no longer were they to be recruited from ship-yards at the end of their apprenticeship, instead they were to be trained aboard ship. Of course the dinosaurs among the engineer fraternity rubbished the concept from the word go, but boy! were they to be proved wrong! One has to be careful in phrasing the difference between the old and new. On balance, let's say that the new trainees were better educated and more forward looking than the majority of their predecessors. When I was serving on Tribulus we had to re-staff the ship at North Shields at the end of refit. I was, at the time still, O.I.C. and had been advised that five apprentices were to join. At the appointed time, three elegant, immaculately uniformed young men came to my cabin and enquired as to where their accommodation was. I assumed they were deck apprentices and was taken aback when they said they were engineers! A little later two objects appeared at my cabin dressed in raindrop suits and bovver boots, they were the deck apprentices! What a contrast. Subtly, over the years the oil and water conflict between deck and engineer officers disappeared - and this was a revolution! These same young men transformed ship and shore management in the fifteen or more years after the inception of the scheme, very much for the better.

My next ship was one of Sir Charles Clore's ships. Charlie Clore, as he was known, was a shoe manufacturer and a multimillionaire to boot (if you'll excuse the pun!) who turned his entrepreneurial talents to shipbuilding and bought a shipyard at West Hartlepool. He built good, functional ships both dry cargo and tankers, and, I assume at an economic price. San Edmundo (my first of two consecutive 'saints') was her name. Her design, as far as cargo systems were concerned, was based broadly upon the T2. Not a particularly flexible ship, but, ton for ton, she was the most powerful pumping ship I had yet served upon. I joined her whilst she underwent refit at Tilbury (London), this is the best time to join a ship, in order to familiarize oneself with the ship and its various systems before resumption of trading. I joined on 6th June 1962 and we sailed for Venezuela on 16th June under the command of Captain R.B. English, a charming Irishman from Cobh. San Edmundo was a black oiler, i.e., crude oil, fuel oil and diesel. Our first cargo was from Punta Cardon to Perth Amboy, New Jersey. On completion of discharge we moved up the Hudson River, above the Roosevelt Estate and Ossingning (the notorious penitentiary, Sing Sing) to load river water for Curaçao. From Curaçao to Puerto Miranda in the Maracaibo Lake to load for Shellhaven and Thameshaven on the Thames, thereafter across to Rotterdam to load for Killingholme on the Humber. To the Caribbean once more to load at Trinidad for Stanlow. Unfortunately, a family crisis of serious proportions arose and I had to leave San Edmundo at Stanlow to attend to the matter - left John Stuart, the Second Mate, somewhat in the lurch I'm afraid. However he coped and he and his lady asked me later to be godfather to their daughter Julia.

I was home less than a month, as I had accumulated little furlough time, but it was sufficient to allow me to help in resolving the family problem before my next appointment to San Fernando. I joined her at

Stanlow on 9th October 1962. At that time, she was a white oiler and we carried out some trading around Europe before drydocking at South Shields at the end of October. The ship, a somewhat embellished example, in appearance, of the standard design 'H' class, was to be changed from white oils to the lubricating oil trade. This trade was quite the 'ne plus ultra' of all conventional tanker operations. The oils vary from axle grease to sewing machine oil and all manner of lubes in between. Shell were absolutely pre-eminent in the business and there was an industry reputation to uphold, with no room for mistakes!

I did not have a particularly auspicious beginning to my service aboard San Fernando. I was allowed to go home from South Shields for a week-end so I hired a car to avoid the day long train journey. Unfortunately I had an accident which landed me in a Harrogate hospital. I had a slice in my scalp, a few broken teeth and a strained back, which wasn't too bad, so I was allowed to continue home by train. I returned to the ship a day later than arranged, so I painfully resumed my duties. Fate hadn't finished with me yet! A day or so after my return, I was checking a work item in the pumproom and because one of the shipyard workers had removed a section of grating, I fell half way down the space! Miraculously, I survived this fall with little more than a few grazes and my car accident injuries somewhat aggravated! My back never recovered from these two knocks, two years later my scalp scar was irritating me and I removed a sliver of glass which had been in my head all that time! Meanwhile, Joan had been invited to resume her teaching career and commenced work at one of the local high schools. Dada and Mama looked after Rhiannon.

Anyway to the business of carrying lube oils. These were complex cargoes requiring a great deal of planning, checking and re-checking. Within the charterer's office, shore staff, mostly ex fleet officers, would calculate and plan the cargo independently of the ship's staff. Having done so they would send a detailed message to the ship outlining the quantities of various grades to be carried, where they were to be loaded and the amounts to be discharged at the numerous discharge terminals. It was quite common to load at six ports and to discharge at an equal number of destinations world wide. This was a global trade. I would calculate the cargo arrangement (i.e. where different grades were to be placed), calculate drafts and ship stress at each port, arrange ballasting procedure.

Paramount was the requirement to keep each grade safely segregated, to avoid hugely expensive contamination - with the ever present fear of termination of employment! Shell's policy was for the people on board to take full responsibility for cargo care (bearing in mind that they had already calculated the feasibility of the proposed cargo operation). Other oil companies had a different philosophy, they would calculate a cargo set-up and instruct the ship on how to load and discharge same. I believe the Shell policy was far more efficient and satisfying.

Our ballast voyage out of South Shields took us to the United States to load at ports in Louisiana and Texas. Each cargo valve had to be tested and proved tight prior to loading. Some grades had to be heated to maintain fluidity, so all cargo tank heating coils also had to be tested - should a coil leak, water could ruin a tank of lubricating oil. Loading lube oils was done by a method known as 'over the top', it simply meant that hoses were placed in the tanks via the open tank hatches (these were the openings on the deck to individual tanks, of which there were twenty seven) allowing the oils to fall into each space, thus avoiding the contamination of the pipeline system. Our first cargo was loaded at Good Hope, Beaumont and Curaçao, a process that took us thirteen days to complete - a long time for a tanker, such was the care taken. Each tank had to be mopped and dried before cargo was loaded and on completion, tank hatches had to be scrupulously tight to avoid any possibility of sea water or heavy rain entering the tanks. A wild card was the Panama Canal! The ship had to be exactly even keel and at tropical fresh water loadline marks - the Canal inspectors were absolutely rigid and exact in their measurements, so it was with heart in mouth that I awaited their examination! As you will have gathered we were bound across the Pacific. We left Panama on 12th December 1962 bound for Cebu in the Philippines, once again the ocean lived up to its name and we enjoyed a very pleasant month crossing this beautiful body of water. We arrived at Cebu on 11th January 1963, having got Christmas and New Year safely out of the way (always a source of anxiety with a British crew, when seasonal merriment could lead to uglier scenes). We dropped a small quantity off into barges at Cebu before going on to Singapore. I shall always remember the trip from Cebu to Singapore! The rainy north west monsoon was at its height and we had to cross one of the world's more dangerous stretches of water, the Sulu Sea. Frankly, it was a bloody nightmare! Captain Robert Annett was in command, an experienced master who was sorely tested with this passage. We were headed for the Balabac Strait, south of notorious Palawan Island. The Sulu Sea is littered with ship wrecks, there are so many reefs, charted and uncharted, that even clear weather navigation requires attention and prudence. The currents are unpredictable and at times very strong. Given these factors and zero visibility in the torrential rain, totally blotting out any radar response, we were virtually blind. We fell back upon a time tested technique known as a 'line of soundings'. I was given this job as the senior navigator, and to this day I know of nothing more satisfying in my navigational experience than that task. Basically, one measures the water depth at regular intervals, plotting the readings against estimated distance run. After a 'run' you try to match your findings with water depths on the chart. I did it! I established our position, well away from where we should have been, and with heart in mouth (once again), we altered course towards the strait and thankfully I was bang on! We went from Singapore to Hong Kong, finishing off at Djakarta. We returned to the Caribbean via Cape Town - wonderful long sea passages with plenty of opportunity for maintenance - a mate's dream!

I am now going to raise the contentious issue of homosexuality. In these enlightened times, differing sexual preferences enjoy almost universal understanding but I'm about to recount matters that occurred in another era and within the confines of an isolated, closed community. Ships have always been a magnet for gay men, the work they did, almost exclusively within the catering and service departments, suited their natures. They were efficient, caring and often very humorous characters. We, in tankers, had always been aware of the odd such man within the ship's company, but they were a rarity in the forties and fifties. With the decline of passenger ship trade in the sixties and onwards - where most gay men had gravitated - more and more of men of this persuasion appeared on crew lists, particularly aboard tankers. It is my experience that gay men allow their sexuality to play a disproportionate part in their day-to-day life, in contrast to heterosexuals, whose sex life, or absence of, is a personal and private matter. Aboard a ship, if the ship's company includes a significant number of gays, then there if a recipe for difficulty. Such was the case aboard San Fernando. The catering department, from the Chief Steward down were either gay or became so during the course of voyage! Some of them were predatory and actively disrupted the ambience of the ship and actually 'turned' some crew members. My comments should not, in any way, be construed as an anti-gay statement but rather an illustration of what uneasiness an active homosexual can create, should he so choose, aboard a ship.

One of my duties as Chief Officer was acting as the medical officer to the ship's company. My knowledge and background in such matters was rudimentary, as was the case with all my colleagues. However, with time, one did garner a certain experience which served one well in addition, one had the wonderfully simple and wise tome "The Shipmaster's Medical Guide" to guide one through most ailments and accidents. The big fear at sea was appendicitis - this could be a killer. Stomach pain was always viewed with caution and apprehension. Some days after clearing Panama during mid December, we had a young seaman suffer an attack of acute appendicitis, this led to the quandary of what action had to be taken - usually this meant deviating to a port to land the patient- however, in this instance we were fortunate and were able to rendezvous with the Liner, 'Southern Cross', which had a doctor and full medical facilities to deal with our young man's condition. It was always with the greatest relief that one saw a similarly afflicted person leave the ship! One of my more serious medical problems, during my stay aboard San Fernando, was dealing with a case of rheumatic fever. In this case it was the Third Engineer. I had to nurse this officer, feed him, wash him, tend to his bodily functions and try to keep his morale positive. He wasn't allowed to move in case the effort would affect his heart, so it was some job I can tell you! He survived and I reckon I saved his bacon because he rose to become the man in charge of Shell Tankers Marine Store in London Docks. My main function, as the MO, was treating men with venereal diseases which meant injecting antibiotics into the upper and outer quadrant of mens' backsides! Although I was the practitioner, the ultimate responsibility was the Master's.

Our next cargo was loaded at Curaçao, a simple delivery of basic lubricating oil stocks to three European refineries at Rotterdam, Hamburg and Thameshaven. We completed that job and sailed from

London on 2nd April 1963, once more for the Gulf of Mexico. I think, on reflection, that this probably was the most complicated cargo for which I was ever responsible. We loaded at six terminals, with stock transfer of grades between one of the American ports and Curaçao, in the middle of the loading sequence! Prior to the commencement of loading at the first terminal, London wished to be advised of the even keel draft at the penultimate discharge port, Bombay! That was some brain teaser I can tell you! We loaded about twelve different lube oils at Lake Charles, Beaumont, Smith's Bluff, Bay Town, Curaçao and Punta Cardon. Our discharge ports were Genoa, Bombay and Calcutta. Bear in mind that the discharge at Genoa had to be done via the single stern pipeline, so that the various grades had to pass down the same pipe. We completed our operation at Calcutta in mid June. Back to Curaçao and Punta Cardon, via the Cape of Good Hope, stopping off at Cape Town for bunkers and mail.

We loaded a multi-grade cargo for Australian ports, viz., Brisbane, Sydney, Melbourne and Adelaide. Now we discharged exactly the same product to a number of oil companies and I remember asking a Castrol representative why was it his company could make such extravagant claims as to the superior quality of their motor oil, when, in fact, it was a Shell lube oil! He replied, quite tellingly I thought, that the analogy would be that a number of bakers would bake bread from the same flour, but the results would vary according to each baker's skill! From Adelaide we returned to Curaçao, once more crossing the Pacific and transiting the Panama Canal to load for Rotterdam and London. This, again, was a relatively simple cargo. I paid-off on the 21st October 1963 to begin a new chapter in my career.

Author, circa 1970.

t.s. 'Tydfil'. Sea Cadet Corps, author standing far right, third row.

*Two ragamuffins -
Apprentices (l to r)
Archer and Williams.
May 1946.*

Ashore in Falmouth. May 1946.

*Dressed to go ashore. Curaçao,
December 1945.*

Shark fishing. Miralda 1947.

Atlantic greyhound 'Hyalina'.

m.v. 'Dromus'.

t.e.s 'Thallepus'.

Our wedding day, July 17th 1952, St.John's Church, Penydarren, Merthyr Tydfil.

Seladang - the Bull.

Seladang - the Bull.

Seladang's Crowd!
(l to r)
Ahdoo (dim as a Toc'H' lamp);
Bosun & Nelson (one eye)

Hemiglypta sailing
through Otago Sound,
South Island,
New Zealand.
25.11.1961.

Master of Asprella,
Swansea Docks 1967.

s.s. 'Melo'

Lepeta alongside at
Kharg Island, loading
Iranian Crude.

Lepeta receiving helicopter service off Cape Town.

Opalia.

Opalia entering harbour, Willemstadt, Curaçao.

Opalia - cadets'
lecture room.
I.C.O. James Deane.

In command -
Opalia.

Opalia - cadets on
gangway watch.

H.M.Y. Britannia passing Opalia during 1977 Jubilee Spithead Review.

Methane Progress having passed Methane Princess for final time, 16.7.1981.

LPG carrier Isomeria in Dover Straits.

Gadinia.

Typhoon.
s.s. Gadila,
October 1981.

Loading crane
at Lumut,
Brunei.

Bee swarm!

Ken Hart with author.

Tectus at Hong Kong, September 1982.

Captain's lady goes ashore from Western Anchorage, Singapore, August 1982.

Joan and I greeting guests at one of the Hong Kong receptions, September 1982

Sharing a joke with Mike Howard (Shell Coal's regional manager)

Tenaga Empat.

Tenaga Dua berthing at Kawasaki.

Farewell.
Presentation at author's
retirement party.
October 1984.

Opalia Lightening VLCC
off Curaçao 1976

Author in conversation with
Marine Co-ordinator,
Mr. D.R. Skinner, on
Opalia 'Open Day' 1975

*Bishop of Singapore
with Captain W.
Irvine, CH Engineer
W.H. Mortimer and
Second Engineer
P. Cavanagh 1959*

*Father and Daughter
1982*

Family: Author, Rhiannon, Owen, Caitlin, Joan & Lloyd. August 1993

CHAPTER TEN

THE GAS MAN COMETH

The year 1964 was to mark a radical change in lifestyle for me. To begin with, I was ashore from the end of October 1963 until the following September. It was one of the more exciting periods in my seafaring life. When one talks about halcyon days - these were certainly they as far as my work as a Chief Officer were concerned!

The transportation of liquid natural gas or methane, was already an established technology having been carried in insulated barges from Louisiana to Chicago through the USA inland water system as early as 1951 An experimental ship 'Methane Pioneer', a conversion from a conventional carrier, had been commissioned by the nationalized British gas organization, British Gas Council, to carry a transatlantic cargo in 1959, from Lake Charles to Canvey. The man who initiated the concept, one Mr Billy Wood-Prince, President of Union Stockyard and Transit Company of Chicago was joined by Continental Oil to form Constock in 1954. Subsequently Shell joined to create Conch International in 1960 - I relate these facts to illustrate the truly transatlantic nature of the venture. Shell International Marine were contracted to supervise the building and operation of the world's first two commercial natural gas carriers, namely 'Methane Princess' and 'Methane Progress', the former being built at Barrow and the latter, Belfast. Concurrently, the French were constructing a carrier to be named 'Jules Verne'. All three ships were to load their cargoes at a new gas plant at Arzew in Algeria, the 'Methane' ships to deliver to a purpose built installation at Canvey Island in Essex, the French ship to Marseilles. These were the small beginnings of what eventually became a huge world-wide trade in moving LNG around the globe.

I was delighted to learn that I was to join one of three teams that would operate the two ships which were to be commissioned later in 1964. After an excellent furlough which included Christmas and New Year, I was instructed to join my fellow initiates at Chester for 'methane familiarization' at the Thornton Research centre (this was Shell's main British experimental/research establishment) for a five day course. Each team comprised five officers: Master; Chief Engineer; Cargo Officer (an engineer), Second Engineer and Chief Officer. The lead teams were as follows: Methane Princess - Commodore Atkinson, Chief Engineer Parsons, Second Engineer Laithwaite, Chief Officer Rodger and Cargo Officer Campbell. Methane Progress - Captain Munday, Chief Engineer Lowe, Second Engineer Another (I forget his name!), Chief Officer Thomas and Cargo Officer Mayhew. The relief team: Captain Swainston, Chief Engineer Waugh, Second Engineer Herbert, myself as Chief Officer and Cargo Officer Crook. Shell Tankers had a certain genius for picking compatible personnel whenever they chose! Certainly this was the case in the compilation of these three teams - which became, eventually, inextricably mixed up as time went on. There were no major personality clashes between any of the fifteen men who originally manned the teams. Naturally as time passed, new officers replaced the veterans and were never as successful as the originals. Of course, as would be expected, there were mutterings in the Fleet at large about elitism - which were justified insofar that I believe we were the 'creme de la creme' in 1964. We all worked together without prejudice - effectively and efficiently, creating a new bond between deck and engine departments that had, hitherto, been absent. This was in no small measure due to the enlightened and enthusiastic contributions made by the intelligent and highly articulate engineer officers, particularly Chief Engineer Lowe and the Cargo and Second Engineer Officers - they heralded a totally new atmosphere of comradeship and co-operation that made serving aboard the methaniers such an invigorating experience. I spent two very happy years with this band of gentlemen before I went on 'to better things', the euphemism for promotion!

The Sunday quality newspapers ran full page advertisements submitted by British Gas, one of which was entitled 'The Gas Man

Cometh' featuring Second Officer Alan Charlesworth's profile, complete with uniform hat at a jaunty angle, emblazoned across the page - hence the title of this chapter. The junior officers, of which Alan Charlesworth was one, were also of a high standard, so the ships operated at a cheerfully high level of efficiency. But, once again, I am somewhat previous!

Liquid natural gas (LNG) or liquid methane is manufactured by progressively cooling the gas extracted from reservoirs located in or adjacent to oil fields and which hitherto had been burnt off by flare as waste. Liquidizing methane reduced its volume to one six hundredth of the volume of the substance in its gaseous state. However to achieve this, natural gas is cooled to minus 161 degrees centigrade (minus 260 Fahrenheit), thus creating the need for specialized equipment for handling and containing the liquid. We entered the field of cryogenics in a huge way!

At the conclusion of the familiarization course, we were all sent to either Belfast or Barrow-in-Furness to stand-by the final days of the construction of the two ships. The stand-by team, of which I was a member, was posted to Barrow together with the 'Princess' team. Here, and in Belfast, we had the experience of working with personnel from Union Stockyard and Continental Oil, who together with Shell people comprised the management of Conch. We became firm friends with all these men, it was an all round great experience.

In the transport of LNG there are a number of containment systems, each designed to provide near total insulation. To describe these systems would be too technical, however it was rumoured that the 'Princess' and 'Progress' required a forest of balsa trees, grown in South America, to supply the insulation walls for the cargo tank range aboard these two ships. And what fine ships they were! Graceful beauties, which still looked magnificent twenty years later.

As I've already mentioned I was part of the stand-by team, headed by Captain Raymond Swainston. He and I now became pawns in a political battle that eventually had to be resolved on the floor of the House of Commons! It had all to do with pilotage. The venerable institution, Trinity House, had responsibility for pilotage in the River Thames extending from Dover to the London Docks. A ship arriving from the west boarded a pilot at Dover who took the vessel as far as Gravesend. If she was bound further up river, the pilot would hand over to another pilot who would take the ship into the Port of London. Many shipping companies had what were known as 'choice pilots', men from the general pool of pilots stationed at Dover (inward pilots) and Gravesend (outward pilots) who were paid a retainer by a particular company to pilot their ships. This gave the companies the comfort of knowing that the men who handled their ships were familiar with their craft and company policy, and, of course in the matter of berthing their ships, possessed a better working knowledge of the ships than perhaps a stranger would. Shell had two such gentlemen at Dover and another two at Gravesend for outward passages. The rule was that you could only be 'choice' for one company. Shell wanted these men, and these men exclusively, to pilot the Methane ships. Trinity House would have nothing of this. They construed that whereas the ships were managed by Shell Tankers (UK)Ltd, they, nevertheless, were owned by the British Gas Corporation and therefore did not qualify to employ Shell's choice men. So Shell stated their intention of training their senior ship's officers as pilots for the restricted area between Dover and Canvey (it was possible under the pilotage bye-laws for coastal shipping officers to obtain pilotage exemption, which was precisely what Shell intended to pursue). My God! talk about shock horror! The bones of departed pilots stirred in burial places around Kent and Essex, such was the commotion the very idea created - it was rumoured that some worthies even lost their appetite for ale in the hostelries in and about Dover and Gravesend! One just does not attempt to change the status quo in such matters as Trinity House tradition! Anyway, we did attempt.

Ray Swainston and I were the guinea pigs! Very willing guinea pigs I might add! Firstly we were briefed on the corporate strategy of the venture by Captain John Rendle, then a young marine superintendent with Shell International Marine who later became Managing Director of Shell Tankers (UK) Ltd. We boarded Shell or Shell chartered ships at Dover and Thameshaven to accompany our choice pilots in the passages through the outer reaches of the Thames and during berthing and unberthing operations. The first reaction by the pilotage community was to send our choice pilots 'to Coventry'! I kept a detailed record of all the ships that we travelled upon, with their dimensions and characteristics, but alas I have lost it and cannot recount the details. Captain Swainston and I had the most interesting and enjoyable time of our sea-lives! We boarded ships of many nationalities and were able to compare varying standards and attitudes whilst familiarizing ourselves with the river and estuary. We spent three months carrying out our training, after which we went home to 'swot' in readiness for our examination by the Elder Brethren of Trinity House. This we knew was going to be rigorous, in view of the raging controversy surrounding our activity in the pilotage district!

Captain Swainston and I became lifelong friends, as indeed did our families. I always showed deference in my dealings with Ray Swainston, although he urged a more relaxed relationship. I knew, however, that I would sail with him as his junior ere long and did not want to create a situation whereby embarrassment could result - being a strong advocate of the notion that familiarity breeds contempt. So throughout I called him 'Sir'! Notwithstanding, we did savour one another's company, enjoying this unusual period to the full. We lived in a private hotel in Southend-on-Sea called the Heath Hotel. We were given an allowance for board and lodging, so obviously we didn't choose the four star hotels! The Heath suited our purposes admirably, it was small but comfortable and we were able to come and go at any time of day or night. The food was good and it was licensed - which was also important! The word 'Heath' derived from the owner, one Mr Heath who was known to the locals as " Mista'eef " so forevermore that is how he was referred to! We employed a local small boat company to transport us from the seaward end of Southend Pier to ships anchored in the Southend and Maplin Sands anchorages awaiting berths at Thameshaven. We would travel to Dover by train to join incoming ships at the Dungeness pilot station and on disembarking outward bound ships, return by the same means. Boarding loaded tankers from the pilot cutter was relatively easy because of the small freeboard (height of main deck above water level) but it was another story getting off the ships in ballast, often dangling precariously above the bobbing cutter, holding on desperately to ladders that, occasionally, were of doubtful integrity, and waiting for the opportune moment to jump into the heaving craft! It was altogether a very interesting and enlightening education in another aspect of ship operation. There were quiet periods when the alert TV observer might have recognized amongst the spectators, two well imbibed seadogs enjoying a wonderful day's cricket at Lords! One of our other pursuits was playing tenpin bowling at the Pier arena during the mornings (with the young matrons of Southend, in adjacent alleys!), before resuming our investigation of the Essex watering holes at lunch - I had my car with me, which helped us in this endeavour!

As I have written, we returned to our homes to prepare for the forthcoming examination - each of us afraid that one would pass and the other fail! We were in daily 'phone contact - sounding out each other as to the other's progress, in so doing we redoubled our efforts to succeed. I believe we would have succeeded in passing any scrutiny of our knowledge of the area, had we been put to the test. James Callaghan, a future Prime Minister no less, raised the matter in the House of Commons! He was acting on behalf of the pilotage association and a question was tabled. In the best British tradition, compromise won the day with Trinity House allowing the Shell choice pilots to berth the Methane ships at Canvey Island. However Ray and I had the dubious distinction of having created something of a furore in hallowed halls of the marine establishment!

Whilst our little drama was unfolding, both Methane Princess and Methane Progress had been delivered to British Gas. The Progress was ahead of schedule so was employed, as an interim and profitable measure, in transporting a cargo of LPG (not LNG) from the Arabian Gulf to Japan. She returned to her home port, Canvey Island, on September 1st 1964, and, we, the stand-by team, joined on that day to take the ship to Tilbury for a clean-up - to get rid of the sand acquired with the Bahraini LPG! We left twelve days later, bound for Arzew in Algeria to begin our designated business of LNG transport. The Princess was just ahead of us and loaded a part cargo, really a test cargo for both installations - Arzew and Canvey. We, aboard Progress, loaded the first full cargo of LNG to be delivered to the UK. The initial cargo loading took longer because the ship had to be cooled down ahead of the loading operation and systems had to be proved. From the commencement, both ships operated extremely successfully - eventually delivering shipments at the rate of some 1,000,000 tons a year - the scheme continued for some twenty years, until North Sea supplies superseded the need for imports. I was to serve, briefly, as Master of the Princess some seventeen years later, so in total I was involved with 43 cargo deliveries by these two remarkable ships.

I have mentioned the calibre of the officers involved in the set-up of the operation. The importance of the scheme was such that the Fleet Commodore, Bill Atkinson, headed up the staff contingent. The other two masters, Jack Munday and Ray Swainston were fine men and a pleasure to work with. Of the Chief Engineers, one was quite outstanding: Dick Lowe. He had been a junior engineer officer in pre-war days and was captured by the Japanese when they invaded Singapore and was incarcerated in Changi Gaol. Anyone who has read 'King Rat' will know what a hell hole that place was. He would talk little of his experiences there, apparently he was the boxing champion of the place, so perhaps his level of fitness helped him survive his ordeal. At the time I am relating, there was little love lost between him and the Japanese! However, subsequently, when Shell undertook a major building programme, later in the decade in Japan, he reluctantly accepted supervisory posting to the Japanese shipyards where he found it in his heart to teach English to children, in his spare time. Such was his magnanimity - the mark of the true gentleman he is. Other outstanding people were Bob Herbert who became a Director, a softly spoken man with a keen intelligence and gentle wit. John Crook eventually rose to be a Director of Swan Hunter, one of Britain's erstwhile great ship building yards. I have mentioned a few of the personnel, but, all in all, everyone was a winner!

There was a popular series of documentary films produced by the Rank organization which were sandwiched between features at cinemas during the sixties called "Look at Life". I think it was while I was serving on 'Methane Progress' during the autumn of 1964 that we carried a film unit who filmed activities aboard the ship from Canvey back to Canvey, taking in the loading operation at Arzew. This feature was entitled "Stepping on the Gas" and was shewn in cinemas around the UK. On the furlough following my stint aboard the Progress, I located a cinema in Port Talbot that was exhibiting the film, so we as a family were able to watch it - it was of particular interest because yours truly was one of the 'stars'! Some years later we were having gas central heating installed in our home and one of the fitters said he was sure he had seen me somewhere before. It transpired that "Stepping on the Gas" was used as a training film by British Gas, and that was where he had seen me!

I spent the best part of the next two years aboard these two ships, a most enjoyable way to complete my service as Chief Officer. Friendships were formed that last to this day. In particular the family association between the Swainstons and ourselves became very strong, meeting as we did at refits and later on a non-ship basis. Ray and Mary, on retirement moved to South Wales where he secured a post as a government surveyor and examiner and so the families became ever closer. I finally left the methaniers in July 1966.

Sadness pervaded my family when my mother contracted cancer in 1965 and for seventeen months we waited for the inevitable, acting out a charade at my father's insistence, that she not be told of her fate. So it was that another phase in my life ended amid personal grief, my appointment and promotion to Master tinged with bitter sweetness in August 1966.

CHAPTER ELEVEN

AN OLD MAN - AT LAST!

In the British Merchant Navy the universal label for the Master of a ship (the Captain), is the 'Old Man'. The title is such an intrinsic part of the shipping industry patois as to be almost an official term and is freely used in conversations at all levels. To the outsider this may seem strange, even comic!

It was with trepidation and excitement that I relieved Douglas Reid of his command of Pallium on 26th August 1966 - by the strangest coincidence, 32 years to the day as I type this paragraph! I thus became her 'Old Man'! This was the culmination of every deck officer's career and the pinnacle of his profession at sea - one could, if chosen, be appointed to shore management which was considered to be further promotion. Most of us aspired to this lofty reward if truth be known, however many factors mitigated against such a radical change in circumstance, a subject I shall dwell upon at a later stage.

I had had a taste of this new world prior to joining Pallium, in that I was treated by agents et al with much more deference than I had experienced hitherto. I flew from London (attired in a sharp Austin Reed suit and expensive suede desert boots, I intended to look the part, if nothing else!) to New York, thence to Miami. I stayed in Fort Lauderdale for a couple of days awaiting the arrival of the ship at Port Everglades, where every wish was their command! Although I enjoyed the newly found status enormously, I was beset by a gnawing worry in that a hurricane (whose name I, alas, forget) of fierce proportions was approaching the Florida coast. So, before assuming command of my first ship, I felt the weight of my new responsibility whilst lying upon my vibrating bed in a Fort Lauderdale hotel of very superior elegance!

For the next eighteen and a half years I was to be addressed as 'Captain'. The final and longest phase in my seafaring career and one in which I rejoiced, although I had thoroughly enjoyed the other ranks, you couldn't beat being the boss! I had witnessed many different masters and had either benefited or suffered under their ministrations and yet I hadn't really formed a philosophy on how I would handle the position. So I decided I would spend my first days in command in reflection and cogitation in the expectation that I would evolve 'my' philosophy. Ha! What pomposity! There's nothing like a hurricane bearing down upon one's ship coupled with the unexpected discovery that we really didn't have sufficient bunkers - to knock such lofty theories out of the porthole!

Pallium was one of a small number of specialized ships built to carry bitumen between Curaçao and the USA eastern seaboard, but equally able to carry the range of 'black' oils in general trading. There were peak demands for asphalt both seasonal (with a much lower requirement during winter months) and a dependence upon current road building programmes. Pallium was state of the art in her designated function, being the latest ship to join the trade. Built in West Germany during the mid sixties she closely resembled the new generation of general purpose ships that Shell had designed and put into service during the late fifties and early sixties. They were handsome ships and Pallium was no exception. I was very proud to have such a smart looking job as my first command! For the previous two or more years I had been involved with the carrying of cryogenic liquid, here I was concerned with material at the other end of the temperature spectrum! The liquid was so hot that any water ingress led to alarming consequences with super hot black froth pushing out of every orifice - this dread reaction was magically calmed by the addition of a tiny amount of silicone to the surface of the liquid! The cargo heating equipment aboard these 'tar boilers' (as they were universally called within the Fleet) had to be in tip top order as did tank integrity (both to prevent any water going near the stuff!). As you can imagine, should the heating system fail, one would be left dealing with a solid tank of highway!

138

It may be apposite, if not in context, to describe to the uninitiated the means by which liquid cargo is transferred from shore to ship and vice versa. Everyone will have gathered that cargo is pumped on or off. The interface between ship and shore is a flexible hose (duly strengthened) or a self-adjusting mechanical arm, universally known as a'chiksan' after the firm that originally developed the equipment. Flexibility is obviously required to withstand the movement of the ship in tidal situations and the lowering of the ship in the water whilst loading and the reverse during discharge. The reason I mention the subject at this juncture is that the most vulnerable place during the transfer of liquid between ship and shore is at the 'manifold' (where the hoses are connected). Terrible accidents have occurred with the transfer of bitumen, with bodies cremated within a sarcophagus of tar at the manifold. Equally awful, but entirely different, consequences would happen with LNG, should someone be covered in the liquid. I have inserted this subject to illustrate dangers that one had to be aware existed.

We sailed from Port Everglades (having discharged a part of the cargo) on 27th August 1966 bound for a place I had never heard of - Kearney Point. What a hole! We passed through New York harbour, the Statue of Liberty, the United Nations Building and Manhattan Island with its familiar skyline on to the New Jersey side to this place. I had never been in a dirtier terminal in my entire life! It was no more than a heap of coal with bitumen tankage stuck between mounds of the stuff. I had grandly invited friends of mine, living on Long Island, to visit the ship! I had no idea that Pallium would be berthed at such a filthy location and was mortified when my guests boarded looking as though they had been down a mine! They were not amused! To go back, the voyage from Florida to New York took three days and we were able to flee ahead of the tropical revolving storm (hurricane in these parts), however I guessed, correctly as it happened, that we would have to deal with her (in those days, a TRS was always female) on our return to the Caribbean. I mentioned bunkers earlier. I was not happy with the amount we had on board and ordered additional fuel at New York - in case we had to deviate to avoid the hurricane. Naturally, fueloil in New York is much more expensive than the supply in Curaçao, so I rationalized the decision by deciding that it was wiser to have too much than to run out of the stuff! Fortunately for me, my principals in London concurred. So we left the Ambrose Light Vessel at the entrance to New York harbour and set course for Puerto La Cruz in Venezuela, a Gulf Oil installation. This, during his first week in command was to be a testing time for this novice!

As I had surmised we had to deal with her! Now there are almost scientific rules for avoiding a TRS, as long as the storm behaves in a predictable manner. There's even a lofty sounding rule called Buys-Ballot Law to enable one to estimate the position of the storm centre. Bear in mind that at this time we didn't have the luxury of facsimile maps, instead a wonderful book called "Meteorology for Mariners" published by Her Majesty's Stationery Office which would see one through. Anyway, Pallium avoided the dangerous semicircle and despite very heavy seas and swells arrived at our destination just a few hours later than estimated. We loaded fueloil at Puerto La Cruz for a delightful place called New Bedford in Massachusetts.

Europeans are steeped in history, with practically every city, town or hamlet having a rich background in one way or another. They tend, therefore, to regard their cousins across the Atlantic as lacking this gift bestowed by many previous generations. Not so! I have rarely been in a place which exuded such a feeling of historical atmosphere, albeit nautical and recent, more so than New Bedford! It had been the centre of the whaling industry in the nineteenth century, and there was no one more adept at this business than the New Englander. I thought it was a charming, colourful little port with memorabilia from those bygone days arranged in tasteful ways, their quaint houses with 'widow walks' all creating a palpable ambience of that era. Oh joy of joys! I was taken to lunch by the Agent! I had watched masters when I was a subordinate, having limousines arrive at the gangway to whisk them away for all sorts of entertainment, with envious eyes. Gordon Bennett, it was now happening to me! I remember the clam chowder and lobster thermidor I had at that memorable lunch with relish! I was really enjoying my new status.

I was born in Merthyr Tydfil. A few miles from my hometown there's a village called Hirwaun. One of this century's great maritime educators and visionaries was born in Hirwaun, one Charles H. Cotter, B.Sc. Extra Master, who taught at the Sir John Cass College in London for many years. He wrote a number of books among them

140

one entitled "The Master and his Ship", a slim but wise volume mainly commending various aspects of seamanship techniques to situations a ship's master might encounter. He was no mean philosopher to boot. Here's a quote from his introduction to this book:

A labourer is one who works with his hands;
A craftsman is one who works with his hands and his head;
An artist is one who works with his hands and
his head and his heart.

Cotter develops the theme in relation to a shipmaster's function. Ideally he should become an artist in his profession, embracing the various aspects of his responsibilities, viz., good shipboard husbandry; dealing efficiently with changing meteorological conditions; the exercise of prudent and precision navigation; to insist upon exemplary safety procedures; to know the legal aspects of business and insurance and to be well versed in the Merchant Shipping Acts; to prepare himself for marine and medical emergencies; to exercise discipline firmly and fairly. Above all to be a wise judge, to be independently minded and kind to all who sail under him. Cotter continues by writing that it is clear that a ship's master should be a man of many parts with a wide scope of interests. Further he should be well versed in several branches of knowledge in order to work his ship intelligently. Finally he should be a well-informed ambassador of his country. Phew! some paragon that man is going to be! However, for a young, first trip master it was an ideal to work for - however pretentious some of the foregoing may seem. In actual fact the ship's commander is master under God, invested with almost absolute power - a burden of responsibility indeed!

After leaving New Bedford in mid September 1966 we made a delivery of bitumen to Savannah, New York and Jacksonville which had been loaded at Curaçao. Our next loading at Punta Cardon took us to Boston. We left Boston on October 20th. On October 21st, that fateful day, I heard from a New York newscast that there had been a tragedy in Aberfan - part of the borough of my hometown - at the primary school where 116 children and 28 adults were overwhelmed by an evil mountain of sludge. Joan had relinquished teaching to care for my mother who was desperately ill, but the realization that had circumstances been otherwise, Joan could have been one of the teachers at Aberfan (she had been supply teaching prior to my mother's diagnosis) was distressing. The following day, on my father's birthday, my mother died. A very sad and disturbing time for us all, I felt very alone and grieved deeply for all the sadness in my family and in my town. This isolation from one's loved ones, in times of sorrow or stress, was always the most difficult burden to shoulder.

Next, at Curaçao, we loaded a cargo of fuel oil and diesel oil for West Africa. Our first call was at Dakar in Senegal, a city in a dry, arid part of the continent where everybody seemed to want to sell you something, apart from artifacts, trinkets and the like they even offered their mothers, sisters or, if your leanings were of a different ilk - their brothers! Our next port of call was Abidjan, the capital of the Ivory Coast, once a French colony. We were obliged to anchor outside the port for a night. This in itself was unremarkable except that the only place we could anchor was on a one mile wide shelf off the lagoon where the port is situated - this meant that we were less than half a mile off the beach in a pretty heavy swell, certainly not the happiest of places to spend a night. Didn't sleep much that night! Actually our stay in Abidjan wasn't a very happy experience for a number of people. As I'm sure the reader will appreciate, there's an industry in port areas that depends largely upon sailors for its success, namely prostitution. Abidjan was no exception. A short distance from the tanker jetty there was a collection of huts which housed local beauties and a few bars to help matters along. We entered the port on the morning of 10th November anticipating departure that same night (as we had only a small 'parcel' to discharge). It didn't take long for our brave worthies to locate the pleasure spot and for them to avail themselves of the amenities offered! Unfortunately, when it came to carrying out a crew check an hour prior to our departure time, half the crew were missing plus one officer! If they didn't return, we couldn't sail, it was as simple as that. Now I had had many years experience in sorting out jolly jack when I was mate and had occasionally resorted to unconventional measures to bring them into line! This night called for 'imaginative' action! I summoned the ship's agent and went to the village and rounded them up like cattle, herding them back to the ship with me in a slow moving car behind them, occasionally getting out to stop stragglers leaving the herd! It was almost refreshing to hear, once more, the oft shouted epithet "You Welsh bastard" in the safe and sure knowledge that my day would come tomorrow! I summarily sacked the officer in question and took the lads for every penny I could. Never had a ha'porth of trouble thereafter! Incidentally, we sailed on schedule!

The West African coast was served by a number of regular liner companies, one of which was Palm Line. My old buddy and flatmate from our early married days, George Holeyman, now in command with Palm Line passed Pallium in his magnificent ship, so we were able to have a long chat on the VHF between Abidjan and Takoradi, Ghana, our next call. All I remember about Takoradi was the fearful swell within the harbour which caused the ship to buck about alongside the wharf. After that on to Lagos and the wharf adjacent to the slaughter house at Apapa still as horrifying as it had been twenty years earlier! We left on 15th November, bound once more for Curaçao.

It was great fun (if you succeeded!) in finding the favourable currents firstly on the Grain, Ivory, Gold and Slave coasts and then on the voyage across the Atlantic Ocean. We were helped, almost entirely, by Current Atlases, which gave the most likely position of the Guinea, South Equatorial and Benguela currents on a monthly basis, together with their counter currents. So the trick was to select courses that you estimated would take fullest advantage of any assistance that a current would provide. It was enormously satisfying to discover that the ship was storming along at 18 knots instead of the service speed of 15 knots. Equally frustrating would be to find that you were down to 12 knots, in the knowledge that you had made a nonsense of things!

We returned to the asphalt business. We loaded for Nassau in the Bahamas, New York, Savannah and Jacksonville which in total took us sixteen days until returning to Curaçao. I enjoyed going ashore in these stylish ports! Nassau was a delight, with its quaint colonial atmosphere, whilst Savannah was redolent of Confederate rule and Southern elegance as indeed was Jacksonville. During the time I served as Chief Officer 'going ashore' was a rare pleasure - in fact it was almost a condition of employment that you didn't! I must say I found this aspect of being a ship's master, very much to my liking! At Curaçao we loaded fuel oil for New York and spent Christmas

Day in Sewaren on New York's West Side. It was the practice aboard ship that one cancelled Christmas Day, if spent in port, and you celebrated at the earliest convenient day once back at sea. This we did and had a magnificent day! We were bound for Puerto Miranda in Lake Maracaibo to load fuel oil for Perth Amboy. En route to Venezuela I had my first experience of life threatening illness as Master, one of the crew members developed acute appendicitis so I deviated to Curaçao on 1st January 1967 (a great start to the year!) to land him for surgery. I will refer to this aspect of seagoing in more detail at a later stage.

From Perth Amboy in New Jersey we returned to Puerto Miranda to load for Europe. We first went to Denmark, discharging at Copenhagen and Fredericia, thereafter to Thameshaven and finally to Dublin. These final weeks aboard Pallium gave me some pretty exacting experience in English Channel and North Sea navigation in dense fog most of the time. There was nothing quite as effective at concentrating the mind than a transit of the Dover Strait under such conditions. Fortunately I had had plenty of passages through the Channel aboard the Methane ships, albeit as an observer, which stood me in good stead.

Joan joined me at Thameshaven, accompanied me to Dublin and thereafter to Cardiff for refit. We sorely needed to be with one another after the tragedies that had happened in our personal and town lives. There was so much to catch up on. It was a source of great pride to me to have her aboard, as the Captain's wife - she had waited and supported, nourished and counselled, for twenty long years, this was some small recompense.

I recorded officers aboard the Methane ships who had done well in later life, we had a bright young junior engineer who served on Pallium whilst I was in command, one Blair McIntyre who is now Technical Services General Manager with the current Shell marine organization, STASCO. I sailed with a few outstanding guys in my time!

Pallium berthed at the tank cleaning wharf in Cardiff on February 17th 1967 and I left on the 20th being superseded by Mike Lee (who impressed me enormously with his entertainment equipment - a powerful short wave receiver, state of the art hi-fi and a portable

144

TV, which was very avant-guard in early '67!) Just couldn't persuade Joan that this was the norm for ship masters!

During the forthcoming year there was a minor revolution in shipboard management and social attitude to officer/crew relationships. By happenstance I landed up in the forefront of these changes. Whereas I had been tentative in my approach to a Captain's function aboard Pallium, not knowing just how to establish a meaningful and useful part in ship operation, the developments in 1967 solved any dilemma I may have had.

CHAPTER TWELVE

A LINER AND TWO TRAMPS

Periods of service were now reduced to about six months, which was a great improvement from the 'old' days. Furloughs were longer in that we were getting about eight days leave for every month served aboard ship. You could say that compared with the pre-war old timers, who served three years and had three months furlough at the end, we were in clover. However, we are all products of the age in which we live and work, and certainly at the end of the sixties, the average professional man ashore would not have regarded our conditions as attractive.

I mentioned, at the end of the Preface, that I am ever conscious of the price we, as a family, paid for the career I followed. Rhiannon, our daughter, probably suffered most. It was totally unrealistic to expect her to be as close to me as other girls were to their fathers. This was an enormous difficulty for me - I so wanted that affection yet knew, in my heart of hearts that as hard as I would try, we, Rhiannon and I could not attain that goal. Yet, there was a point when she was about thirteen years old when I thought I had achieved it! She came home from school, a day before I was to return to sea, plonked herself on my lap, threw her arms around my neck and tearfully said "Why can't you be an ordinary man, Daddy?" I had never heard anything so poignant and I haven't since.

We had a lovely Spring leave, the weather was good and my batteries were fully recharged! Yet again I was to have interesting work to do

146

- another new field to plough. On April 8th 1967 I joined Asprella at Rotterdam. Asprella was Shell's chemical carrier, one of the relatively new 'A' class ships to which I have previously referred, suitably adapted to carry mainly benzene from Puerto Rico to Europe. Now benzene is seriously dangerous material to handle! Its main hazard is its carcinomatous properties which had to be stringently guarded against. Not a drop of the liquid was ever to touch the human body nor were benzene fumes to be inhaled. To monitor everyone's health, blood samples were taken from all hands on each return to the Europe for laboratory analysis - such was the seriousness with which Shell regarded this product. Additionally, it was a highly volatile spirit, but this was something tanker men knew all about. To my knowledge, I was not aware of any Asprella crew member contracting cancer as a result of benzene contamination.

Apart from the need for extreme care in cargo management, Asprella was a wonderful ship. Now I appreciate the common perception of a 'liner' is that of a passenger ship, but the strict interpretation of the word would be a ship employed on a regular run between regular ports. Once again it would be stretching the meaning of the word to describe Asprella thus. However, she was the nearest approach to a liner that Shell had in those days. She loaded exclusively at Guayanilla on the south coast of Puerto Rico and discharged at one or more of the following ports: Antwerp, Rotterdam, Thameshaven, Swansea, Stanlow or Grangemouth - to the initiated it would be apparent that we delivered exclusively to a selection of refineries operated by either Shell or BP.

Asprella was the first ship within the Shell group to conduct shipboard weather routeing. She possessed a prototype facsimile weather map machine which enabled the navigation team to assess the most economical route across the Atlantic to achieve the best possible passage time with the least likelihood of weather damage. We, as a team, became quite successful at this advance in passage planning technique and concrete advantage was evident with an improvement in voyage performance. In its infinite wisdom, the Shell organization decided to employ a Dutch meteorological service to route all its owned and chartered ships across the Atlantic. The service was considered to be very professional and would undoubtedly prove its value in the long term. However, we too considered ourselves pretty

147

competent at this routeing game, giving, as we did, our undivided attention to 'our' needs. An edict was issued that we no longer were to conduct our own routeing but to follow the advice of the shore organization. I remember well the voyage that we first availed ourselves of this service (compulsorily). We had discharged at Rotterdam, Thameshaven and finally at Grangemouth and up until the last day I had not received orders to utilize the Dutch routeing instructions. Consequently, I had observed the weather prognostications some days prior to our leaving, upon the mistaken assumption that we would continue to route ourselves. I had prepared a passage to head south through the English Channel to avoid the Atlantic track of a hurricane that was about to embark upon its trail of destruction. We, at the last minute, were told to follow the meteorological service routeing plan. This had Asprella going north through Pentland Firth and thence into the Atlantic. I profoundly disagreed with these instructions and advised my principals of my uneasiness with the advice received. To no avail. We suffered the most violent passage in my experience, having to heave-to to minimize damage and stress in the teeth of the tropical storm. Joan, who was accompanying me on this particular voyage, and I were marooned in the 'midships accommodation for the best part of two days! She had the distinction of having witnessed the worst weather I had endured. The whole object of so called weather routeing was to avoid such a situation and I subsequently wrote an acid report criticizing the Dutch met office for its ineptness - this later elicited an apology.

Socially, the ship was most enjoyable. We, the staff and crew, had a most fruitful liaison with the people at Guayanilla where we established a good working relationship in addition to a mutually valued social link between the ship and shore management. The drill was that a party was held on board during one visit and ashore the next - in fact Asprella became an notable venue in the social calendar of Guayanilla and Ponce, certainly Shell's image was enhanced. We had a memorable voyage when the Company's Chief Medical Officer, one Dr Johnson, accompanied by his wife, made a round voyage partly on business (assessing the medical risks associated with benzene) and partly for pleasure. We were given carte blanche to entertain them at our very best. So we sure enjoyed that month! I have, ever since, had a fearfully expensive taste for Puligny Montrachet - the good doctor's favourite table wine! Of course Joan and I had a marvellous round voyage together, despite our frightening experience in mid-Atlantic. This was one of the major benefits of being master, having time to be with one's loved one, without the daily hassle of the mate's job. Then of course, during my sojourn, Asprella visited Swansea on three occasions. I was able to hire a car and was in Merthyr within the hour, so she was a very happy ship as far as I was concerned.

I became actively involved in quite dramatic change within ship management and the social structure aboard Shell ships. We had an imaginative Managing Director, Bernard Blakeley who decided to transform the traditional practices that had existed aboard ships for eons and he chose Asprella as the forerunner for these developments - in essence a test bed. Traditionally, cargo ships and tankers were ruled by two men, viz., the Master and Chief Engineer with little or no liaison between these two all-powerful people. More often than not, power was delegated to their immediate subordinates, the Chief Officer and Second Engineer Officer. There were many Old Men and Chiefs (the common reference to a Chief Engineer) who regarded their elevation to the top rank as a reward of, say, twenty years as dogsbodies with the attendant hard work and therefore felt no necessity to inject their knowledge and experience into the shipboard ambience - "Let them get on with it, I've done my stint!" attitude. Tales abound of these senior men having opted out totally from the running and operation of their ships and engine rooms. They were nothing more than expensive ballast. There was one legend concerning a chief engineer who in the course of one year's service never left his accommodation (apparently he was excused lifeboat and fire drills on the grounds of ill health) and when the time arrived for him to leave, he had become so fat that they had to enlarge the doorway to release him! (his nickname was 'Tiny'). Others, power hungry and resentful of their years as underlings, became martinets and crushed initiative and ruled with a rod of iron. Neither example was to be extolled. Fortunately, the majority of men conducted shipboard affairs somewhere between these extremes. To an observer, however, it would be manifest that 'this wasn't the way to run a railroad'!

Nowadays, the concept of management teams is old hat. Then, in the late '60's, it was almost revolutionary! So we, aboard Asprella, formed the first shipboard management team in Shell Tankers (UK) Ltd. The

149

team consisted of myself as chairman, the Chief Officer, the Chief Engineer Officer and the Second Engineer Officer with a junior officer as secretary. We were all afforded the opportunity to voice our opinion about any subject appertaining to shipboard affairs. There were dire mutterings about 'you cannot run a ship by committee' and the like, but the whole venture was entirely successful and one of two breaths of fresh air that enlivened the shipboard ethos. The success was due, in no small part, to the people involved initially. Chief Engineer Mike Holderness, who later aspired to top management and now operates a thriving marine consultancy, embraced the concept enthusiastically. Brian Oliver, the Chief Officer, who was teetering on the edge of promotion was also a wholehearted advocate. John McCallion, then Second Engineer (who also rose to dizzy heights within Shell Tankers management) with his incisive mind, completed the team. It should be mentioned that the committee meeting discussions were formally minuted and filed.

In parallel with the management team experiment we were asked to form a shipboard welfare committee with the express purpose of operating a crew bar. Ever since Nelson was a little lad, crew members had been issued with 'bond'. The word derives from the bonded store where beer, cigarettes and spirits were stowed with additional security (i.e. an extra padlock) to comply with customs requirements. Bond night was a big feature in the lives of crew members when they could purchase whatever their allowance of beer may be (this depended upon the judgment of the master). There were those who didn't drink (few and far between!) who would draw their quota and flog it to one of their mates. Aboard tankers, in Shell anyway, there was a weekly rum issue when each crew member would draw a tot from the Chief Steward (usually on a Sunday) and more often than not take it back to his cabin. Additionally, whilst tank cleaning, those involved were entitled to a tot of rum (ostensibly to displace the petroleum fumes the man may have ingested - which was a load of old tosh in reality!) and the laddos really valued this perk. Ha!Ha! They would save it, and also add the non-drinkers' tots to their reservoirs. On 'bond' nights, they would give credence to the adage that ' work is the curse of the drinking classes'! The fact of the matter was that the men were not being treated in an even handed or dignified manner. Bernard Blakeley could clearly see this social imbalance, thus the change in management attitude. The crew members constructed a very creditable bar in their messroom and so began a new era. In tandem with this change, social evenings were organized for all hands - quizzes, bingo nights, whist drives and the like which proved wholly successful. The ship had an laudatory mention in the National Union of Seamen monthly journal "The Seaman". The Company constructed a 'proper' bar when the ship docked for its next refit and extended the facility to all other British crewed ships in the fullness of time.

I look back upon my stay on board Asprella with satisfaction and a sense of achievement. I left her at the end of October 1967. We, as a family, had a great leave which included Christmas and New Year. I well remember taking Joan to a New Year's Eve dance in one of the local dance halls and then falling victim to 'flu on New Year's Day . This in itself is unremarkable but for the fact that I had to join my next ship at Bremerhaven the following day. I travelled to Germany feeling awful, and, as soon as I boarded promptly went to bed for two days!

The ship was Hemicardium. A bird by another name - she was San Fernando in her new Shell guise (see Chapter Nine) and still employed carrying lubricating oils. Anyone will tell you that ships have 'atmospheres'. Depending upon the mix of individuals, an atmosphere could vary from sensible and businesslike to almost lunatic in nature. The latter applied in the case of this appointment. As I have written, I joined (in freezing conditions) with a raging fever and within minutes of my arriving in the master's accommodation I was almost accosted by the Chief Engineer and Mate! I daresay I had, perhaps, established a reputation in the short time I had been in command, which was not to the liking of some but which, hopefully, would be welcomed by others. The ship had been at Bremerhaven for some time, undergoing refit, and had been left under the supervision of the Mate and Chief - the previous Master having left on arrival at the yard. Anyway, I was issued with a list of ground rules on how I was to conduct my stewardship of Hemicardium! This also happened later in my career, which I shall refer to in a subsequent chapter. I was in no mood to suffer such idiotic nonsense and sent these two guys packing with a few choice expletives to help them on their way before retiring to my bed. The Chief was a very clever man, intelligent, well read but so idiosyncratic and unstable as to be a constant concern to me. Throughout the Merchant Navy there was a well known condition called 'tankeritis' and this officer evinced all the symptoms of this fabled condition. Apart from his efforts to subvert my authority, he would clown around the ship in fancy dress, crawling along the flying bridge on all fours as we were berthing alongside a jetty and embarrassing me to the point of fury. The Mate, a huge mountain of a man with a dour unsmiling countenance, somehow found the Chief amusing and foolishly thought he could intimidate me in some manner. As soon as I had recovered sufficiently, I interviewed these gentlemen, established my authority and immediately instituted a management team, which took the wind out of their sails forcing them to behave like responsible leaders.

I served aboard Hemicardium for six and a half months, during that time we made voyages from Curaçao to south east Africa and Europe, finally circling the globe. Fortunately, I was well versed in the transport of lube oils so was able to help plan the complicated cargoes and actually load our final cargo during my tenure when the Mate had to leave through ill health. From Bremerhaven we called at Southampton for spares en route to Curaçao where we loaded for Lourenço Marques and Beira. Two totally disparate features of these visits stand out in my mind. One was a meal and the other was being taken to account by HMG. I went ashore in Lourenço Marques and landed up in what was known as the People's Restaurant where I enjoyed one of the most memorable meals in my entire life! It was simple and delicious - a large plate of freshly fried prawns accompanied by crusty bread washed down by cool Portuguese rose wine, I've never forgotten it. The other experience was of a much more grave importance. We delivered gas oil to an installation at Beira (having temporally been taken off the lube oil trade). This was the time when the British government was blockading Beira in an effort to prevent shipment of cargo to Southern Rhodesia, which was in a state of insurrection having declared unilateral independence from Britain. After being challenged by a Royal Navy frigate, we entered port and I was summoned to Her Majesty's Consulate at Beira to swear on oath that the eventual destination of Hemicardium's cargo was not to the Smith regime in Southern Rhodesia. This I did with a clear conscience, knowing nothing more than that the bills of lading consigned the cargo to Shell in Beira. Subsequently, I had my suspicions that perhaps, inadvertently, I had told a porky!

152

We returned to Curaçao where we loaded for Rotterdam and Stanlow. Joan and Rhiannon visited the ship at Eastham Lock (the entrance to the Manchester Ship Canal) travelling up canal to Stanlow, leaving the next day when Hemicardium completed discharge. These visits, although short, were wonderful interludes and kept our batteries charged. Apart from the obvious happiness of being together, it afforded Rhiannon the chance to see some of what life aboard a ship meant. Our next loading port was Curaçao (gets a bit boring, doesn't it ?). However, en route, I had to divert the ship to San Juan, Puerto Rico, to land two sick crew members. If there was ever an anxiety that consumed my thoughts it was the preservation of a human life under my care. In the course of a career as master I think I had to deviate to land eight cases of appendicitis, a severe case of pancreatic, a bowel obstruction and two incidents of severe scalding. Among other experiences I had to clear a bladder obstruction with a catheter, replace a dislocated shoulder that was half way down the man's side.

We loaded a multigrade cargo of luboils at Curaçao and Punta Cardon in Venezuela, departing on 16th April 1968 for Durban, Singapore, Djakarta, Hong Kong and Yokohama. Again I had to deviate to Port Dickson in Malaysia to land an apprentice with appendicitis. Now, the decision to deviate was entirely the Master's - no reference to the action was ever made by management, so one always prayed that the decision was correct. One didn't take this decision without express medical advice, however the doctor relied entirely upon the picture the master painted. In later years one could examine a patient in his cabin using the cabin 'phone and speak directly to a doctor in a hospital by short wave or satellite link and follow his instructions explicitly. Anyway, enough of this subject. We completed the final discharge of our cargo at Yokohama on 6th June. Unfortunately, the Mate had to be discharged on medical grounds and we sailed short handed. I took the mates's watch (4 to 8), organized the tank cleaning and the planning of the next cargo. Once again we were bound for Curaçao which entailed a trans-Pacific voyage of twenty days' duration, a Panama Canal transit plus another two days in the Caribbean before reaching our destination on 29th June - some two and a half months after completing our previous loading.

Assisted by the deck staff, who in fact did all the leg work, I loaded the next cargo. The new Chief Officer (the Mate, I keep switching titles) joined at the latter stages of the loading operation, much to my relief. I was so pleased to see him, I was almost inclined to help carry his bags on board!

A strange change of subject, but its relevance will soon become apparent. I am now going to describe anchor cables and their stowage with particular reference to Hemicardium (ex San Fernando, as already mentioned, formally an Eagle Oil owned ship, having minor differences in appearance and design from the standard Shell 'H' class ship). Anchor chain is pulled aboard by a windlass and disappears into the fore peak space into a chain locker. Nowadays and then, chain lockers are/were self-stowing and certainly this ship should have had no problems in this regard. However, this particular sub class of 'H' boat certainly did! The lockers (one for each cable) were too small for the amount of cable she carried, unless stowage was helped physically by a man or men carefully flaking the incoming cable neatly within the locker using cable hooks, the locker would fill before all the cable was on board Now our first discharge port was Tenerife in the Canary Islands and we anchored off the port of Santa Cruz in deep water. We discharged our parcel into barges at the anchorage which didn't take long to complete. Practically all the cable was out, because of the depth of water and when the moment came to sail, we experienced great difficulty in lifting the chain on board, the windlass just couldn't manage the job because the vertical weight of the chain was too great. By dint of careful manoeuvring to ease the strain and using maximum steam pressure on the windlass, we slowly recovered our cable. In the excitement and concern over our little difficulty, the new Mate remembered that he had to attend to the stowage in the locker. Unbeknown to me he went below to check that the rating who had been given the task of stowing the chain and found he was was running into problems, so he (the Mate), very foolishly, went into the locker to clear a kink. Next thing, the pile of chain settled and pulled him into the compartment and started to cover him. The rating raced up to the foc'sle head to stop the operation and succeeded in quick time. I left the Bridge in charge of the officer of the watch and went forward to see what I could do. We reversed the direction of the cable movement and very slowly extricated the Mate from the cable pile. This guy was a tough 'un! He appeared OK, bloodied, bruised and very dazed. I landed him in hospital for observation, retrieved the cable and sailed, once more, short handed, to Rotterdam. He re-joined us there, fortunately in rude health! After Rotterdam we completed our discharge at Shellhaven and I left for my summer holidays on 20th July 1968.

We had a wonderful summer furlough, spending some time in Tenby, our resort of dreams. This was a time when we, as a family (with Rhiannon between the age of eleven and fourteen), so enjoyed our valuable time together - particularly on such holidays. We three would spend glorious days on the wonderful Pembrokeshire sands, Rhiannon and I would swim to a nearby island and we would all walk the coastal paths together. We stayed at the best hotels wherever we went, which gave our girl a taste for the finer things in life. It was a time of great contentment.

I flew to Curaçao on 5th October to await the arrival of Amastra, my next appointment. I had a couple of days at the Avila Beach Hotel during which time I managed quite successfully to cripple myself. I went swimming from the hotel beach which had shark nets, so I felt quite safe from that hazard but succeeded in stepping on not one, but two, sea apples! Fortunately only one foot was affected, other-wise I would have been unable to walk. Under other circumstances, I might have enjoyed the cure the beach waitresses administered, but I was in excruciating pain with my foot rapidly swelling with black threads inside the flesh. They literally turned me upside down and poured hot candle wax over the affected foot which alleviated my suffering remarkably! I went to the doctor's and received further treatment, but it took weeks to recover. So I joined Amastra with a bandaged foot and a crutch!

I had a relatively short stay aboard Amastra, interesting nevertheless. She was a 'white oiler' (aviation spirit down to heating oil). My first cargo took us to Los Angeles and Seattle (but, once more, I had to divert to land a sick seaman at San Diego) which I found very pleasant - including two transits of the Panama Canal. Our next delivery was to west Africa, Accra, Lagos and Douala, by now almost familiar ground to me. Back to the Caribbean to load for two instal-lations in New York. After my final loading at Curaçao we took a cargo to Kingston, Jamaica, Nassau in the Bahamas and Bermuda. Whereupon I was relieved for 'better things'.

I should, perhaps, relate that whilst I was serving aboard Hemicardium, I applied to Silver Line for a post as Marine Superintendent - principally involved with the carriage of chemicals and lube oils which I considered I was eminently qualified to fulfil. I had a most apologetic letter from their management advising that I had been too late in making my application and that the post had, by that time, been filled. There was almost an air of regret about the reply. Whilst I was home after Hemicardium I was invited by Shell International Marine to join their shore staff as a Marine Superintendent. Now there was a crucial difference between Silver Line's post and that offered by Shell. Silver Line was UK based, whereas Shell's was an overseas appointment after six months in London. This meant, that at the age of eleven, we would have to send Rhiannon our daughter to boarding school. The young lady had already suffered enough with my being away so much that it was unthinkable to Joan and myself that we should subject our girl to the unknown experience of being sent to a public school, so I declined the appointment on that basis. Had I taken the post I suspect I would have landed up relieving Bob Allen in Australia. (Bob, a legendary figure in our organization, wrote "Wartime with Shell" a wonderful tale of his exploits during the war years). So I returned to sea.

A word or two about the term 'tramp' In seafaring parlance, a tramp is a cargo ship that seeks a cargo wherever and whenever it can. This could not be ascribed to a tanker, however the effect was similar in that both types of ships really didn't know where they were going to next. Hence the title of this chapter.

CHAPTER THIRTEEN

" BETTER THINGS "

Up to this point in my 'recollections', the narrative has consisted, largely, of a log or diary of my movements interspersed with the occasional viewpoint or observation. From this juncture onwards such a record would be both boring and uninteresting. The type of trade with which I was involved from 1969 onwards (with notable exceptions) was in the transport of large volumes of crude oil or liquid natural gas - often from one open sea berth to another. This is about as exciting as watching butter melt! The previous chapters covered 24 years of my career, the remainder of my story spans the final 15 years.

As I recounted at the end of the previous chapter, I left Amastra at Bermuda. I flew to the UK by British Airways on the night of 15th January 1969. The little I saw of Bermuda impressed me with its quiet pace of life (maximum road speed 20 mph!) and gentle folk. On the overnight flight I had the curious experience of sitting alongside a then famous British boxer (a Cockney, and feather-weight champion, whose Christian name was 'Terry') who was alleged to have contacts with the 'mob' in Miami. The flight had started at Miami. By the time the Bermuda passengers boarded, this guy was completely stoned and just a mite aggressive. He insisted upon calling me 'Curly' (I had dead straight hair) which was a familiarity I found perturbing but being an arrant coward suffered his increasingly truculent manner with a benign accep-tance! I was glad to leave that aircraft unscathed.

I cannot recall anything of note occurring during the short furlough that followed my brief stint aboard Amastra. Joan and I continued to make the most of every available opportunity to enrich our time together, to give Rhiannon as many experiences as possible - which usually meant taking her to London in winter or Bournemouth and Tenby in summer. My father never recovered from my mother's fearful death. He was a single minded man who devoted himself exclusively to his much beloved Hilda and was ill-prepared for life without her. Although Joan and I did all we could to alleviate his grieving, he gradually lost interest and his zest for life. A constant concern to us all, but with my brother, Tom, following a new career in Canada, the responsibility devolved upon us and Joan in partic-ular. Another impediment imposed by seafaring.

The 'better things' referred to in the title of this chapter represent my 'promotion' to bigger ships. I have already alluded to this euphemism in the last chapter, but this was but one of a number of 'in' phrases that comprised Shellese - almost a language in its own right. Whilst mentioning the subject, two famous expressions are worthy of record, viz., "We fail to conceive" would presage an ominous response whenever corporate disapproval was about to descend upon a hapless ship. The other: "We are pregnant with despondency" showing their displeasure in another form. A wag from one ship commenced a letter thus: " We too, are pregnant with despondency at your failure to conceive"! To return to 'better things'. I'm sure that the expectancy was that bigger would be better, but alas, such was not the case. The next 21 months were to be the most taxing in my career as master.

I welcomed my elevation with huge enthusiasm, not at the time real-izing how misplaced this was going to prove. The experience I absorbed during these months aboard three ships, although painful in some ways, was a valuable learning curve and stood me in good stead in crisis management and coming to terms with 'ennui'. Two ships: Donacilla and Daphnella were the vehicles for the first lesson and Opalia the second.

Donacilla and Daphnella were sisters - British built at yards in the North East - fine modern craft of some 70,000 tons deadweight driven by Sulzer motors (a seagoing paradox was that Sulzer was a

Swiss firm nestling at the foot of the Alps, hundreds of miles from any port, manufacturing the finest of seagoing propulsion units). They possessed two flaws that so affected my equanimity during this period. The first, and potentially the most critical, was the inability of the water producing plants to perform efficiently. The second, which landed me in more hot water than I would wish upon my worst enemy, they didn't have sufficient anchor cable.

I was on Opalia on three occasions. I refer the reader to Chapter Four, when I served aboard the original Opalia. On my final appointment to the successor, she was a Cadet Training Ship an entirely different experience about which I will wax eloquent in a subsequent chapter. This chapter will deal with my first assignment to the 'new' Opalia. She was the most beautiful of ships, the finest example of British shipbuilding one would ever witness. Built at Cammell Laird's in Birkenhead in the mid '60's, she was the last of the luxury ships - built to a specification and then paid for on a 'how much?' basis. Apart from the highest technical quality, she performed like a dream and never gave the slightest operational concern during my stewardship. The accommodation was lavish with beautiful wood panelling, spiral staircases, luxurious furniture with expensive prints scattered here and there. She was a steam turbine driven ship of about 50.000 tons deadweight, a handy middle range tanker. I found her during this period, despite the opulence, a desperately lonely ship.

I served aboard Donacilla from March until August 1969, Opalia from October '69 to April 1970 and Daphnella from June until December the same year.

Donacilla was almost my nemesis. After a restful few days at the Raffles Hotel in Singapore awaiting her arrival, I boarded to take command on 5th March, little knowing that the following four days were to be little short of a living nightmare. Hitherto, my biggest ship had been less than 20,000 tons, here I was in control of a monster nearly four times bigger. That in itself would have been sufficiently daunting for anyone, particularly as we left the jetty at Pulo Bukom in the small hours of the morning. However, as we were being towed off the berth the engine failed repeatedly to start so we, with considerable difficulty, anchored in the Western

159

Anchorage. When the fault was remedied, we recovered our cable, and, in so doing succeeded in jamming the anchor in the stowage pocket. There was nothing we could do, under the circumstances, so we proceeded on passage to our destination, Mina al Ahmadi in Kuwait. Naturally, I remained on the Bridge until we cleared into the Malacca Strait. I well remember savouring the jungle scents carried by the off-shore breeze, so evocative of years spent in Indonesian jungle rivers, feeling at peace with the world in anticipation of rewarding months aboard this fine ship. It was a Friday morning and Heaven disintegrated into Hell!

At 1000, the ship blacked-out, we lost the boilers and the emergency generator failed to start. Instantly we became a hulk and a dangerous one at that! No power meant no water, no ventilation, no cooking, no washing and no cold beer. We had battery power so were able to communicate our predicament to Singapore by radio. Singapore, in turn, contacted London. I was reluctant to disclose our plight to other ships or shore stations for fear of having salvage vultures descend upon us. Remember, one of our anchors was jammed in its pocket, so we only had one in order to secure our position should the ship be in unavoidable jeopardy. I called up a passing Shell ship on VHF (a British ship at that) requesting that she stand-by until a rescue was organized. The master refused, much to my consternation, little does he know what grief he caused me - I did meet him later, but wisely refrained from tackling him.

We drifted up and down the Malacca Strait, fortunately clearing shoals so we didn't contemplate having to drop our remaining anchor. The ship possessed a charcoal brazier which enabled the Chinese crew to boil rice and we, to brew tea. Otherwise we ate tinned food because the cold rooms were warming up and the frozen contents were defrosting in the tropical heat. The most uncomfortable inconvenience was not being able to bathe other than by dipping a bucket into a water tank and washing oneself by that means. Fortunately we were able to flush toilets with sea water, again using a bucket.

In the event, the Company engaged a deep-sea tug to tow us back to Singapore on a commercial contract rather than on a salvage basis. This exercise was very interesting and occasionally worrying,

160

particularly when traversing the Philip Channel (part of the Singapore Strait notorious for its strong tidal streams) with Donacilla yawing wildly at the end of a tow line. We reached the Eastern Anchorage and after further difficulty in getting our 'free' anchor cable to run, anchored safely. Nothing, but nothing, went well for us in those early March days in 1969.

We presented a pretty scruffy and fetid image to those who boarded at the anchorage. The smell of unwashed bodies, by now unflushed toilets had added to the pervading odour, the main refrigerators had defrosted and food had begun to rot making another contribution to the general foulness. A very welcome visitor was Shell Tankers' Personnel Manager, Ron Howell. He was on a tour of the Far East, assessing Fleet morale and conditions. He considered a visit to a ship 'in trouble' a valuable adjunct to his work experience. We provided him full measure with full visual and aural accompaniment plus more than a smidgen of rankness! The expression 'warts and all' comes to mind.

The plant was repaired, ample water supplied, the ship cleaned up, bodies washed and powdered, clothes laundered and the 'stuck' anchor pulled out of its pocket by a tug. New provisions were supplied so two days later we were on our way, once more, Arabian Gulf bound. We loaded at Kuwait for Sydney and Geelong. The Chief Engineer, who was on the verge of a nervous breakdown (and I kid you not), was relieved by a stout hearted Geordie lad named Charlton who came aboard like a breath of Northumberland fresh air (or maybe it was Durham - one has to be careful, they're nearly as prickly as the Welsh!). At some point, later in this narrative, I will relate how Chief Engineers became comrades and friends. Ron Charlton was, after Mike Holderness and James Flett at this point in my career, as good a friend and colleague as they had been. One can always tell a seafaring friend (and I write of colleagues and obviously not of subordinates) if you can insult one another in the most outrageous terms without rancour by either - then you are indeed friends (nowadays, I suspect, the term would be 'male bonding' or some such high flown expression)! This, in the rugged atmosphere of a troublesome motor ship, meant a lot.

Despite Ron Charlton's buoyant confidence, half way across the Indian Ocean we ran out of water. The reason was that these ships possessed inefficient water distilling plants (which normally produced enough fresh water for all purposes by distillation of sea water) and once more we were in trouble. The ship had to be stopped (because the main engine piston jackets used fresh cooling water) and lo and behold, the emergency generator failed to start yet again and we became a hulk once more! We collected rain water with tarpaulins for domestic use, although as we were in the middle of the North East Monsoon, there wasn't much of that either. Fortunately, repairs were effected to the distillation units and the boiler flashed up by burning cabin doors and gasoil and slowly coaxed into life, as was the remainder of the engine room equipment. Another uncomfortable and anxious couple of days. Water remained critically short for the remainder of the voyage and was strictly rationed, no showers only buckets, so we stank our way to Australia! Our hearts were in our mouths, particularly as we crossed the Great Australian Bight with its fearsome weather, for fear of another catastrophe. We made Sydney on the 16th April 1969. I have two excellent photographs of Donacilla majestically sweeping past the embryo Opera House en route to Gore Bay. We looked a picture of quiet efficiency, what a false impression - nerves were like piano strings! From Sydney (with a plentiful supply of fresh water) to Geelong to complete discharge and to carry out further repairs. The Shell resident superintendent at Geelong was none other than Bob Allen. This kindly, jovial man injected a large measure of cheer into this daunted floating community, in his inimitable manner - which is why he has been such a beloved character throughout the Fleet.

My in-house Editor (Joan) tells me, amongst other things, that I must not continually go on about trials and tribulations. Unfortunately, aboard Donacilla there seemed little else. Anyway, I take her point and will write about diverse matters.

I had been in command for something less than three years, which made me little more than a neophyte in the business of managing a ship. For the last ten years I had sailed with British crews exclusively, Donacilla was manned by Hong Kong men. There's an entirely different psyche with a Chinese crew, they do not respond to the direct, sometimes robust approach one used with the Brits. More a subtle, circuitous technique was effective in one's dealings. Whatever one did, one did not allow loss of face to occur. One of my precepts since becoming Master was to ensure that victualling was of the highest achievable standard. So much depended upon the ability and good-will of the Chief Steward / Victualling Officer and cooks, plus, the quality of provisions. However, a master could impact effectively upon this standard if he showed interest and knowledge. I always strived to have 'a good feeder'. Whereas there had been a degree of integration between officers and crew aboard British ships in recent times, language and culture prevented such a wind of change aboard Chinese crewed ships. Some five years later I experimented with a modest and occasional social 'party' between officers and crew, in addition to the traditional Chinese New Year Party which was always a memorable occasion. So one adapted oneself to the differing ethos, be it British, Chinese, Filipino and subsequently, Muslim. One had to regard oneself as the mayor of a community and tend to all social needs as well as the technical operation and disciplinary requirements of a ship.

Donacilla needed a firm, compassionate hand at the helm. Morale was fast plummeting after two debacles, so I fostered the odd party (clearly understood, only in safe waters), where additional libation was sanctioned and men released their frustrations by acting the fool (charades), games (horse racing) or arm wrestling (for those who remember, I retired undefeated champion of the Fleet at this sport of kings. John Leach - eat your heart out!) and plenty of good eats. I've mentioned John Leach who was Chief Officer, because paradoxically some years later he became marine superintendent, and my boss to boot.

I have to get back to disaster I'm afraid! This particular event affected me personally and landed me in hot water, although at the time I didn't suspect so. From Australia we returned to the Arabian Gulf to load at Umm Said in the Kingdom of Qatar. The loading point at this port was in an open sea berth where one used the ship's anchors in the mooring operation. Once in position, the cargo pipeline was picked up from the sea bed and connected to the ship's manifold. Unfortunately, Donacilla did not have sufficiently long anchor cables for this particular port. This was an original design deficiency. To be even more technical for a moment, the operation was termed a running moor (or sometimes referred to as a 'flying moor"). The ship was positioned precisely then one of the anchors was dropped whilst the ship steamed forward, dragging the cable out as she moved to another position, when theoretically by braking the cable the ship would be stopped, whereupon the second anchor would be dropped and its cable run out while the first cable was hove in. Ignore these details if they are too mystifying! The long and short of it was that we lost both anchors and cables in two attempts at berthing. Each time the 'lost' cable was found by divers and picked up by the ship. However you will appreciate that the 'bitter end' (the origin of this expression, by the by) of both cables had been wrenched out of their securing mounts (clenches), damaging them beyond repair. This was a calamitous situation. The only ameliorating feature of this predicament was that no one had been injured during these incidents. Imagine, if you will, the picture of a cable roaring out through its hawse pipe, scattering mud and rust thus creating a black/brown cloud over the area and then as the brake was applied, sparks and flames as the brake lining almost disintegrated before the spectacle of a clanging, bucking cable end rearing high above the men and disappearing overboard. Not once, but twice. One thing was sure, the ship could not berth after these incidents - because neither cable could be secured. I decided on a radical solution, I had both cable ends shackled to one another - each cable pile providing the security for the other. I apologise to those non-seafarers who may find this detail too difficult to comprehend, I can find no other way of explaining the nightmare. Anyway, the ruse succeeded and we berthed without further incident. Nothing of interest happened thereafter, we returned to Sydney and Geelong and back again to Kuwait, thence to Port Dickson in Malaysia. On the ship's return to Kuwait I was unexpectedly relieved. In searing heat on August 1st 1969, I flew to Beirut with two colleagues for some much appreciated R & R during a stop-over at this civilized, cosmopolitan city, in pre-war days.

My references to hot water and my unexpectedly early replacement had not, as yet, become apparent to me. Even after a heated exchange, by telephone, with one of the desk mariners at London office concerning the gambit of joining both cable ends together, no alarm bells rang in my head! I was summoned to Shell Centre. I had no inkling that this bidding was expressly to investigate my competence before a disciplinary committee. Ingenuous me. When the seriousness of my position dawned upon me I had no time to reflect. I suspect my total unpreparedness and the firm belief that the steps I had taken were appropriate, if not innovative (for which, I had expected commendation!), carried the day. The arm chair navigator, to whom I have already referred, was my chief interrogator - but frankly I was able to spiritedly counter all his cross-examinations, such was my incensed state of mind. No fault was ascribed by the board, which included our Managing Director, so I left with a clean sheet if feeling somewhat perturbed by the turn of events.

We, Joan, Rhiannon and I had an excellent leave, despite the upset. At that time, when one felt at the top of one's effectiveness, one threw off worries easily. We had two wonderful summer months which included a week in Tenby. We continued to enjoy the company of my mother-in-law and father-in-law, whose interest in our doings and their unstinting support in times of trouble were a great consolation. My father seemed to be tolerating his widowerhood with a little more acceptance, he became increasingly more involved in Free Masonry as time elapsed, which gave him comfort.

What a beautiful name - Opalia, it rolled off the tongue so readily. This was not the case with some of the other Shell ship names, however they were stylish and distinctive. The company, Shell, was singularly esteemed - a fact clearly recognised worldwide. At the time that I was appointed to Opalia in early October 1969, another era in tanker transport was being established - I refer to the advent of huge crude carriers. Known by the wholly unprepossessing initials VLCC's (very large crude carriers), these leviathans were mainly used for carrying big volumes of crude oil from the Arabian Gulf around the Cape of Good Hope to Europe. The Suez Canal was being widened and deepened to take these monsters in ballast so that the 'empty' voyage would be shorter and therefore the economic equation more favourable. However, in the initial days, the return voyage was also prosecuted via the Cape. In December 1969, two of Shell's VLCC's suffered catastrophic explosions, the first 'Marpessa', operated by our Dutch colleagues, sank on her maiden round voyage (the biggest ship to sink). The second, 'Mactra', was severely damaged. Both ships had fatalities and people with severe burn injuries. The next day a Norwegian ship 'King Haakon VII' (not a Shell owned or chartered ship) suffered a similar disaster as Mactra. It was a very anxious time for shore and ship management - there was, however, a common factor in that the accidents took place whilst tank cleaning on the ballast voyage. More of this some other time.

165

I suffered from 'back' trouble. It was particularly bothersome in my thirties and forties and probably resulted from a car crash in 1962. Anyway, I had a severe and disabling bout just prior to my appointment to Opalia. After my 'interview' I was determined that I wasn't going to miss Opalia because of a dodgy back, otherwise I might have landed up on a grotty 'H' boat! So I flew in agony to Singapore, barely able to sit let alone walk. They must have wondered what the apparition was coming up the gangway when I joined. More a limping question mark than a man! She was beautiful! Graceful, luxurious, well-maintained and trouble-free. I was so glad I had made the effort and not cried off sick. However, two swallows do not a summer make.

I've mentioned the opulence of the accommodation, but it was also spacious and vast. We were just nine officers (which in those far off days, was a small squad) so we rattled around like a sprinkling of peas in a large bucket, with a host of empty cabins. Beneath the officers' quarters were the petty officers and ratings also sparsely spread over their available accommodation. With people on watch on the bridge and in the engine room, one felt as though one was aboard the Marie Celeste, such was the eerie silence that pervaded the housing! Another factor was the quietness of the main engine, which should have been a relief after the noisy Donacilla, but somehow aided the feeling of isolation. I merely describe these circumstances to create the sense of emptiness, if you like.

I've mentioned my association with chief engineers. My misfortune aboard Opalia was that I had little in common with the incumbent when I joined. He was accompanied by his wife, whom he kept in a state of almost purdah. I suspect Mrs C/E would gladly have welcomed some social activity, however hubby kept her cloistered within his palace whilst he indulged in his favourite pastime of freeing and greasing nuts and bolts. Not the most stimulating of colleagues. Rumour had it that he spent his furloughs freeing and greasing nuts and bolts in his garage! Anyway, outside of meal times, I had no contact with them except for a table tennis joust, to aid digestion, after the repast. The bitterness that some Eagle men felt, lived on, he forever muttered about halcyon days as a bird man. When his reminiscences became too tedious, I threatened to recommend his next appointment to a motor ship, which used to give him sleepless nights (particularly after my lurid tales of Donacilla)!

166

Navigation was my most taxing preoccupation. Initially, there were no problems on this score because we retraced familiar sea scapes between Singapore and Kuwait thence to Sydney and Geelong in Australia. I well remember a notable evening spent with Celia and Bob Allen when we docked at Geelong. I was invited to their home for dinner where the conversation was bright and humorous - a contrast from Opalia's top table, and I went back to the ship feeling refreshed. We returned to Kuwait to load for Tabangao in the Philippines. We began trading in arguably the most dangerous waters at the most difficult time of the year. Let me expand. To get to Tabangao, Opalia had to negotiate the much feared Palawan Passage, which is north of Borneo and part of the Philippine archipelago. The southern end of this passage is affected by strong tidal movement and can unexpectedly sweep the ship one way or the other, off the course track. The Palawan is lined with vicious reefs - the graveyard of many a hapless ship. Later in life I traversed this area on a weekly basis, but with the aid of satellite navigation which remedied the problem. I mentioned the time of the year, December, this month heralded the commencement of the North West Monsoon, with its periods of unceasing, heavy rain. We possessed two radar sets, but the best radar in the world is of little use in impenetrable rain. Additionally, celestial navigation was very difficult in such hostile circumstances. By hook or by crook we had to establish a reliable position before entering the Palawan. Between the last weeks of December until the beginning of February 1970, we transited this passage nine times on a run between Miri (Sarawak) and Tabangao. I recall, with a mixture of anxiety and relief, the Christmas Day forenoon. We, the navigation team, stood on the bridge wing for hours with our sextants poised to catch a shot of the sun whenever it fleetingly appeared in a cloud break, as we approached the southern entrance to Palawan off Balabac Island. Lowering skies, sweeping rain were our contenders but magically by persistence, we all managed to obtain altitudes and then at midday, a radar image of Balabac. Position established, great hilarity as we tumbled down the companionways to enjoy a good Christmas lunch!

Our New Year's cargo took us from Miri to Whangerei in the North Island of New Zealand. Instead of the Palawan Passage, we turned eastwards through the Balabac Strait onwards via the Sulu Sea to the Basilan Strait - another dangerous crossing with reefs and currents to contend with. We crossed the Celebes Sea into the Pacific and thence north of Papua New Guinea through little charted waters (chart soundings every few hundred miles). This is the loneliest damn place in the world! No ships, no radio reception because of the area's remoteness. Just silent isolation. Whangarei was a welcome breath of New Zealand cheerful air. Back to Miri, on to Tabangao. As with many Philippine ports, life can be pretty precarious! Tabangao was no exception. Situated near Batangas, this was one of Shell's major refineries in the Far East. Everyone, including the ship chandler, sported a gun which they would use with small provocation - the Filipinos are possessed with the shortest fuses of any nation in my experience.

Prior to my leaving Opalia, I made two more voyages to the Antipodes, both to Sydney and Geelong via the moonscape route with a welcome cargo transfer from Geelong to Sydney which qualified us for a voyage through the marvellous Great Barrier Reef passage. I finally left in April 1970 at Geelong.

Two matters arose during my service aboard Opalia, which affected me. Firstly, my father suffered a severe coronary on March 1st which left him without any will to continue - really all he wanted was to be reunited with his beloved Hilda. Joan immediately gave up her supply teaching to sustain him. As far as my family was concerned they had an angel for a daughter-in-law, not even a daughter could have been more caring and attentive. The other matter was the appointment of Peter Redfern as Chief Officer. Peter and I, together with our respective wives and children had been good friends since Methane Princess and Progress days, some six years earlier. I mentioned the horrific accident that occurred aboard Mactra earlier in this chapter - he was the Chief Officer who was serving aboard that unfortunate ship at the time. The mishap had left him scarred and untypically, nervous. When it came time for his next appointment after his furlough, he asked to sail with me - in the belief that a friendly face would help him through his 'convalescence' and restoration to normalcy. Peter had, at a young age, become prematurely bald. So to set the tenor, I immediately referred to his large parting when we met and made frequent references to his fine head of skin! He spoke endlessly about the accident which enabled him to ease his continuing sense of shock, and, with sympathetic ears

168

prepared to listen, he settled down well enough. Of course he had a job to do, which was therapeutic in itself.

We, as a family, had a relatively short furlough together before my following appointment to another floating horror story. I don't think we did anything particularly noteworthy, I seem to recall that I spent most of the time in house maintenance as Rhiannon, now 13 years old, was at school the whole time I was home. I do recollect having to bolster my father's confidence after his heart attack, with little success I regret. I flew out to Kuwait in mid June to join Daphnella, accompanied by Glanville Jehu the relief Chief Engineer and Ryan Thomas, Engineer Superintendent - three Taffs.

Daphnella was a repeat performance of Donacilla. She had precisely the same problems with water production and the emergency generator. Fortunately for me I arrived at the end of the play and didn't have to suffer the trauma of having to contend with another series of calamities. We lay at anchor off Mina al Ahmadi for five weeks undergoing repairs, carried out by a flying squad of shipyard workers from the UK. It was Ryan Thomas's function to oversee the repair. I won't belabour the reader with details, however firm friendships were forged between Glan, Ryan and myself, it seemed that the staff aboard the ship were completely demoralized by their misfortunes, so firm direction was needed and provided by the Welsh trio! We left Kuwait, after loading a full cargo of crude oil, for Bandar Abbas in Iran to pick up a portable emergency generator which we stowed in the swimming pool. We finally waved 'good-bye' to Ryan and his team on July 29th 1970, bound for Port Dickson in Malaysia.

As I indicated in the last paragraph, morale was at rock bottom. En route to Malaysia, the engineer officers who had been aboard prior to the ship's arrival at Kuwait all succumbed to a mysterious gastro-enteritis type of illness which decimated the engine room watch-keeping squad. I was quite baffled by the disorder because it attacked the engineers exclusively. I suspected there was an element of psychosomatic hysteria, but the symptoms were real enough! I reported the outbreak to London and Port Dickson - in case it heralded a more serious condition. My anxiety was echoed by both the Company and the local health authority at Port Dickson, who temporarily quarantined the ship on arrival. To this day I believe it to have been 'all in the mind'. However, in the energetic figure of our Chief Engineer and his healthy scepticism of such matters, plus a few changes, the ship soon became an efficient, hard working concern. We returned to Kuwait and loaded for Genoa, where Joan and Celia Jehu joined, together with the welcome appointment of the irrepressible Jack Beaumont as Chief Officer who replaced a particularly useless drongo. Life hereafter was, to quote the old phrase, 'a bowl of cherries'. Joan stayed with me for the next two months which included a long stay at Greenock whilst undergoing refit. From Genoa we went to Es Sider in Libya and loaded for Teesport after which we proceeded to the Clyde for drydocking. I have to tell you that I had one of the most unnerving experiences of my navigational life on the latter coastal voyage. For those of you who are unenlightened in the matters of tidal streams around the UK, take it from me that the strongest flow a ship will experience will be during spring tides in the Pentland Firth (around the northern extremity of Scotland). Now the clever master will judge his passage through this channel by adjusting the ship's speed prior to arrival at either the east or west entrances, to take fullest advantage of a favourable tide, and not the reverse! I prided myself on being fairly competent in these matters and succeeded in making a complete 'balls-up' of this calculation. Two factors militated against success, firstly the hull was extremely 'dirty' (barnacles and weed accumulated after two year's service) and for whatever reason we were unable to run the main engine flat out during tank cleaning. My calculations were too optimistic, consequently we arrived at precisely the wrong time with the full force of a spring tide flowing against us. We were a pretty big lump of ship, all 70,000 tons of it, and if I were to tell you that for about ten minutes, in the centre of the Firth, we went astern (backwards) with the engine at full power ahead, would you believe me? It happened!

We had an extensive refit at Greenock. Time and tide wait for no one, if you'll look again at Chapter 4 you'll recall my first meeting with Matthew Gillespie. By the strangest of coincidences, he was the Engine Manager at the ship yard - I was so delighted to see him again. Our reunion was a bitter disappointment to me, we no longer seemed to have anything in common and were quite unable to re-establish that early rapport. I think he had immersed himself in a new family and didn't wish to be reminded of his first marriage and was totally at a loss to learn that I was not a Freemason! This latter involvement meant so much to him that I suspect any friendship outside the Craft was too difficult to sustain. I have, in fact, noticed this growing away of friendship between school pals and myself, precisely for this reason. For me, it was sad. Notwithstanding, Joan, Rhiannon and I had a very pleasant period together despite the rain falling horizontally practically throughout our stay in the Clyde! We very much enjoyed Greenock (with its unexpectedly excellent restaurants), Glasgow and Edinburgh.

We left the Clyde in early November 1970 bound for Nigeria. The ship ran well under the vigorous ministration of Chief Engineer Jehu, and, I believe, performed efficiently thereafter. We had one distressing incident when the Fourth Engineer was trapped in the bilge space and was badly scalded in his lower abdomen and upper leg area. I'll never forget his screams as we lowered him into the hospital (yes, every ship had a hospital) bath to relieve his agony, with his genitals in tatters and his eyes wild with pain. We landed him in Las Palmas where he recovered, thank God! Other than this there were no noteworthy tales to tell. We loaded at Bonny for Tranmere on the Mersey where Glan and I left for Christmas furlough - we've been friends ever since.

CHAPTER FOURTEEN

BEHEMOTHS

Between January 1971 and October 1976 I was in command of five Very Large Crude Carriers (VLCC's) with five appointments to other ship types in this period. The next three chapters, including this chapter, will dwell upon these ten assignments. To begin I'll describe my recollections of service aboard these sea leviathans. Undoubtedly, in the early seventies, these ships were at the cutting edge of crude oil transport when 'size mattered'. Shell's British VLCC's varied in size between 196,000 and 318,000 tons deadweight (whereas Shell's French fleet operated two, half million ton ships). The statistics were staggering. I quote the data for Lepeta, which was one of the bigger class and the biggest ship type built in the UK: Length 1153 feet (to all intents and purposes a quarter of a mile, give or take 160 feet); 180 feet wide (Seladang was only 141 feet long!); the hull was 94 feet deep (greater than the height of Buckingham Palace); the top of the Signal Mast was 223 feet above the keel; the main engine turbine produced 36,000 shaft horsepower; the cargo pumps could deliver cargo at 17,000 tons per hour; the propeller was 30 feet in diameter and perhaps the most popular statistic, three football fields could be accommodated on the deck space - which took 500 gallons of paint to coat!

My first appointment, at the end of January 1971, was to Marisa, one of the smaller VLCC's, and for the following two and a half years I was in command of a further three ships of this class, viz, Melania, Melo and Mangelia. I have described this class as 'smaller', but they were three times bigger than Daphnella and eleven times the size of any ship that I had commanded previous to Donacilla. They were big hunks of metal. The prime objective was the self evident function of carrying large volumes of crude oil to Europe, and, to a lesser extent, to the USA and the Far East. To be a trifle unkind, they were ocean-going barges with little or no character.

However they were not easy ships to successfully operate. The main problem area was a human one. Often the ship traded between one sea mooring, out of sight of civilization, to another equally remote discharge point. On a typical voyage around the Cape to and from the Arabian Gulf, the ship would be serviced at Las Palmas and Cape Town by helicopter (where stores, films and personnel were delivered and exchanged) and at Ras al Khaimah at the entrance to the Gulf, by a service launch, - so our enlightened employers did all they could to sustain their ships and the people who sailed thereon. Notwithstanding, one had to combat ennui (to which I have already alluded) and an almost sloth like apathy that crept into everyone's disposition resulting from weeks at sea. I found that at a point about three days before arrival, at either end, I had to 'ginger' everyone up with a few judicious rollockings (seafarers, substitute 'b' for 'r'), they in turn applied the same treatment to their subordinates, thus creating a reasonable state of readiness!

Conditions of service in the seventies had improved out of recognition. Officers served on board a ship for about six months, later reduced to four months. They were allowed to be accompanied by their wives with the company paying two air fares per year. The newer ships had excellent facilities. There were well outfitted bars for both officers and crew, recreation rooms with table tennis tables, cinema facilities, fully equipped laundries, a gymnasium with cycling machines and punch balls, and a well appointed outdoor swimming pool, plus the traditional Seafarers' Education Service library. The living accommodation was luxurious, by any standard, with individual bathrooms and w.c.'s, cabins even had 'phones (which enabled individuals to speak to their families from the privacy of their cabins) and radio speakers. Victualling was of a high standard, so all was provided that could possibly cater for the welfare of the ship's company. However, being isolated for months on end, away from society and the occasional run ashore, caused discontent. Life was akin to that of a paid prison stretch! It actually suited some people! There is a type of man, normally a bachelor, of a quiet disposition who would keep himself to himself, who joined the Merchant Navy for the structured routine a ship provides. All he asks is a book of his choice, three square meals, a modest beer or two and the BBC World Service. Although, perhaps, his salary would be modest he would nevertheless save money assiduously and in time become wealthy. He would spend his time ashore in one of the Missions to Seamen establishments and be perfectly content. The VLCC suited this guy! Anyway, the majority were not quite as enamoured, so we would organize quizzes and bingo nights to give some variety to the humdrum weeks in the Indian and Atlantic oceans.

I wouldn't describe myself as having a fitness fetish, but I had realized the need for keeping one's self in reasonable health. Since the early sixties I had followed the Royal Canadian Air Force exercise routine and endeavoured to eat wisely - as I had a distinct tendency to gain weight. Aboard these big ships, keeping fit was relatively easy, if one jogged around the deck four times you ran a distance of two miles. Using the gym and playing some table tennis also contributed.

Life at sea aboard these ships was a feast and a famine (as indeed one could describe a seafarer's married life). If one regards the ocean voyages as the famines, then the activity at the voyage ends was almost frenetic by comparison and represented the feasts in this analogy. The loading end, primarily within the Arabian Gulf or Oman - which lies to the south west of the Straits of Hormuz (the entrance to the Arabian/Persian Gulf) was a relatively straight forward operation, but one that might be undertaken at two ports. When you consider that these ships loaded at rate of around 20,000 tons per hour, simple mathematics will show that we were alongside these terminals for a very short spell. The loading structures were purely functional - without any recreational facilities whatsoever, so the wish always was to leave as soon as possible! The main terminals were at Sea Island (Mina al Ahmadi in Kuwait) literally an island constructed of steel with wooden sheathing capable of loading two VLCC's simultaneously. Kharg and Halul Islands were similar, situated on the south coast of Iran with Ras Tanura in Saudi Arabia as a another likelihood. In Oman, ships loaded at Mina al Fahal at a single buoy berth. All of them not in the least attractive. The weather in winter months is quite pleasantly cool, but the cauldron like heat and humidity of summer was intolerable with the added hazard and discomfort of impenetrable sand storms. To be crude, if the world has a rectum, it has to be here!

At the cargo discharge end, usually in western Europe, a whole different set of circumstances faced the arriving ship. On one occasion I took a fully laden VLCC through the English Channel to Rotterdam. These craft draw up to 70 feet of water, and the English Channel does not sport too many areas of sufficient depth to accommodate this draft. One had to stage the transit to take advantage of tidal rise, one ensured that the ship was upright and even keel - a single degree of list would increase the draft on the low side by 18 inches; five degree list, 8 feet! Another factor was a phenomenon known as 'squat'. In shallow water a ship will lower its bow and generally squat as soon as it moves forward thus reducing the under keel clearance. The amount of squat is directly proportional to the speed at which the ship transits a shallow area. The Channel transit necessitated precise timing, a warning broadcast to all shipping and a zig zag set of courses to weave in and out of sand banks and other underwater obstructions, speed reduced to limit squat in critical areas and pray like hell that you didn't have fog! I can tell you it's a nerve jarring experience. Although 36,000 horse power sounds huge, when you're in confined waters, the engines are on 'stand-by' conditions, so you have something less that two thirds of maximum power at your disposal and it takes a lot of oomph to shift these ladies around as you would wish, particularly in powerful tidal conditions The reader should also remember that there may be as many as fifty ships on the radar screens at any one time. Another floating nightmare - particularly after the soporific influence of a month or more trundling around the Cape!

The more usual contact would be with a 'lightening' ship. This was a distribution technique largely developed by Shell to put a smaller, specialized ship alongside the VLCC and relieve her of 70.000 tons of crude oil. At the end of the operation, both ships would go their own ways to different refineries - a most efficient and cost effective means of servicing at least two refineries in one delivery. Another major benefit was that it enabled the VLCC to enter ports that would have been barred to her at loaded draft.

The operation entailed the two ships making a rendezvous in a specified lightening area. There were a number of these zones chosen for their suitability, mainly for shelter and accessibility to the eventual destination of the VLCC. The procedure was under the command of the master of the lightening ship who controlled both ships. In brief, the ships berthed alongside one another with large pneumatic, rubber fenders between their hulls and when they were secured, the VLCC would anchor and hold both ships during the transfer program. The men manning the lightening ships were specialists, and, as such, developed an attitude that could be described as individual or in some cases, cavalier! They worked consistently hard at the business and, occasionally, showed little regard for their almost supine brethren aboard the mother ship. This was a major operation with two large ships with a combined deadweight of nearly half a million tons attached to each other by moorings and pipelines, and to my knowledge, in many thousands of such operations no major accident occurred - which is totally to the credit of the lightening boys.

When a ship is at sea, at full power, there's no question of reducing that power - other than in dire circumstances or for heavy weather. Approaching a port, seagoing conditions systematically give way to manoeuvring conditions. With a VLCC, this is a long and tender process. Imagine the weight of cargo (say, 300,000 tons) plus the weight of the ship at about 130,000 tons and you have a substantial mass to bring to a stop. A controlled approach spans 20 miles! That begins with an hour's notice to the end of passage. The engineers will then change over from voyage parameters to port entry conditions during that hour, at which time the ship will be able to manoeuvre. Say the ship travels fourteen miles in that time, it will take another six miles to slowly reduce and stop the engine before running the engine astern to bring the vessel to a complete standstill in the water. In ballast, in a flying light condition, with strong winds, these monsters were very difficult to control with a very high freeboard acting as a huge sail. I well remember having joined Mangelia at Shellhaven the previous day, the embarrassment I suffered when the pilot was disembarked at Dungeness in the early hours of the following morning, I lost control and ran over the Sandgate buoy in gale force winds. I was mortified! On that ballast voyage, after clearing South Africa and the Mozambique Channel I had the ship tipped to expose the propeller, and to my horror there was a nasty nick out of one of the blades. Fortunately, the ship's performance didn't suffer.

176

All was not gloom however! Joan joined Marisa at Tranmere (Birkenhead) in mid April 1971 and spent a month with me, most of the time spent in Lisbon, which was the preferred refit port for VLCC's. She and I had a wonderful time. We had a chauffeur driven Mercedes at our disposal whenever we required transport. We would go into the city for dinner or down to Cascais for the evening and be regaled with beautifully rendered Fado (Portuguese folk singing) by our driver on the return to the ship - for us, it was quite unforgettable. We entertained the managers and their wives for lunch on successive Sundays, I was fortunate in having Mr Whitty as the Catering Officer who excelled in wining and dining guests. Both Joan and I were struck by two impressions: the first was the poverty we witnessed outside the shipyard, situated on the south side of the River Tagus in contrast to the prosperity in the city; the other was the preponderance of soldiers who had lost limbs - I believe in Angola. It was a memorable period in our lives and came to an end too soon!

I joined Melania in October 1971, travelling to Bordeaux with a party of officers and wives. Our flight from London was delayed by fog so instead of arriving in mid afternoon we got there at about eleven o'clock. We were all famished because for whatever reason we had had no food throughout the day. The point I'm about to make is that, for the first time in my life, I ate horse! We rushed to this restaurant before it closed and ordered steak and chips. To obtain steak as we knew it, we should have asked for bif steak. We ate it with relish until I twigged its origin, whereupon our enthusiasm was tempered somewhat! Melania berthed at Le Verdon at the mouth of the River Gironde, a VLCC berth serving the Paulliac refinery (where, as I have indicated, the refinery effluent did wonders for the Baron's Mouton Cadet!). I took over at Le Verdon from whence to Gothenburg in Sweden where another gastronomic experience awaited me. I was taken to dinner by the agent and sampled the rather adventurous Scandinavian convention of drinking schnapps with one's meal. One tossed back a mouthful of this liquid fire after each bite of solid food rendering me a little less than capable at the conclusion of the main course! By the time I left Melania in March 1972, we had delivered two cargoes to Europe from the Arabian Gulf.

Melo provided an interesting change in trading patterns. I joined at Ras al Khaimah at the entrance to the Arabian Gulf in June 1972, thereafter we loaded in the United Arab Emirates and Kuwait for Chiba in Tokyo Bay. The challenges for a deeply laden VLCC, during this voyage, were twofold and disparate. Firstly there was the Malacca Strait transit which had to be staged to ensure safe under keel clearance. The second, and by far the more worrying, was piracy. I write this account twenty six years after my time aboard Melo, when this hazard is much more widely known (and, it seems, persisting and intensifying in scope and menace), then little publicity attended this threat to life and limb.

I have already written about our having to combat piracy and thievery whilst serving on the 'small' ships in the Far East. We formed defence teams armed with staves and cudgels to deter and fight, if necessary, any intruders. The problem existed in many parts of the world, notably in Indonesia, the Philippines, West Africa and Brazil. The VLCC is a choice target for these criminals, particularly as the lumbering old girl battles with the tides and streams in the Singapore Strait, with the ship on stand-by power and therefore travelling more slowly and having to keep strictly to a set course to avoid stranding on reefs. These swine (the pirates) wait for the tanker to pass their hideouts (and remember, navigational warnings are broadcast to warn shipping that a VLCC is about to transit the Strait, so everyone knows) and then slip into the ship's wake and rapidly overtake their victim - having highly powered light skiffs as their chosen vehicles which can move at phenomenal speeds. Using bamboo poles with hooks which they attach to the poop railings or shear strake the clamber aboard armed to the teeth. They know exactly what to do! Nowadays, they are inclined to hijack a ship, but then they would rifle cabins and steal everything of value in a systematic sweep - without the ship's crew being aware of anything being amiss. Should they be challenged, they wouldn't hesitate to kill or maim. The British crew (who relished the task) were formed into guard patrols who made themselves altogether visible in the fully floodlit decks and accommodation housing. Such high visibility preparedness was suffice to deter would-be miscreants, coupled with high pressure hoses playing overside, made the prospect of invasion unwise. On the return from Japan, the ship's freeboard (vertical height of the deck above the waterline) was too great for any jiggery pokery.

Taking a deep drafted VLCC into Tokyo Bay was no tea party either. The volume of shipping entering and leaving the Uraga Channel is probably the densest one will experience at any port in the world. Subsequently I oversaw entry scores of times, but aboard much more responsive ships than an underpowered barge! We returned to the Arabian Gulf to load at Ras Tanura in Saudi Arabia on a Texaco charter to Milford Haven and Brunsbuttel on the Elbe. Anything for a change! Joan visited at Milford Haven so we went to our favourite resort, Tenby, for an evening meal in our favourite hotel - what a lovely interlude it was. En route to Germany in early September 1972, in densest fog, our spirits were lowered even further by the tragic events unfolding at the Munich Olympics. It was a most trying passage from Milford to the Elbe, however greatly eased by the routeing system now well established through the English Channel and southern North Sea (largely developed by Shell International Marine and the Royal Institute of Navigation in conjunction with various European maritime authorities). I finished off by loading at Kuwait for Singapore where we discharged at a single point buoy mooring near Pulo Bukom. These mooring buoys were a wonderful development after the nerve wracking multi-buoy berths we had had to use in open sea berths, hitherto. The buoy incorporated the discharge pipe and the mooring point in one unit, so simple and effective. A post script, after I left at Singapore, the ship repeated the voyage and on the second visit to the SBM at Singapore, my successor was attacked by bandits, tied up and at knife point obliged to hand over a large sum of money plus all his valuables. There, but for the Grace of God...........!

Two personal anguishes affected me after my leaving Melo. Whilst on furlough my father died after sustaining a stroke. I was glad to be home to deal with our loss jointly with my brother, Tom (who flew from Canada for his funeral) and of course, dear Joan, who had borne the brunt of our family misfortunes previously. The second was a tragedy. My dear friend and much loved father-in-law, suffered the cruellest of blows a deaf person could bear - he became totally blind. It was such a appalling thing to happen to this fine, courageous man - he who had sustained us so well and selflessly. It placed a huge burden upon my mother-in-law and of course, our ever supporting Joan.

My last 'M' ship was Mangelia. During my service we loaded two cargoes of Arabian Gulf crude oil and one Nigerian cargo - all discharged at Tranmere after lightening in the Irish Sea. I will write at some point later in this narrative about my associations with Chief Engineers, it is however worthy of mention that aboard Mangelia I met my greatest seafaring buddy, Ken Hart, who was of course, Chief Engineer. He had been Second Engineer aboard Mactra at the time of the explosion, more to the point, in this context, his wife Barbara was also on board that fated ship. She was on the Monkey Island (the deck above the Wheelhouse) sunbathing when the eruption took place. The flash went over the Bridge leaving her desperately burned, in fact her body outline remained on the steel deck after she was removed. She survived and was hospitalized at Beira in Mozambique. Her back, the back of her head, neck and legs were severely affected, to compound her awful predicament she received infected blood during a transfusion and went down with malaria. It was a desperate time in their lives. As you can imagine, when she recovered after a long recuperation, she was nervous of any ship and particularly of a "M" class ship. So aided by tranquillizers she returned to seafaring aboard Mangelia. I went out of my way to ensure that they enjoyed their time together, she was and is a spirited, brave lady and the perfect foil for my East Lothian mate! We sailed from Tranmere and back via Forcados in Nigeria.

It was whilst serving aboard Mangelia that for the only time in my career I experienced a mutiny! The ship was manned by a Hong Kong crew. Their conditions of service were far different from those enjoyed by officers or European crews, in particular with respect to length of periods of service. It should be stressed that Shell's conditions of service in the context of the Hong Kong seafaring community were probably second to none. However, a year's aboard a VLCC was pushing even the Chinese renowned patience to the edge. For whatever reason, Shell were unable to replace Mangelia's crew at the appointed time and continued to extend their service beyond reasonable expectations. Whatever the Cantonese expression is for 'enough is enough', half way through my stint they announced that they would take the ship no further than Kuwait. Panic! This was almost unheard of. The Crew Department in London quickly sussed the situation but were unable to accede to this threat - loss of face would be catastrophic. A compromise had to be agreed upon. After lengthy negotiations between myself and practically every crew member, it was agreed that, upon my word that I would honour the agreement, they agreed to sail the ship to Ras al Khaimah, and no

180

further. This was done, we anchored and discharged our merry men - only to discover, to my horror, that the joining crew refused to come onboard because the cabin crew of the aircraft that had brought them to RAK had rifled their personal baggage and nicked their cameras etc. etc. (it was a Kuwait Airways). Back to the negotiating table! I then had to guarantee that everything that had gone missing would be compensated for. We were delayed for two days as a consequence - without a crew at that. So we brought the old British stand-by, the frying pan, into commission and survived on a fearfully unhealthy diet for a couple of days - ever resourceful we Brits!

On the way to Nigeria, one of the engineer apprentices had, what appeared to be appendicitis. The diagnosis was confirmed by a doctor at a hospital in Weston-super-Mare - such had technology advanced that I was able to speak to this doctor by 'phone from the young man's bedside and follow the doctor's instructions in examining the patient to enable him (the doctor) to form an opinion. He recommended immediate diversion to the nearest port. Now you just cannot take a quarter mile long ship into any port! The nearest likely port was Freetown in Sierra Leone - but even this was a marginal choice, because this place had never had a ship of this size within its port limits before. So I had to decide whether or not I should jeopardize the ship or possibly lose a young life. We deballasted to reduce our draft to the minimum consistent with an ability to manoeuvre and took the gamble, but to this day I tremble at the thought! In the event, matters proceeded satisfactorily but having the distinction of having taken the biggest ship into that port, is no comfort.

I sailed aboard Lepeta on her maiden voyage in 1976. I relieved Commodore Stanley Dean (who had stood-by the building at Belfast) at Ras al Khaima, and took the giant to Iran and Oman to load her first cargo. A beautiful ship - if you liked ULCC's (Ultra Large Crude Carriers), significantly bigger than the 'M' class and, of course, at the cutting edge. We took the cargo to Rotterdam, via Lyme Bay for lightening. After the discharge, my relief, Byron Davies, accompanied me to Las Palmas where I was lifted off by helicopter. I enjoyed a short furlough prior to returning to the cadet training ship. Lepeta was the final appointment to these huge vessels, not a type of ship I would have gladly returned to, as a class of tanker they were my least favourite.

CHAPTER FIFTEEN

DISTAFF, FRIENDS AND THE PECTEN

Before I continue with my life's saga I thought it appropriate that I describe the peripheral aspects of being a seafarer together with a mention of the friends I made, particularly in my later years.

The most important influence in my life was, of course, Joan. I was so fortunate to have her as my life's companion. Not everyone was as blessed, and there can be little criticism of women who just could not manage the huge responsibilities, the loneliness and frustrations that they withstood as a seaman's wife. Those who were able and those who made themselves able were undoubtedly women apart. I would, therefore, pay homage to them. As time went on in my career, women became ever more evident aboard ship. In my last years in command I had a number of female officers on the staff who in addition to officers' wives meant there could be ten or twelve females on board. Most ladies behaved impeccably and had a leavening effect for the better, men were obviously more contented and the women imbued an air of civility that perhaps would otherwise be absent. Their favourite pastime was sunbathing, which added to the atmosphere around the pool, one could almost imagine oneself aboard a passenger ship at times! Through their husbands, women could exert considerable influence on social activities in particular. Female officers were good, nay excellent in most instances because they had more to prove and were inherently above average intelligence. They overcame their physical limitations with charm, causing the men to leap about opening and shutting valves for them. One of the accepted conventions that developed aboard ships in the seventies and eighties was the relaxation in dress code after the evening meal, I confess I never quite became accustomed to the Third Mate tripping around the Bridge in a frilly dress!

You may think that, with so many females in a confined and largely male community, occasionally things could go wrong. I sailed with a number of 'rogue' ladies in my time who made life, as we knew it, very difficult. Some were provocative and others promiscuous with the occasional nymphomaniac thrown in for good measure. I cannot relate the astounding incidents I detected during my term in command, and before, for that matter! Suffice to add, that these happenings whilst spectacular, were rare.

It became inevitable that the majority of seafaring friendships made whilst I was in command were Chief Engineers. It was difficult to sustain a friendly association with a subordinate because of the occasional necessity to differ with them. However there were a number of Chief Officers with whom I had good and lasting relationships. I will write at some length in a subsequent chapter about my experiences aboard Cadet Training Ship 'Opalia'. It was aboard this ship, carrying out this function, that I established my closest links with these younger men, mainly because the ship's objectives demanded team work of the highest standard. Of these John Gyles, David Pringle and Roger Firth and Manny Longmore stand out in my memory. I had a particularly warm and humorous acquaintance with Dave Pringle, he and I shared an eye for the ridiculous and we would ape people's idiosyncrasies, much to our mirth! Amongst the other ships, I warmly remember Peter Redfern, Jack Beaumont, Brian Oliver, Doug Renton, Malcolm Wilkie, Alan Charlesworth, Fred Croxon, John Grisdale and Jim Petty. These men represent 20% of the total of mates with whom I sailed as Master. With all these guys I shared a particular rapport.

To continue. For obvious reasons Masters and Chief Engineers were likely to associate more closely with each other because of their rank, and, the physical fact that under modern circumstances they lived in adjacent accommodation. With the advent of the engineer apprenticeship scheme which had evolved during the 1950's, the oil and water syndrome gradually lessened and almost disappeared by the time I attained command. Shipboard ambience benefited enormously as a consequence. So it is that I now count among my best friends, assorted ex Chief Engineers - out of a total of 48 Chiefs (I sailed with some a number of times) I should like to mention those whom I enjoyed sailing with most.

It is perhaps invidious to single out one colleague and at certain moments, adversary. As I've indicated previously it has to be Ken Hart. Glan Jehu, Dave Hill, Tony Morton, Chris Camp, Mike Holderness and James Flett were others with whom I had very enjoyable relationships.

I first met Ken Hart aboard Mangelia and sailed subsequently with him on two 'G' class ships. Although he hadn't been a Shell apprentice, I awarded him the status of 'honorary Shell Cadet' because such was his agile, fertile mind, he deserved it! From East Lothian, he was, in some ways, your archetypical Scottish Chief Engineer - commanding, fiery with a healthy hatred with all things to do with the Deck Department (or so he said). Not one to suffer fools gladly, he was nevertheless possessed of a bright intellect and a great sense of humour. Although we enjoyed each other's company, nevertheless we often fought (metaphorically) to a standstill over a shipboard matter and frequently, politics. However time flew and one's mind was forever stretched by this Kitchener-mustached, gingery bald, messiah-like apparition that would appear at my cabin door with steely blue eyes glinting dangerously, and address me as 'Captain' - then I knew trouble was brewing! Normally we were on Christian name terms. Occasionally, we would share a private meal of ox-tail jardiniere and a bottle of good red vino and put the world to rights! I remember him with great affection. Joan also enjoyed his lively company.

I have already written about my time with another good and steadfast friend, Glan Jehu, whose first job as Chief Engineer was with me aboard Daphnella. Unfortunately, his being certified only to operate motor ships meant we had no further opportunity to serve together, most Shell ships being steamers. We've been good friends ever since our sailing together. David Hill was also a great favourite of mine. A most intelligent young man bringing his sharp intellect to bear on ship operation, not much good at table tennis, but one hell of a good fellow to sail with! I cherish the memories of Sunday drink/lunch sessions with Dave, his thinking was considerably to the right of Ghengis Khan so the contrast in our opinions made for lively conversation, again Joan found him a great companion. Subsequently, our families have met frequently and we have stayed in each others' homes.

Tony Morton and I sailed together on three occasions. As well as being an excellent engineer he was also a painter of note - and had picture exhibitions displayed at various locations. Possessed of a keen Merseyside humour, he'd have everyone in stitches. Although I count him as one of my friends, he always maintained a distance in his official dealings with me. Unfortunately he retired prematurely from Shell employment, because of an incident at a Japanese shipyard where he was exonerated from blame, but, being the man he is, accepted responsibility and resigned. Last heard he was sailing as a watchkeeping engineer aboard a Cross Channel Ferry. We exchange Christmas cards.

Chris Camp was something else! I sailed with him aboard Opalia in her cadet training role. Another bright star who, being such an individualist, found it somewhat tedious conforming to the strict codes prevailing aboard the ship at that time. However he did conform and contributed well to the milieu. He had a sharp, quirky sense of humour which took some understanding. Bright lad though. I subsequently met him in Kobe in Japan where he was on an assignment as I was joining a ship. We had drinks in my hotel and he ordered a large Jack Daniels. Now I wasn't at the time familiar with this beverage but did my stuff as host and bought the drink which cost me about ten quid! I let him know in the friendliest manner that the next time we met he would owe me a case of beer . The point of this episode was that later he arrived back in London and sent Joan a bunch of flowers with a note signed: 'Jack Daniels'! Now Joan was even less likely to know who "Jack Daniels' was and she returned the flowers to the florist. The florist investigated the source and again delivered the bouquet - now this caused considerable mystification and some concern, because Joan didn't want to accept flowers from an unknown suitor, given her longstanding liaison with me! Anyway, it was sorted but it illustrated Chris's eccentric humour!

I mentioned two others: Mike Holderness and Jimmy Flett. They were figures from my early days as Master. Mike was a young, energetic Chief Engineer with whom I sailed aboard Asprella. Now he had been an engineer apprentice with me when I was Mate of Tribulus, and had led the engineer battle against the deck brigade - completely ousting the latter! Anyway, as Chief Engineer he was of great assistance in the setting-up of the new shipboard structure aboard that ship. He now operates a very successful marine consultancy firm. Jimmy Flett was older than I (which was unusual), and I mention him because he had a wise head and kind nature. I enjoyed his company and very nearly mastered the Aberdonian dialect, because Jim took no hostages in this matter, you understood his broadest Aberdonian or you missed out altogether!

I want to conclude this short chapter with comments on my lifelong employer: Shell Tankers (UK) Ltd., as it was known during the latter years of my career, and upon those who sustained us in London, Singapore and other outposts.

My political leanings developed, over the years, into something loosely social democratic, but I was always prepared to lean further to the left if it meant balancing the fearfully right wing sentiments of my brother officers! It would be perhaps logical for a person such as myself to be intensely critical of an archetypical capitalist organization such as The Royal Dutch Shell Company. Such a conclusion would be entirely misplaced. I always had an intense loyalty for the Pecten and never doubted Shell's moral probity or the enlightened management it showed in all its worldwide operations.

To proceed to Shell Tankers and to its mother organization Shell International Marine. We, aboard ship, had a professional technical back-up second to none. Although very much an engineering biased support (which logically should be the case) we nevertheless had exceptionally good marine/navigational help whenever needed. Some of the personalities who figured large in my career span were: Captain Ian MacLean (brother of the famed author, Alistair) whose firm and kindly stewardship was much admired by this writer and Captain John Rendle who was awarded the CBE, a remarkably astute and clear minded gentleman, and indeed a true gentleman, with whom I had dealings over a period of twenty one years.

I have made fulsome reference to the amalgamation of Shell Tankers and Eagle Oil - I hesitate to use expressions such as take-over

186

because I could never decide who took-over whom! One of the blessings of this marriage was in the form of a cheerful, very kindly soul called Geoff Shakespeare. He was taken ashore into shore management and used his exceptional PR gifts in both the marine, safety and personnel domains. He was a much admired figure throughout the Fleet and to my certain knowledge, there was never an unkind thing ever uttered about him! Some people get all the luck - and he was a Bird Man, there's no justice!

My final tribute goes to the Fleet Personnel Department. Other than actually going to sea, there was no less enviable job than being the person who appointed and relieved those who did! I can only write about those men who impinged so strongly upon my life and those of my family. Not only did these wise men have to deal with the seafarer but also with angry or distraught wives and mothers who wanted to know...! People such as Ron Howell, Frank Keepax, Bert Barker figured large in my life, not only did they contribute to my destiny they almost controlled my peace of mind. Talk about unsung heroes, these were they. As I am now in my early seventies and memories become less certain, please forgive any omissions.

CHAPTER SIXTEEN

HEAT FROM COLD

This chapter is all to do with the numeral "7". There were seven ships with names beginning with the letter 'G', the seventh letter of the alphabet, and I served seven times aboard ships of this fleet which transported LNG from Lumut (near Kuala Belait) in Brunei to Japan. In total these 75,000 cubic metre carriers (equivalent in size to a 100,000 ton deadweight conventional tanker) transported five million tons of LNG to Tokyo Bay and Osaka each year. The scheme was originally given a life span of twenty years, it still operates successfully twenty eight years after its inauguration. Surely one of the great industrial/maritime achievements of this century. It fact the total concept was a truly magnificent example of international co-operation. The main companies were the Royal Dutch/Shell group and the Mitsubishi Corporation. The supplier was the Brunei Shell Petroleum Company and the receivers were Tokyo Electric, Tokyo Gas and Osaka Gas. The liaising company was called Coldgas, with offices at St. Georges, Bermuda. The liquefaction plant at Lumut, together with jetty and loading equipment were built to Shell's design by companies from the USA, Holland, the United Kingdom, Japan, Korea, Switzerland and Singapore. Finance was facilitated through American and Singapore banking organizations. The ships were built at three shipyards in France under the supervision of Shell International Marine and they were operated by Shell Tankers (UK)Ltd - that was us, of course. Anything more global than this set-up would be difficult to find!

My involvement started at the end of 1973, after a furlough (post Mangelia) in which we, as a family, had to come to terms with my father-in-law's blindness - but, being the courageous man that he was, he helped us to deal with the new situation. He quickly acquired a skill in reading our messages using a finger to write on his palm, later he learned a form of Braille. However it added to the strain that my mother-in-law, Ethel, and Joan had to accustom themselves. In fact, Ethel succumbed to a terrible attack of shingles in her face which was a cruel burden. It was a sad year between this and my father's death. However, Joan, Rhiannon and I managed to have our last holiday together - Rhiannon was now sixteen years old and almost too old to spend her vacation with a couple of old fogeys! We went to Bournemouth, staying at one of the best hotels and thoroughly enjoyed ourselves. There was a snag however, prior to our holiday I 'did my back in' and whilst at Bournemouth I discovered I had a floppy left foot - which transpired to be foot drop. I went to my next ship armed with springs and assorted exercise techniques to repair this defect, at which I was only partially successful.

When I joined the scheme, there were just two ships in service, viz., Gadinia and Gadila with a third, Gari, entering the trade during my first stint. It was two years later that the program became fully operational with all seven ships plying between Brunei and Japan. There were two class acts available to senior men in the seventies, one was to join that intrepid coterie of steel nerved men known as 'lighteners' (those in command of the lightening ships) to which I suspect I was not psychologically suited and the second an appointment as a 'Gee Man' to command the new LNG carriers. Once again, my natural enthusiasm for anything new made my involvement a pleasure.

We considered ourselves as 'la creme de la creme' in those days! Elitism, within a large company such as ours wasn't entirely a bad thing. I realized, at the time, that the remainder of the Fleet were sceptical and given to sneering at the 'G' men; this was to be expected and we tolerated their comments with a quiet sense of superiority! It provided the stimulus to excel. Anyone who has worked closely with the Japanese will tell you that the association between the two cultures requires a deal of understanding, patience and unfailing courtesy. Not only does one have the oblique (in Caucasian terms) Oriental approach to discourse, but with the

Japanese one meets the fierce and rigid ethos of absolute competence - which is a hallmark of the race. In passing, I believe it would be correct to say that we, in STUK, met every demand placed upon us by this somewhat inflexible yardstick. I have heard it said that the Japanese customers were wholly impressed by our fleet - perhaps we were not as fulsome in our responses!

My first year in this liner trade was spent aboard the original carrier, Gadinia. My service was in two stints, October '73 to March '74 then July to November 1974 with a wonderful late spring, early summer furlough in between. Perhaps the single outstanding visage of the undertaking was the unique loading crane at Lumut. Poised at the end of a 4.5 kilometre jetty like a giant preying mantis, all 42 metres high, it slowly dropped and engaged with the ship's loading platform situated abaft the stern on a lattice support. A wonderfully successful piece of engineering it serviced thousands of loadings without defect. I always felt it was the weak link in the scheme, should terrorists or damage have put it out of action, a number of major conurbations in Japan would have been seriously affected. I understand the system has now been superseded by a conventional loading system. However, in my time, the crane was all.

Liquid natural gas is highly volatile stuff, although at a temperature of minus 160 degrees centigrade it boils! As with any liquid that is at boiling point, it gives off vapour. Now this vapour has to have space or be disposed of in some manner. Burning was the solution. At Lumut whilst loading, the vapour was sent to a flare stack close to the loading platform, providing near daylight conditions during the hours of darkness - such was the light intensity. Radiant heat could often be felt aboard the ship, particularly if the flare spurted. En route to Japan, the ships' boilers burnt the 'boil-off' from the cargo - up to a maximum of 90% of requirement (the classification society, Lloyds, insisted that at least 10% fuel oil be burnt in the boilers at all times). Likewise, on the return ballast voyage, a small quantity of LNG was retained to keep the tanks cold and to provide fuel for the boilers - almost perpetual motion!

We delivered cargoes to three installations: Negishi (Yokohama), Sodegaura (Chiba) and Senboku (Osaka). The ships berthed conventionally, i.e., alongside a jetty using chiksan arms to transfer the LNG. We, aboard ship, had truly excellent support organizations in Japan. Our 'umbrella' establishment was known by the unprepossessing cipher - IMR. Staffed by Shell superintendents of the highest calibre, under excellent managers such as Arthur Findlater, Phil Owen and Sandy Tosh. The Agencies provided first class service, but the quite exceptional organization was one Fuji Trading who would supply any conceivable thing a ship requested. A character called Mr Mitsunaga will ever remain in our minds as a genius at discovering the location of the most improbable items!

The ships were magnificently equipped in every respect. Fast and manoeuvrable, they were a joy to operate and handle. Soon after my assignment to these ships we were supplied with satellite navigation equipment (sophisticated stuff in those far-off days) which made transit through the Palawan Passage a doddle and later we had satellite communication equipment. It goes without saying that we had state-of-the-art radar installations, which were used continuously. We fed like fighting cocks, with top quality provisions from Japan. So we were well equipped to deal with the vagaries of the Far East.

The loaded voyage took six days. We arrived at Lumut in the early morning at daylight, quitting the berth in the early hours of the following morning. The berthing operation was specific and never deviated from. Ships were secured to a series of five buoys with the stern (and loading platform) under the crane - no connection, other than the crane, was established between ship and platform, this enabled the ship to make a quick getaway should an emergency arise, the crane could be quickly disengaged automatically. At the Japanese end, we invariably arrived at the pilot stations at a specified time in the early morning. As far as I was concerned, the two days in and out of Tokyo Bay or the Inland Sea approach to Osaka were the most intense in any one round trip. Shipping density was extraordinary and because of the nature of our cargo one had to be wholly committed to meticulous navigation and traffic avoidance - a mistake was unthinkable.

I was 'on' and 'off' the "G" class ships, as I've already mentioned, seven times. During that period, up to early 1982, I delivered fifty cargoes in what was a very rewarding period in my life. It seems pointless and tedious to list all the spells I spent on these ships or with whom I sailed. Better, I think, if I extract some highlights from my ever failing memory before they're lost!

Between voyage ends the big impediments to my peace of mind were: typhoons, fog, and one earthquake. I'll describe the latter incident, first. I cannot recall which ship it was but Joan was sailing with me at the time. We were off the northern tip of Luzon (Philippines) and we were about to retire for the night, it being about 2300. I had already been to the Bridge to chat to the Third Mate and to leave my written 'night orders', it was a lovely clear, starlit tropical night and all seemed well with the world. I went down to my cabin to join Joan, who was already in bed. I changed into my pyjamas and was about to join her when there was an almighty heave and thud and my head hit the deckhead (ceiling)! I had no idea what had happened, I literally flew back up to the Bridge to be greeted by an ashen faced young man, who also had no idea what caused the ship to lift bodily as she had. My first thoughts were that we had hit something, but this seemed unlikely, then I thought of an uncharted reef, but this too was patently not so. I contacted the Engine Room watchkeeper who had suffered a greater fright than we because the bang reverberated through the cathedral like space, causing great alarm. The possibility of an underwater disturbance then percolated through my thoughts. I contacted Tokyo who confirmed that there had, indeed, been an ocean seismic upheaval in the area, so that was that!

Whilst on the subject of earthquakes Joan and I experienced a worrying day when the ship, I believe it was Genota, was berthed at Sodegaura, near Chiba. Whenever a ship berthed in any of the terminals, a minibus was laid on to take people ashore to the nearest city. That meant the wives sallied forth to spend money! On this particular day, in the late afternoon, the ship started to move violently with mooring wires twanging and chiksan arms bucking like horses - we stopped discharging immediately and made speedy preparations to quit the berth. This was one of the ultimate nightmares of being in a Japanese port. The old girl (the ship!) settled down, so we remoored her and waited for confirmation that danger had passed before resuming the cargo operation. This happened within the following hour so we picked up from where we had left off. I was sick with worry because Joan was ashore and there were tales of damage in Chiba. I was so concerned I stood on the fo'cas'le head for an hour or more awaiting the minibus's return, and I was never more relieved to see it appear at the jetty end and Joan get off unscathed. She had had the unnerving experience of being shooed out of a department store with everything shaking and rocking, with chandeliers swaying wildly, I don't think she realized what was happening until she reached the street. Thank God none of our wives or crew members were harmed.

Not being of a superstitious nature, I found it difficult to believe that Joan was a Jonah! A Jonah, in seafaring parlance is someone aboard, who the crew consider is bringing bad luck to the ship. I mean two earthquakes - the only ones I experienced - and who was with me? The most bizarre emergency also occurred when Joan was with me! You won't believe this, but the ship was brought to an operational standstill by bees! The ship was making routine preparation for loading cargo at Lumut, going through all the safety checks and system proving when a huge swarm of ferocious jungle bees settled firstly on the aft loading platform and later at the 'midships cargo manifold. Both of these locations had to be accessed physically, despite the fact that the loading operation was centrally controlled, if for no other reason than safety. We were unable to commence loading! Now imagine, if you will, a desk driven cargo man in London giving credence to the reason for the delay as 'bees'! We were nonplused as to how to deal with the problem. Desperation drove me to lead a team of heroes, wrapped in swaddling and boiler suits (in steamy heat), armed with a high pressure water hose to disperse our visitors. What a spectacle! As soon as we directed the jet at the swarm they zoomed down the stream of water and attacked us, so we ignominiously fled in disarray leaving the hose bucking around like a bronco and receiving the full attention of the bees! The little sods would not go elsewhere so we had to call in a squad of pest exterminators from Kuala Belait to deal with them. We lost hours before they were dealt with. For days afterwards we had to be very careful because the decks were carpeted with dead and dying bees and quite capable of inflicting a nasty sting. Do you think it was Joan? The cargo archives in Shell Centre are the repository for the cargo statement containing the preposterous reason for the delay as 'a bee swarm'!

There are two meteorological conditions that are worse than fog: impenetrable rain and blinding snow which totally obliterate radar response and make visual surveillance physically impossible. Although we had our share of these two phenomena, fortunately they were not, as a rule, as persistent as fog. Epitomised by one I later experience crossing the North Pacific when I was obliged to be on the Bridge for the entire voyage! However, I now write about taking 'G' boats in and out of Tokyo Bay and through the Inland Sea. One had to have every hair on end, with streams of ships coming from all directions and worst of all, the most undisciplined craft afloat - and a law unto themselves - Japanese fishing fleets. You touch one of those guys and you're in deep trouble, believe me! My worst experience occurred in May 1978 (the height of the fog season) when just having cleared the Uraga Channel and discharged the pilot, the Second Engineer, Richard Parnell, collapsed with severe abdominal pain. There was no doubt in my mind that I had to return to the pilot station to land Richard - and it was just as well I did because it was subsequently diagnosed as acute pancreatitis, a very dangerous life threatening condition. We were in thick fog and I had to cross from the outward route to the inward route which meant going broadside to the traffic flow in each direction to change lanes, and the same again when we landed Richard. That night was an absolute nightmare! However it saved a life, and that was all important.

Then there were the 'big winds', the literal translation of the corrupted Chinese word 'typhoon'. These tropical revolving storms were of great importance in this trade, avoiding them was essential. In my day the typhoons were given women's names, starting at the commencement of the season at the beginning of the alphabet. In 1980 I served aboard two 'G' ships and during the twelve months there were that many storms, the names went through the alphabet almost twice. Now obviously not every storm affected the particular ship you happened to be aboard, but one had to consider every storm and the likely influence it may have upon voyage planning or upon one's stay at a Japanese port. I frequently had to divert through the various passages in the Philippine islands to avoid typhoons which added distance to the length of the trip. It was not considered prudent, in any event, to be caught up in the heavy swell that followed the path of a storm because the cargo tank membranes (the containment structure consisting of dimpled stainless steel sheet that enclosed the liquid natural gas) might become distorted by the hydraulic surges of the tank liquid. If one happened to be in port with an approaching typhoon likely to hit the area, one got out and went to sea to dodge the storm. This only happened to me on one occasion. My most poignant memory of a typhoon was when Joan and I joined Gari in Osaka in late September 1980 and the joining staff (including the Captain's wife) of the Bibby ship 'Derbyshire' were in a hotel in Yokohama, awaiting her arrival. As most people will remember, Derbyshire went down with all hands in typhoon 'Orchid' a dreadful tragedy which saddened us deeply.

I have referred to elitism, being a 'G' man. This was sponsored, to a degree, by our being able to buy 'G' Boat hats (which I wear to this day, and in Canada they look nothing unusual- being typically North American in style) and tee shirts - it all led to a sense of being part of a club (I had better not say 'exclusive' for fear of offending my non 'G' boat friends!). Of course I was moving to different ship types in between service in this liner fleet, which I shall describe as I go along in this narrative. However I thoroughly enjoyed my seven stints in the nine year span that I was in command of these fine ships.

CHAPTER SEVENTEEN

CADET TRAINING SHIP "OPALIA"

Cadet training ships had been plying the oceans for many decades. In the British Merchant Navy such ships were owned by cargo/passenger companies such as the New Zealand Shipping Company and the Federal Line. These were ships with ample accommodation with a tradition of cadet training, carrying out this function in a time honoured manner. The young gentlemen were cosseted to a degree in that there was always a nucleus of ratings to man the ship's operations, be it as helmsmen, port preparation, mooring and unmooring and any other work involving seamanship. The cadets led a structured life with an emphasis upon practical training.

In the early seventies concern was being felt at the ever dropping success rate of cadets attaining their certificate of competency at the conclusion of their training - this despite the enlightened education regime that was in vogue at the time. Cadets, then, attended nautical colleges pre, during and post qualifying sea time - which was in stark contrast to the rudimentary grooming afforded previous generations of trainees. Also, it was thought, within Shell Tankers that there was a diminution in professionalism which could, if allowed to go unchecked, give rise to a lowering in standards. Thus the concept of 'Opalia' developed, very much the brain child of a young, charismatic Chief Officer called John L.Gyles, who almost single handedly evolved the project. John was one of a new breed of officer who obtained university degrees in addition to the standard nautical qualification. Shell Tankers' management, enlightened as they were,

196

decided to proceed with the creation of a cadet training ship of an entirely different ilk. Opalia was chosen - an inspired choice - with ample accommodation and space for construction of lecture and training functions plus liberal room for eating and recreation facilities. Perhaps, without it being considered at the time, the attraction of the ship to young men was that she was a general trader, and not dedicated to a fixed role, which gave them a measure of excitement in seeing interesting new ports and meeting people (aka girls!). Opalia was converted to a training ship at Hamburg during the latter part of 1974. The refurbishment provided a fully-equipped classroom, a study and technical library plus a seamanship workshop for practical instruction. The cabin configuration was amended to accommodate 28 cadets. A large Mess Room provided ample seating for all cadets and they were conferred the privilege of being supplied with, and allowed to operate, their own Bar. A large area of the Boat Deck, adjacent to a capacious swimming pool, was netted off for the lads to work off their excess energy in ball games and where facilities for boxing were also provided. A boathouse under the Fo'cas'le Head housed two 14 feet 'Wayfarer' sailing dinghies, plus a small fleet of kayaks. It really was a brilliantly thought out conversion, which together with expert pre-planning made the scheme hugely successful from its very inception.

Opalia sailed from Hamburg in November 1974 under the command of Commodore Robert Lumsden - the fact that the Commodore was appointed to the ship indicated the importance with which Management judged the venture. Opalia, although she was expected to meet all her commercial and operational objectives, was, nevertheless, a 'personnel' ship. The eyes of the fleet and those of the Department of Trade were upon her. The Personnel Director was one Peter Davenport who maintained a careful watching brief. However, there was little doubt as to who was the power behind the throne! John Gyles of course. He was aboard as Instructor Chief Officer, carefully nurturing his project through its early days.

I imagine that everyone, in whatever career they pursue, has what they consider a pinnacle in that career. Mine was my appointment to Opalia on 24th January 1975. I flew to Dakar in Senegal to relieve Bob Lumsden for furlough - he had spent months at Hamburg during the conversion, so was due for 'the off'(MN slang).

He and I shared the command of Opalia for the next two years. It was a great honour. Our styles were dissimilar in that he projected a genial, avuncular demeanour (disguising a steely resolve, when needed) whereas I tended to be acerbic and demonstrative. When John Gyles left the ship after his first stint, he was asked to characterize the difference between the two masters and he likened us: as one being Lord Hailsham and the other as Anthony Wedgewood-Benn (sorry if any non-Brits miss this one) - I leave you to figure it out! Anyway, I was thrown in at the deep end.

Bob Lumsden stayed with the ship for three days, leaving off-shore at Las Palmas - so I had a very good handover. Prior to my joining I had, of my own volition, accompanied my friend and ex-boss Ray Swainston, in his capacity as Department of Trade Nautical Surveyor and Examiner (to which post he had been appointed in Cardiff, after his retirement from the Shell Tanker fleet), aboard one of the New Zealand Shipping Company cadet ships to get a sense of their organization and training schedules. I had also obtained a copy of the Opalia training manual whilst at home, so I had a good idea of what to expect. Ideally, one would have wished for an uninterrupted open ocean voyage, to get oneself properly familiarized with the ship. Such was not to be the case! Firstly, I was faced with the prospect of an English Channel passage to the Thames where there was to be an Open Day for Management and parents of the cadets at Shellhaven. Thereafter the Deputy Chief Examiner of Masters and Mates, Captain A.M.Jestico was to board at Shellhaven to carry out a voyage of inspection to certify the suitability of Opalia in her new role. Should the examination be successful, official status would be granted.

During these early days, another personal sadness was unfolding rapidly at home. My father-in-law and dear friend Ted Morris was slowly sinking towards his final day. I was most fortunate to have Joan come to the ship for Open Day, where she so charmingly and competently carried out the function of hostess. This was a boon to me because it was a huge social occasion. All the big wigs from Shell Centre, including the Marine Co-ordinator (and Managing Director of Shell International Marine, our mother organization) Mr D.R.Skinner, other directors and so down the hierarchical ladder. Most importantly we had fifty or more parents to entertain and discuss their little lads' futures. Exacting just wasn't the word, however the day was carried - in no small part due to an excellent staff, headed by the urbane Mr Gyles.

Unfortunately, because of her father's deteriorating condition, Joan had to leave the following day. We remained alongside for six days because of a tug strike. Captain Jestico boarded immediately before our departure and so began another period of intense anxiety because the good Lord had decided to make things as difficult as possible - we had dense fog all the way to the Western Approaches, via Rotterdam!

In the introductory pages of the Cadet Ship Training Manual an admonition states thus: "It is the responsibility of the Master and all concerned on board to ensure that the vessel is managed and operated with the most stringent observance of the highest professional standards." In other words we had to be an exemplary model, and, in effect, teach by example. This was, of course, the guiding principle we followed throughout, be it in tanker operation, safety, navigation or personal rectitude. A difficult act to play - it sharpened everyone's wits, but it succeeded.

Back to Captain Jestico. He was a most courteous man, but observant and perceptive so you knew that bulls..t wouldn't baffle brains! It was a harrowing time, chiefly for personal reasons, but also professionally - in the knowledge that everything had to be done 'right'. We had loaded bunkering fuel at Rotterdam for the Canaries and Cape Verde Islands thence to Dakar and Gambia. Tony Jestico left us at Las Palmas on 18th February 1975 and flew to London following a ten day stay. My friend Ted Morris died on my daughter Rhiannon's birthday, 15th February, such a sad passing for all of us - I missed him forevermore, but, as the saying has it 'it was a blessing'.

Opalia had a wonderful staff on her maiden tour as a training ship. Chief Engineer Eric Satterley, with whom I became friendly, accepted the ethos enthusiastically and ensured that the engineer officers followed the strictures, formalities and requirements of a CTS with particular attention to dress code. David Pringle, the Chief Officer, was a first class officer. A humorous, gentlemanly man and just the sort of man the cadets could well emulate. Second Officer Chris Rowsell, also a BSc, was another outstanding young officer who impressed. Finally, and the officer closest to the cadet body, Third Officer Tim Charlesworth, standing a lofty six and a half feet with a personality to match completing the Bridge Team. The Instructor Chief Officer, whom I have already described in glowing terms augmented the Deck Department. At some early point, I can't remember when, John Gyles was superseded by James Deane as ICO. He was an older man, having served with the Kenya Marine Service and subsequently as a college lecturer, who made the ideal replacement as he was well versed in academic and teaching skills if not displaying quite the charismatic image his predecessor projected! In addition to the normal engineer officer complement Opalia carried an extra officer in the role as Safety Officer and to carry out any engineering training that might be needed. The ship also employed an extra petty officer for training purposes. Opalia carried 14 crew ratings, specifically utilized in the Catering and Engine Room departments. In current merchant ship practice she had a large complement at 61 people.

Cadets! 12 Phase II cadets and 16 Initial Sea Phase cadets - henceforth referred to as P2's and ISP's. P2's possessed both Efficient Deck Hand and Lifeboat certificates, constituting the basic legal manning. I've referred to 'traditional' training ships - Opalia was not. The deck department was manned solely by cadets without assistance from older ratings, under the surveillance of a Chief Petty Officer and an Instructor Petty Officer, all operations subjected to the scrutiny of the Safety Officer. At any one time, at sea, two P2's would operate a tandem navigational process alongside the officer - of-the-watch (OOW), filling in log book details and virtually navigating the ship in a dual operation. An excellent teaching technique. During a watch period one P2 would navigate whilst the other maintained a look-out, changing function as arranged. ISP's, sixteen year old youngsters in the main, comprised the maintenance work force, under the tutelage of P2 supervisors.

In my day, the very prospect of having a squad of cadets to clean, chip, scrape, wire brush, prime and paint decks and superstructures would have a been a mate's nirvana. Imagine having eager, enthusiastic and compliant hands to attend to your every instruction. A dream - that's what it would be. Reality was somewhat different! As I was at seventeen years of age, they were awkward, untutored and un-coordinated, and anyway, "w o r k" was a four letter word which was something their FATHERS did!! So if any of us anticipated a miraculous improvement in the ship's appearance we were to be sorely disillusioned!

The cadet body was split into three divisions - somewhat uninspiringly designated: Red, Blue and Green, each comprising four P2's and five (or six) ISP's. However, this categorization made for efficient organization in the allocation of operational, instructional, maintenance and domestic duties. It also led to a certain degree of competitiveness which was fostered in all fields, be it professional or leisure. The cadets looked after the cleanliness of their accommodation and public rooms. They were given full officer status in their Messroom, they dressed correctly and received full steward service, no smoking was allowed at meal times. Any infringements in this area was swiftly attended to - it would be too easy to allow a creeping lowering of standards to set in with a bunch of lively young fellows. Four cadets were invited to sit at the Master's table for Sunday lunch, on a rotational basis. I won't belabour the reader with the minutiae of the intricate organization that went into the ship's operation, other than to mention that it was detailed and complex.

It was a marvellous ship to command! There was an intelligence about the ship that didn't exist elsewhere. As Master, one had to have one's wits about one to ensure that everything was correctly and professionally carried out - woe betide if one slipped up! The cadets had an elected group known as the Cadets' Council where suggestions were made to the Management Team via the ICO, during which any slip-up in any field that may have been noticed by a cadet was aired. Now they were, always, a bright inquisitive and sometimes mischievous bunch of youngsters. There were three bars aboard: Officers', Crew and Cadets'. They were democratically 'allowed' to be invited to the other two bars. Naturally there was a strict limit on what they were allowed to drink, no alcohol for those under eighteen years of age, but the little beggars used to try circumventing the rules by 'arranging' for someone to invite them! I used to spend considerable time scrutinizing bar records each day to ensure there was no jiggery pokery. At various ports I would arrange for coaches to take them to places of interest and enjoyment. At the end of my two year stint in command, their Bar was full of souvenirs which had been lifted from ports all over the world! I remember one occasion when I arranged for a contingent to visit South Rampart Street in New Orleans where they filched so many items from bars and streets that I was thankful to clear the Mississippi delta before a posse of police squad cars descended upon the ship! We used to have the most enjoyable social evenings, be they 'dances' (the young and not so young wives loved it) or quiz and bingo nights. Joan just loved spending as much time as she could arrange aboard Opalia.

There's one prank that deserves specific mention! Somewhere, somehow the young beggars acquired an American Bald Eagle chick. Now the Company's ruling, and indeed international health regulations, prohibited the carrying of animals of any description. I used to carry out formal and informal inspections of the ship and found nothing in this instance. The little sods used to ferry this bird around corners ahead of me as I approached and then follow the inspection team from behind, carrying the thing in a cage they had constructed, with a bandage around its beak to prevent any squawks! When I was safely out of the way the bird was put in its room - wherever that was! Of course there was never an eagle that ate better, in fact it was over fed to the degree that it could hardly move - it sat in its cage like an ample based cone! Eventually I discovered the bird and assembled the cadet body at 'divisions'. I laid into them in my most sarcastic and livid manner (secretly, nearly bursting with mirth - especially as this bloody bird was present at divisions) telling them they had two choices: one to kill their pet or to starve the thing and exercise it somehow so that it could fly, and when it could, to release it. Now we were bound for Europe so they took the second option and succeeded in trimming the thing right down, he/she was a magnificent creature. The sequel to this story is almost unbelievable! They released the eagle in the Western Approaches and it disappeared into the mists off Southern Ireland. Some years later, an ornithologist in Eire was astonished to observe what he thought was an American Bald Eagle near the south coast. This was reported in a naturalist magazine... Shhhh.

On the serious side. The training regime aboard Opalia was second to none. There can be little doubt that professionalism amongst future tanker deck officers was greatly enhanced. Certainly the academic standard and examination success improved significantly

202

as was witnessed by the increase in obtaining certification. Captain Jestico conferred official approval upon Opalia as a training ship which brought the bonus of reduced qualifying sea time to those who served aboard the ship.

Commodore Lumsden served aboard Opalia from November 1974 until November 1976 when he retired from active sea service (he subsequently became Marine Manager with Dome Petroleum, working out of Calgary, Alberta). During that period I was his 'deputy'. So, whilst he was in command. I had to go elsewhere to earn a crust. In between times I went for tours to 'Gari' and 'Lepeta'. My times there have already been recounted. Incidentally Lepeta, during my time there became a 'mini' cadet training ship, with a much smaller complement of cadets.

My final period in command of Opalia was from November 1976 until June 1977 - just prior to her striking appearance at the Jubilee Spithead Review. It was my most difficult term. John Gyles had disappeared from the firmament and there was, with changing management, a subtle change in attitude. To appreciate the particular role of Opalia, and the problems thus engendered, one had to have lived with her since the days of her inception. New faces were now bringing unreasonable perceptions to bear upon the function of the ship. There was an impatience abroad with the emphasis upon training and a demand that conventional considerations be given greater credence. Anyway, I was determined that during my stewardship, the ship's training programme would not be diluted by opinions unsympathetic to her primary purpose.

From the interest aspect, this period was the most fruitful. Joan and I flew to Hamburg and I assumed command on November 17th 1976. A presentation of a silver plated model of Opalia was made to Bob Lumsden, in recognition of his contribution to the scheme, by the ship's company whilst we were in Hamburg. From whence we proceeded to Piraeus for refit where the ship stayed for nearly a month. In that time the cadets, except for a nucleus, were sent home on furlough. Meanwhile the officers were accommodated ashore in a hotel which was very pleasant. Joan and I were able to visit all the wonderful archaeological sites in Athens and Poseidon before she had to return to Merthyr. The repair yard manager hailed from a village in hills above Piraeus, he invited the officers to a traditional Greek evening meal at his home which was held in the village square. I have never forgotten that wonderfully simple repast - a lamb roasted on a spit accompanied by the most delicious apples, washed down by a robust wine.

All good things come to an end. We went into the most testing period of my sojourn aboard Opalia. The ship was stored and outfitted at Piraeus when we received our new intake of cadets, largely new to the ship and younger on average than any previous intake. Ideally, it would have been better to have had an ocean voyage in prospect to settle in this bunch of white faced, pimply boys. No such luck. We had to be commercially viable, so no favours were asked for, or given. But! We received orders to load crude at Wadi Feiran in the Gulf of Suez. We left Piraeus on December 22nd and arrived at Port Said on Christmas Eve, transiting the Suez Canal on Christmas Day getting to Wadi Feiran on Boxing Day. Bad weather prevented the ship berthing in the open buoyed sea berth, although we made a number of attempts. Imagine, if you will, putting this fairly big ship into such a berth with these little untutored lads having to handle huge eight inch wires which we pulled up from the seabed - most of them quite unused to the ship, let alone the intimidating experience of a training ship and all the complex rules that went with it! They had already brought the ship through the Suez Canal. After all, it was Christmas! I secretly felt so sorry for them, but there's no compassion in ship operation. The now famous Truman saying applied "If you can't stand the heat, get out of the kitchen!" We did berth, we managed to have some sort of Christmas celebration, we loaded and returned to the Suez Canal, arriving, as you may have guessed, on New Year's Eve! Another canal transit, going north this time on New Year's Day. Those boys were three years older and ten feet tall by the time we returned to the Mediterranean! We discharged at Marseilles where we were visited by the 'new' disinterested and squeaky clean operational superintendent, who wanted to know why the ship looked dirty - I ask you! We repeated the voyage to Wadi Feiran and back then loaded in Tunisia at La Skhirra for Port Arthur in Texas. At last we were able to settle down during a sixteen day trans-Atlantic voyage.

We had another outstanding Instructor Chief Officer, who had already sailed as Chief Officer, one Roger Firth, he was succeeded by another elegant guy: Peter Shefford. So in my time we were well blessed by high calibre ICO's. When I re-joined at Hamburg there was a no-hoper as Chief Officer who fortunately was relieved by Manny Longmore who put his heart and soul into the job. At the end of my stay, Peter Redfern my old friend, was Chief Officer. It was during this time that Chris Camp was Chief Engineer - the person I referred to in a previous chapter, and a laugh a minute! It was a very happy voyage, socially. Joan re-joined at Port Arthur, our daughter by now in college and not needing her mother's ministrations, so from that point of view, things were good.

I have referred to the voyage being interesting. It was also instructive. We had already completed four transits of the Suez Canal which was more than some people experience in a lifetime. Later we made two transits of the Panama Canal, taking a cargo from Curaçao to Balboa at the Pacific end, which was a great episode for the lads and Joan! In addition, we lightened two VLCC's off Curaçao, which gave the cadets a valuable insight. However, the ship was mainly running flat out on the American Eastern Seaboard, a punishing trade, especially as we were then informed that Opalia would be one of two merchant ships at Spithead and we were expected to bring the appearance of the ship up to a high standard. Forget it! It was impossible, despite our operating superintendent's exhortations.

The months passed quickly enough. Cadets each spent a four month period aboard Opalia, earning them one month's remission. No cadet was allowed to serve more than two terms, the maximum permissible reduction in sea service being two months. On the whole cadets loved the ship because they regarded it as theirs and enjoyed the structured routine with opportunities for superior academic and practical tutoring and a happy social environment. There were those who rebelled - Reluctant Opalians - nothing about the ship suited these young men, they found the discipline tedious and the 'organized joy' onerous. Of course, there was huge scepticism within the Fleet, with many detractors and some active enemies. Once again, a price for elitism or whatever one would wish to term something different. However the 'proof of the pudding is in the eating' and there was ample evidence after two years in operation that Opalia had made a significant improvement to the pass rate of Shell Tanker cadets when sitting for their Second Mate's

Certificates. During my span, two hundred cadets received training and not only did they improve academically, I'm positive they were better tankermen when they went down the gangway.

I had to stay in service for seven months because of the impending attendance at the Spithead Review and the requirement that Commodore Simon Darroch, RD, RNR, take command for the Review (I was 'piggy in the middle' or if you wish 'ever the Best Man, never the Groom'!). My last port visit was at Rouen, where I distinguished myself by being collision with a train! We sailed up the Seine to a turning basin in Rouen, which transpired was too small for Opalia. In our manoeuvrings our bow demolished railway carriages on the deck of a moored cargo vessel, so that's how the legend of Dick Williams's collision with a train arose!

Joan and I were delighted to attend Her Majesty's Jubilee Review as guests of Shell Tankers (UK) Ltd. It made everything so worthwhile. I was immensely proud and emotional to witness the event and to know that Admiral Sir Henry Leach, KCB, C in C Fleet sent a signal to Opalia stating, simply: "VERY SMART", just one of two such commendations of the whole Review.

CHAPTER EIGHTEEN

NEW SHIP - NEW VENTURES

Every Captain or Chief Engineer hopes, that at some time in his career he will commission a new ship. I did not achieve that distinction until late 1977.

I left Opalia on June 1st and, together with Joan spent a few days in Portsmouth before and after the Jubilee Review which was held on June 28th. By this time Rhiannon was studying for a degree in education with a view of becoming a teacher, she was now a lovely young woman of whom we were justly proud. Joan and I celebrated our Silver Wedding in July so, with Rhiannon's help, we had a very happy event at one the local hotels at which all available family members attended. My brother, Tom, flew in from Canada and a number of seafaring friends came along. So it was great night. Soon after the party Tom returned to Toronto and a little later Rhiannon joined her uncle for summer holiday. Meanwhile Joan and I had a wonderful tour of Scotland which satisfied our love for exploring the British Isles. Rhiannon was studying at a teachers' training college at Cyncoed in Cardiff. She had met a Canadian student, whose Welsh parents had decided to have him educated in Britain (as indeed they had his older sister). This had been a casual meeting from all accounts, but I suspect he had been smitten. When Rhiannon knew she was spending the summer vacation in Toronto, out of sheer boredom (having to spend long days alone whilst Tom was at work) she contacted this young man. His name was Lloyd Lewis. Boy! Are we glad they met! He became our much loved son-in-law, one of those fortuitous happenings that occasionally bless us.

In mid September 1977 I flew to Halifax thence to St. John, New Brunswick to stand-by the latter stage of building of the first of a new generation of product carriers. She was named Erinna. She was being built by Irving Shipyards, part of a Canadian conglomerate whose activities embraced amongst others, oil refining and gasoline sales in the Maritime Provinces. This was an unusual area to have a Shell tanker constructed - the first such contract in fact. The ship class building programme was split between Canada and Japan, so the Canucks had stiff competition from the very experienced yards in Japan. I suspect they acquitted themselves satisfactorily, although I witnessed some innovative building techniques that would have been frowned upon elsewhere. I spent a most pleasant six week stay in this Bay of Fundy port. It was in the midst of a beautiful fall with the most glorious panoply of leaf colouring one could imagine - Canadian Autumn colour is one of the more spectacular visual experiences to be found anywhere in the world. St. John is noted for its reversing falls. The St. John River pours down falls during ebb tide and such is the strength of the flood tide, the water appears to fall in the opposite direction. As most people will know the world's greatest tidal range exists in the Bay of Fundy - reminiscent of the Bristol Channel, which runs a close second. Another interesting feature of this part of New Brunswick was the existence of a section of the population known as Loyalists. These souls were more British in sentiment than we were! In fact the feisty harbour pilot was such an Empire Loyalist that he refused to fly the Canadian maple leaf ensign when the ship was under Irving ownership (prior to Shell's acceptance) instead flying an older N.B. red ensign. These people had gone to the Maritimes during the American War of Independence and had remained fiercely British in outlook. We threw a party at the acceptance ceremony for all those connected with the building and outfitting of Erinna, together with representatives from the Agency. This occurred after builders' trials had been successfully completed with omissions and faults ostensibly rectified. The party was lavish with champagne, caviar and the works. Once again, the loyalists among those present, were full of praise for we Brits - intimating that only we could have put on a show of such quality - it made one feel good, but one knew differently. Once we accepted the ship the real business of commissioning and proving

208

began. The acceptance transaction took place on 21st October 1977 and we sailed for owners' trials on the morning of the 23rd. These done we sailed for Rotterdam on the evening of that day. This was my first experience of sailing in ballast in an easterly direction across the Atlantic. The voyage was uneventful except for some foul weather towards the latter part of the crossing - when everything was practically turned upside down. We called at Falmouth to board superintendents, who came to check performance and plant proving. We arrived at Rotterdam on the first day of November. Three grades of cargo were loaded (avtur, gasoline and gasoil) successfully for Bonny in Nigeria.

Erinna provided me with my first experience of 'driving' the ship from the Bridge. One controlled the engine by use of a 'combinator' - varying engine speed in conjunction with changing the propeller pitch. Quite a tricky business, until one became accustomed to the technique. When we arrived at Bonny there was a queue of ships waiting to berth, in fact we anchored for more than three weeks. This gave us the opportunity to paint ship and to carry out manoeuvring trials to pinpoint characteristics and performance. We eventually berthed at Bonny on the 4th December (32 years to the day of joining my first ship). Jack Beaumont relieved me for furlough - or at least that was the general intention! Before I was able to get home I had to plan my escape from Nigeria.

My first 'episode' was my transport from Bonny to Port Harcourt. This entailed travelling up river in a dugout canoe, admittedly propelled by outboard motor but the wash from other passing dugouts did a good job of soaking both my baggage and myself. The next experience was my hotel at Port Harcourt where I arrived hot, damp and creased. The building was quite modern but everything was a facade! To begin, there was a notice in the 'en suite' warning everybody not to bath (particularly females) for fear of small critters entering one's body via one's orifices! I kid you not. So one took a quick, smelly shower whenever it was absolutely essential to do so! Every room had a smart telephone which was attached to thin air. The food was atrocious, so I ate at a nearby Chinese restaurant (this race defines the meaning of 'ubiquitous'!) where the fare was reasonable. Then there was the huge problem of getting out of the damn place. The agent booked my flight to Lagos, but omitted to tell me that every flight was grossly overbooked! After one failed attempt to get aboard a plane, I twigged that one had to employ someone to fight for a seat! I paid a large local lad an obscene sum to ensure my departure. Arrival at Lagos, after an awful flight in a cramped Fokker Friendship, heralded another nightmare! There was no one meeting me at the domestic terminal, so having extracted my luggage from a huge pile of baggage which included various containers of livestock, I then had to struggle in a melee of frantic, sweating bodies to transfer my belongings to a taxi. Any movement from A to B within this terminal costs big bucks. I had to pay to have my bags moved from the carousel to the terminal entrance (one could not, of course, leave anything unattended) and a taxi. In between times, I was cajoled and threatened to spend time (once more) with everyone's girlfriend, sister, wife etc.,etc.! I took a car from the domestic terminal to the international terminal, some 100 metres or so, at a cost of ten pounds! I won't belabour you further with the rest of the saga, sufficient to say I did eventually escape via a British Caledonian 'plane - believe me when I write that I was never more heartened to see those lovely British girls in their colourful kilts as I boarded their DC10, bound for London. Phew!

Another family milestone happened during this leave. We met our son-in-law-to-be. Now I had been brought up in a formal 'be seen and not heard' manner by my parents and naturally being in the type of life that I had followed subsequently, I tended to espouse a British approach to new acquaintances - allowing familiarity to flower in due time. Got a bit of a shock with this tall, disarmingly amiable young man. His very first words to me were: "Hi Dick, good to meet you"! His candid approach, despite my rather stuffy preconceptions, won me over in a trice - and he has been a wonderful friend to me ever since. He now ranks alongside my other cherished friend Ted Morris as one of my staunchest companions. He too, is not much cop at arm-wrestling!

So 1977 was, in the main, a good year - one of pride, celebration and welcome. In February 1978 I returned to the 'G' trade, joining Genota at Yokohama. During my spell aboard this ship, Joan was able to join me for a period - she couldn't spend more than two months with me because of her responsibilities to Rhiannon and her aging mother. Life at sea was so much better in these times and this led to an ever increasing contentment amongst the officers. This appointment is covered in Chapter Sixteen.

210

Obviously, the new ship in the title of this chapter refers to Erinna, the new ventures were in an entirely different area of sea transport. Post Genota, I headed a team to Antwerp to take over Shell Tankers' first bulk carrier, the good ship 'Canadian Bridge', owned by the Bibby Line. Thirty three years carrying liquid cargoes of one sort or another, now we were going to load and discharge coal, iron ore or even wheat! Not one of us had any experience whatsoever in this field. Nor were the officers of Canadian Bridge too inclined to help us to any great degree (which I suppose was a natural reaction at losing a ship to another company), so it was 'cold turkey'. As soon as ownership was transferred to STUK, the ship was renamed 'Tectus'. Her size was 120,000 tons deadweight - between a Shell 'D' and 'M'.

Fortunately we had a keen bunch of people with Chief Officer John Hovington and Chief Engineer John Jones in the lead. We had eleven days in which to get to grips with all the new practice and techniques that we would have to adopt. The stability equations, both vertical and longitudinal, were vastly different from those in a tanker - in need of very careful appraisal and calculation. We were ever mindful of the tales of disaster that had befallen other bulkers, (as tragically occurred, subsequently, to Tectus's sister ship Derbyshire) so we really researched our subject as a matter of survival!

Shell Coal was formed in 1975 (I think) in a diversification programme, then a prevalent corporate policy amongst international companies. Cargoes were, until the advent of Tectus, carried in chartered tonnage. Shell had always espoused the principle of maintaining an involvement in any form of sea transport so that the organization could never be beholden to outside interests who may otherwise have held a monopoly. Hence Tectus and subsequently a series of new bulk carriers plus a couple of VLOOS (Very Large Oil/Ore carriers). The Shell Coal slogan was 'Tomorrow's solution to-day" - a sentiment I found difficulty in relating to! Anyway, it was not for us to reason why.

We sailed from Antwerp on September 15th 1978, in ballast, for Richards Bay in South Africa. The ship was in a bloody awful state! She had been laid up in Loch Striven for many months prior to moving to Antwerp so no maintenance or cleaning had been done in that time. The last cargo had been iron ore so the ballast voyage was taken up with removing the residue from that cargo and in cleaning a filthy engine room. She was a depressing sight with massive shards of thick rust on deck and in the holds - it took a long time to whip this number into shape. I will not tax you further with the negative side, but this appointment was no picnic for any of us. We arrived at Richards Bay on October 5th. The lengthy voyage had given us time to 'swot up' on the business ahead - a radically new concept for us.

Richards Bay is a fine natural harbour situated in the province of Natal, about 100 kms north and east of Durban. It is the main South African coal export outlet, operated by South African Railways, also handling chemicals and sulphur. The coal is delivered from the interior by 4000 ton train loads, and a normal monthly export quantity is in the region of one million tons. The coal wagons are picked up and emptied onto a conveyor to a stack (a small mountain of coal) reclaimers transfer the coal from the stack to the shiploaders by another conveyor system. When operating at capacity, 11,000 tons can be loaded in one hour - an impressive quantity.

Fortunately for us, the reclaimers were out of commission, so we had a delay of some five days alongside while they were repaired. A number of us took the opportunity to visit the famous Umfolozi National Park - a rare chance for we tanker men to sightsee such a natural wonder, I'll never forget the sight of a secretary bird holding a snake in one of its powerful claws whilst chomping the reptile's head off. We were hoping to see some of the 'cats' that rove around the park, but were unlucky on that day - we had to content ourselves with watching buffalo, wild pig and baboons and the secretary birds.

We sailed with a full cargo on October 11th for Aabenraa in Denmark in what was the former Schleswig Holstein. It was the first delivery of Shell coal in a Shell ship to any receiver. It therefore merited fairly fulsome entertainment and general jollification with luminaries joining the Management Team for cocktails and such. Whereas the social side went very successfully, the operational demands were not without difficulty - but that would require a laborious technical essay- suffice to write that we spent five days discharging 75% of our cargo. The arrival of Tectus caused a furore among the anti-apartheid brigade in Western Europe who threatened dire consequences should we dare spill a nugget of coal ashore.

The demonstrators were thwarted by lack of transport, however the political atmosphere was, at best, uncertain! The Baltic Sea and the eastern North Sea were blanketed in dense fog, so our journey to our second port, Hamburg, was wet and miserable. The Germans (in usual Teutonic efficiency) whipped the remaining 25% of our cargo ashore in record time. We set sail on our next new venture on November 11th 1978.

Coal, as everyone knows, is dirty stuff. Each of us was filthy after leaving Europe, the accommodation was covered in coal dust, cabin carpets were badly marked, the external white superstructure was grimy. However the stuff has the advantage of being readily removed and cleaned off, but restoring ourselves to acceptable Shell standards took time. Another feature of coal is its huge desire to burn spontaneously, cargo fires are commonplace if due attention is not paid to vigilant ventilation. Anyway, enough of this boring old black stuff. Our next loading was to lift another black/brown/grey commodity - iron ore, from a place called Sepetiba Bay in Brazil.

Iron ore is really dense - try lifting a plastic bucketfull of the stuff, it'll just about pull your arm out of its socket! A normal loading rate, at a modern loading port, is in the region of 20,000 tons in an hour. The ore thunders into the holds, making a huge thudding noise as it hits the plates, which was quite disconcerting to we uninitiated tanker men. Specially strengthened holds are normally used to contain the material, but on this occasion, we had to spread the stuff over the whole range - because we had to lift two types of ore. If you looked down into the holds, all you would see would be a tump of ore not even covering the floor. If you consider the effect of these small mounds of extremely heavy ore all along the length of the ship, you can visualize that all the weight is at the bottom. This makes a ship 'stiff'. A stiff ship is an uncomfortable ship, with short swift and sometimes violent movements in a sea. So we sailed from Brazil at the beginning of December bound for Kure in Japan.

The voyage was something of a nightmare to me. I was ill at ease with the sharp motion, even in a moderate seaway. I think when you take command of a ship you 'live' it, you identify with its every mood or movement and you sense distress or discomfort in the lady in your care. As I've mentioned before, I was very mindful of not putting Tectus in jeopardy as a result of hostile weather - purely because of the cargo we were carrying and the stress the ship could suffer if put in harm's way. Our route took me into realms I hadn't entered before. The South Atlantic didn't hold any terrors, but rounding the Cape of Good Hope with the huge swells and the dreaded 'holes in the ocean' were not to be dismissed lightly. I should perhaps briefly describe the 'holes'. When certain climatic conditions pertain in conjunction with the Agulhas Current (the southerly current along South Africa's south easterly seaboard) enormously steep swells can be created that have engulfed ships. Then there was always the fear of tropical revolving storms across the Indian and Pacific Oceans. Our route took us from Good Hope to the Lombok Strait (east of Bali), thence to the Pacific via the Celebes Sea. As matters transpired our 34 day voyage was uneventful, arriving at Kure on January 5th 1979.

I was superseded at Kure by Jim Forbes. I took the opportunity of going to Hiroshima and the museum commemorating the first dropping of an atom bomb. It was a very moving event and left me with much food for thought. I travelled to Osaka by the 'Bullet Train' - an experience in itself, so impressively efficient and luxurious. From Osaka I flew to Amsterdam and on to Cardiff, arriving in Merthyr on January 8th. I was glad to be home. I assumed I would return to either of my 'core' specialities - gas or oil. In a way I did, but not in the form I imagined!

As an additional arrow to their quiver, Shell Tankers (UK) Ltd had formed a consultative company known as Tanker Fleet Services, offering their expertise to any marine undertaking that was prepared to pay a fee for their services. One of their ventures was to operate two combination carriers for the Norwegian shipowner Hoegh. A combination carrier, commonly referred to as an OBO (Oil/Bulk/Ore), is a most versatile vessel capable of transporting crude oil, black oils, coal, ores and even wheat. Multipurpose they may be, but they are very difficult ships to operate - changing from one product to another. This difficulty is exacerbated when the ship in question is a clapped out mobile heap! As you will have surmised, my subsequent appointment was to one of these ships, curiously named 'Vega Seal'. Although now registered in Britain, previously she had been run by Norwegians under their national flag. I always harboured an admiration for the manner in which Scandinavians operated their fleets, I have to say that this sentiment suffered a reappraisal as a consequence of my ghastly experience running that ship. I won't go into detail, but equipment and standards were severely wanting. The fact was, we Shell men had been cosseted by the ethos of an international oil company whose standards and ethics were vastly superior to those in other sectors of the shipping industry - this realization had been amply demonstrated by both Canadian Bridge and Vega Seal.

I joined Vega Seal on September 8th 1979 at Kakogawa, near Kobe in Japan, and travelled to Singapore with my predecessor, Bill Snowdon, in order to familiarize myself with the new set-up and another form of sea transport. The ship had completed the discharge of iron ore in Japan and we were now stemmed to load crude oil at Ardjuna in Java. Our call at Singapore was to take on spare parts prior to proceeding to Ardjuna, where we arrived on 21st. We anchored for ten days awaiting cargo before proceeding to Rotterdam to deliver the crude oil. One of the disturbing characteristics of an OBO was its propensity, when handling an oil cargo, to list violently as a consequence of 'free surface' (for those who don't know what it is - remember, if you will, the difficulty in carrying a wide, full bowl of water), this arises whenever there's a large surface of cargo and ballast occurring simultaneously during the loading or discharging operations. This could be quite alarming. However, these little frights were nothing compared with the horrors in store.

At Rotterdam we back loaded a cargo of Iranian crude (which had been lying in storage tanks at Pernis for God knows how long) for delivery to Portland in Maine. We left Rotterdam on May 7th 1979, a fateful day for the British Merchant Navy, when Margaret Thatcher came to power and so began the nemesis of our proud industry.

Vega Seal was run on minimum cost - Tanker Fleet Services weren't cheap, so we had to be very expenditure conscious to make the employment of the venture, viable. We had a basic 'pool' crowd, who were not of the standard to which we had become accustomed with a Shell contract crew. So, in a way, it was a return to the bad old days. The mollifying feature was that we were endeavouring to make a new concept (for Shell that is) work, so therein lay a challenge. Unfortunately, many things militated against success. Firstly, and most disturbingly, the Chief Engineer was progressively becoming an alcoholic and had taken to drinking with crew members. This was disastrous from a discipline standpoint. This officer left in Portland to be replaced by John Jones, an outstanding officer - who commissioned Tectus. To digress, our trans-Atlantic voyage took Vega Seal across the Newfoundland Banks at the height of the iceberg season, so we navigated this dangerous area in dense fog that did nothing for my peace of mind! We received instructions prior to our arrival at Portland that on completion of our crude oil delivery we were to prepare holds for loading iron ore at Port Cartier in Quebec.

We looked forward to tackling this task with enthusiasm! This was going to give we Shell professionals the opportunity show our worth. However it was Shell that scuppered that fond hope. The cargo of Iranian crude oil contained mountains of sand and wax which was left after the discharge, across the hold bottoms. Apart from a huge difference in what we should have delivered and what was actually pumped ashore we were stuck with this mess to clean before we could load iron ore. The long and the short of it was that we could not handle the amounts of sludge because our slop tank capacity was too small (slop tanks were those spaces to which tank washings were stored). As soon as our slop capacity was reached, we had to go to Port Hawkesbury to discharge this gunge, then back to sea to complete the hold cleaning. Then when we eventually berthed at Port Cartier, the ballast pumping system failed! Because Port Cartier is tidal, a ship was loaded 'over the tide' - that is loading had to be completed before low water. We weren't able to do this because of the ballast retention, so we loaded less than we should have in order to quit the berth before we grounded! Another charming feature was that most of the crew were drunk - so I had to get all available personnel, be they engineer officers, the radio officer, catering and engine room ratings to unberth the ship before disaster befell us. Our record, in the minds of Heogh, the owners, therefore, was lamentable.

We took the ship back to Rotterdam where I was almost ecstatic to be replaced in mid June 1979, after another fogbound voyage amongst icebergs to complete my horror story.

216

CHAPTER NINETEEN

THIS AND THAT

With one brief exception, the remainder of my seafaring was concerned with the transport of gas. Hitherto, my gas experience had been in the carriage of natural gas. During this phase, however, I was appointed to one of Shell's LPG ships (liquid petroleum gas, viz., butane and propane), Isomeria by name. Also in this period I served aboard all the other LNG ship types that Shell operated or managed - the Methane Progress and Methane Princess, Gadinia, Gari and Gadila and two of the magnificent Malaysian government (Malaysian International Shipping Corporation) ships, Tenaga Empat and Tenaga Dua. I will describe my involvement with these latter two ships in the next chapter.

After my stint aboard Vega Seal, I had a short summer furlough before my appointment to Methane Progress. During this spell ashore I persuaded Joan that we should buy a more up-market residence. She wasn't too keen, knowing that the responsibility for the move would rest on her shoulders. However my enthusiasm, and particularly that of Rhiannon, carried the day and we purchased a lovely house with a magnificent view of the Brecon Beacons. I returned to sea and Rhiannon went to Canada to work as a nanny in a Toronto doctor's household (with the ostensible reason of 'making sure' Lloyd was the man!) - leaving poor Joan to do the business. From our lounge window we had the uninterrupted panorama of one of South Wales' most beautiful sceneries - the vista changed every few minutes, and it proved to be one of the loves of our lives.

Almost fifteen years to the day that I had first joined Progress as Chief Officer, I returned as her Master at Canvey Island. Although my experience in the LNG trade was as extensive as anybody else's. I was, nevertheless, required by British Gas to do a re-training voyage with my predecessor, David Mortimer. As far as I was concerned, this was great! I had a week's cruise before assuming command, enjoying Dave's company enormously (he was an outstanding man, yet he chose, almost exclusively, to serve aboard the methaniers). I assumed command on September 8th 1979, at Arzew. Progress returned to Canvey and repeated the voyage. Thereafter she was withdrawn from that trade, had a short wait anchored in the Thames Estuary, before proceeding to Skikda (formerly Phillipeville) to begin a shuttle service to Barcelona. In my time Progress delivered seven cargoes to this Catelonian port, with only a day between terminals this could have proved to be a taxing trade, however there were frequent lengthy delays at the Algerian end, so the run wasn't too onerous.

Meanwhile Joan was battling with the move between houses. Being the efficient person she is, she organized the transaction and physical move with competence and began the creation of a new and much loved home. About all I could do to sustain her was to write and 'phone as frequently as possible. Because of her involvement she was unable to accompany me during my stay aboard Progress. I left in high spirits on December 15th looking forward to Christmas in our new home.

Joan and I had just about the busiest leave we had ever had! There was so much work to be done in our new home with new equipment to install, we used to go to bed late at night exhausted. A surprise was loosed upon us, during this time, by the unexpected announce- ment by Rhiannon that she and Lloyd intended to wed the following year! This threw us into a paroxysm of activity because she wished to marry at Vaynor, in a beautiful small church nestling in a hollow near Merthyr. As a family we were Anglicans, and whereas Rhiannon had been confirmed in the faith, Lloyd hadn't. Although, once more (!), the major responsibility would devolve upon Joan, I was determined to help plan and aid her as much as I could before returning to sea. We had to seek permission from the Archbishop of Canterbury, no less, for these two to be joined in holy matrimony!

It was a labour of love. We were so delighted that Lloyd and she had decided to tie the knot, we would have gone to the ends of the earth to make it possible. We were assisted and guided (?) by one David Walters, the Rector of Vaynor. David was a saintly, shy almost timid man whose forte had nothing to do with ceremonial organization (in the pulpit he was transformed into a formidable orator with a delightfully humorous weave in his sermons), consequently leadership had to be exercised by Joan. She did a cracker of a job. You will undoubtedly have noticed that throughout my story she provided the backbone for everything we did or achieved - a rare and lovely lady. At the end of February 1980 I flew to Japan to take command, once again, of Gadinia.

Between having to complete the setting up of home and the organization of the forthcoming wedding, there was no opportunity for Joan to join me. In fact she was desperately lonely without daughter or husband and all the responsibility resting upon her slight shoulders, still as ever she came through with flying colours - always aided and guided by Ethel, her mother. The wedding was arranged for July 12th. I arrived home during the last week of June. Apart from a pleasant stay in Yokohama during a refit earlier in the year, I have nothing to retell - in any event my time aboard the 'G's is covered in Chapter Fifteen.

The wedding went wonderfully well. Lloyd's parents and my brother, Tom, flew in from Canada to complete the family circle, so it was a very happy time. The newlyweds honeymooned in the Lake District before leaving for Canada to their new life together. We were well content. One of life's major anxieties for parents is the dilemma posed by grown children when they decide to 'live' with another, thankfully our little bird made her nest with the man of our choice, as well as hers!

During the third week of September, Joan and I flew to Osaka to join Gari. Prior to the ship entering port we had a few days in one of Osaka's wonderful luxury hotels - this one had a rivulet running though the dining room. However, a minor disaster had befallen Joan. One of her suitcases had gone astray - it was located at Toronto (we felt sure that there was a significance in the fact that it had gone to this place!) and it was going to be 'touch and go'

219

whether or not we would retrieve it in time before joining the ship. Consequently she had to take the precaution of buying additional clothes - in case her baggage didn't arrive in time. That was some job! All Japanese clothes were too small, so she was in something of a pickle. However, in the event, her case arrived in the nick of time. When she boarded, someone said it would have been OK because she could have worn shirts and shorts from the ship's football team kit! Imagine! The other notable event, of such a tragic nature, was the loss of Derbyshire which I covered in the final paragraph of Chapter Fifteen. Anyway, Joan stayed with me for a couple of months before returning to her mountain eyrie. Just as well she did because she had to deal with a fearful winter with mountainous snow drifts, and to care for her widowed mother. Never mind, the cavalry, in the form of yours truly, came charging up Swansea Road on January 25th 1981!

My next appointment was to Methane Princess. She operated exclusively between Arzew and Canvey Island during my short stay. I had made travel arrangements to visit Canada in August of that year, so I had requested a brief tour, which Shell granted. I have said quite categorically that I do not consider Joan a Jonah, despite the similarity in names. Now I've related my experiences with earthquakes and swarming bees when Joan accompanied me. Joan was with me for a couple of short voyages aboard Princess and whilst vacuuming our cabin one Mediterranean morn, she heard what she thought were 'popping' noises outside. Indeed she was correct! We were being fired upon by an Algerian naval vessel! Incidents, such as these, only ever happened when her ladyship was with me. Now, is she a Jonah, or not? To be serious. The Algerian authorities had promulgated warnings on voice radio, in French, warning international shipping to avoid specific areas at certain times. We listened on international radio frequencies but not on voice frequencies and certainly our French would not have helped interpretation much either! One of the 'prohibited' areas lay right in our track towards Arzew and we gaily entered the area, quite innocently. The upshot was a fusillade of machine gun fire across our bow! Now that's something of a wake up call in anyone's book! We were quite nonplused and not a little anxious. Communication was established with the gun boat and we veered off to the north, not knowing quite why. I immediately advised London of the incident, with the result that HMS Dido made full steam towards us to defend our national honour. Anyway, with alarm bells ringing around the world and the BBC trying to cajole the Radio Officer to persuade me to be interviewed by them, matters became quite hectic for a short time! Issues were sorted and we eventually completed our voyage, albeit a tinge late. I was interviewed by a sinister officer of the Algerian Secret Police (donned in a long leather coat, would you believe ?) as to reasons for our straying into a prohibited zone, a look of innocence and a spot of Scotland's best did the trick. There was a funny little smile on Joan's face though.

Joan and I had the most fabulous holiday in Canada during the late summer of that year, 1981. At the time Lloyd was working at a correctional institute, and whilst we were there changed to another job with a health support company. Rhiannon was selling shoes at Simpsons. They lived in a small apartment in an area of west Toronto, known as Islington. We thought it was great, they kindly gave up their bedroom to us and they slept on their floor. The apartment complex was air conditioned, there were wonderful facilities with a swimming pool and a variety store - all terribly North American, but so impressive to this couple of Taffs! When we weren't with Rhiannon and Lloyd we spent time with my brother Tom. We stayed with him at his house in Cabbage Town (at the time, a much sought after location for the upwardly mobile). He took us to Stratford and to museums, as well as staying at his home for a few non-airconditioned sweaty days! We also had very happy times with Lloyd's parents at their home outside Brampton, near Bolton. The highlight of this vacation was a long weekend in Quebec City where we stayed at the Chateau Frontenac. We had enormous fun on the train journey to Quebec playing mime (there was a popular TV programme in vogue whereby team members had to guess what another team player was endeavouring to portray, the name of which, unfortunately, eludes me!) - much to the amusement of our fellow passengers. We've never forgotten that happiness. Little did Joan and I know that when we bid Tom good-bye, that was the last time we would see him alive.

Anyway, at that juncture in our lives, we were well content. I was then sent to Brunei to join Gadila, my seventh and last 'G' appointment. It was Shell's policy, and a very wise one at that, that Masters and Chiefs were sent to their joining ports in good time so that they were reasonably well rested at a hotel prior to taking over their particular function. So I looked forward to a civilized takeover.

You're sitting comfortably, feeling relaxed after a handsome gin and tonic, the flight attendant hands you your supper and you're about to eat prior to slumbering the night away en route to Singapore. Suddenly and unceremoniously, your tray is whipped away and thrown into a black refuse bag, together with everyone else's unfinished meals! Next, the Captain makes an announcement, in studiously couched calming tone, that because of a technical uncertainty the 'plane had to put down in Munich. There was absolutely no need whatsoever for concern! One had only to look at the pale faced and agitated attendants to realize that this was a load of codswallop. We were instructed to fasten seat belts and to prepare for immediate landing, women were whimpering, men were looking strained and the attendants assumed a posture of supreme nonchalance - this was British Airways and one expected nothing less than the proverbial stiff upper lip! We landed safely, much to everyone's patent relief but another drama started to unfold. We taxied to an area that was floodlit at the edge of the airport. We were instructed in a peremptory manner to get off the 'plane immediately, to leave our hand luggage on board and to move as quickly as we were able away from the aircraft. Dare I say that we all felt our bowels become a little uncertain? A bus rushed us to a darkened terminal building which was cold and damp. The airport had shut for the night as it was a provincial field, so we had to wait until personnel were brought in to light up the building and to provide us with vile sweet cake and warm beer. We could see a flurry of activity around our aircraft and continued to wonder. Clarification finally materialized when the Captain addressed us in the lounge. Someone aboard the 'plane, or someone else at Heathrow, had left a note in one of the 'plane's washrooms stating that there was a bomb on board! It was signed by 'Black September' the terrorist group that had been responsible for the massacre at this very city, Munich, in 1972 during the Olympics. There was a code word apparently that validated the authenticity of the note, London accordingly instructed the Captain to put down as soon as practicable. Next we had to identify our baggage on the tarmac, which was opened and searched by security people, then our personal cabin bags were searched before we returned to the terminal. After some hours, the

222

aircraft was declared safe. Apparently, Black September had taken to perpetrating similar hoaxes on other flights, so this form of disruption wasn't entirely new to airlines . We arrived at Munich at 10.30pm, we took off at 4 o'clock next morning to return to Heathrow, because the crew had exceeded their flight duration limit! Much to Joan's surprise, she received an unexpected 'phone call from me (which, initially, she thought was from Singapore) at breakfast time! Nothing further occurred, we changed 'planes and succeeded in getting to Singapore unscathed but slightly in shock and very crumpled. So much for my leisurely appointment to Gadila! I was rushed to Brunei and plonked on the deck, a dishevelled heap! Once again, my time aboard Gadila is recorded earlier.

I now come to the 'brief exception' that I mentioned at the opening of this chapter. Shell Coal were spreading their wings and a particularly important contract had been signed to supply a power station in the New Territories in Hong Kong. Tectus was stemmed to inaugurate the scheme. There were local misgivings within the marine establishment at Hong Kong concerning the ship size, the professionalism of a 'tanker' company in this field and indeed the expertise of the men and women (yes, frilly skirts had arrived) who manned the ship. So, in its incomparable style, Shell mounted a public relations exercise to establish confidence within the business and marine communities in the Colony. However I travel too fast. The ship required some stringent sorting before anything could be undertaken. I joined at Richards Bay on July 20th 1982 to discover a ship with an 'atmosphere'. I think I have mentioned this phenomenon in a previous chapter, a small detached community (a ship) quickly develops its own ambience depending upon the personalities that create it. This was a party ship with 'goings-on', wives not maintaining their allegiance and so forth. I was taken aside by a senior member of staff and told that I would not be expected to change 'things'! Now this had happened aboard Hemicardium (Chapter Twelve). My response was as unequivocal in this instance as it had been then! So we all began to regard our vocation a little more seriously. We were bound for Singapore, and during the 17 day voyage understandings were established and those who had most enjoyed the partying, left at Singapore.

We lay at anchor in the West Jurong Anchorage for three weeks carrying out maintenance and cosmetic work in order to prepare the ship for the Hong Kong visit. Joan joined me as soon as we arrived at Singapore so she had a great opportunity to tour and sightsee. Rosemary and Colin Stewart were very hospitable during our stay, Rosemary took Joan around the Island and they both entertained us royally at their home. Colin was Marine Manager for Shell International Marine in the far East, stationed at Singapore. I was filled-in on the almost hostile atmosphere that prevailed within the marine community at Hong Kong towards our impending visit, and we planned our strategy in co-ordination with Michael Howard, Shell Coal's regional manager and Bob Strick (SIM's Hong Kong representative and an old colleague of mine, having served as Second officer aboard the Cadet Training Ship). We determined to put on an exercise of professional competence and to entertain a cross section of the Hong Kong establishment at two receptions. Whilst at Singapore, Joan and I entertained the Stewart family (including their two charming daughters), Johnny Johnson and his wife and children (he was Shell Tankers' Superintendent, an incisive Rhodesian with whom I had also sailed - it was he who introduced me to the tasty African chew, biltong). Colin announced the morning of our luncheon party that he was bringing along an old friend of mine who wished to remain anonymous. He turned out to be Bob Lumsden, my former co-captain of Opalia, now Marine Manager for Dole Petroleum. We had a memorable afternoon!

Our visit to Hong Kong, delivering the largest cargo the port had ever received, was an unqualified success. Not only was the ship commended for its smartness and professionalism, but I think we astounded many people with our social performance. Apart from the planning and back-up by Mike Howard and Bob Strick, I was greatly helped by Joan's gracious presence as hostess. It really was one of the highlights of my career. The comment made by the Director of Marine that his problems would be halved if all vessels were operated in a manner similar to Tectus was adequate reward!

We commenced discharging our cargo at Castle Peak in the New Territories on 9th September after a week's social activity whilst at anchor in Hong Kong harbour. This was another wonderful time for Joan and myself and we were indebted to Marie and Bob Strick for their attention to our welfare. Lunch at the Royal Yacht Club, well ... I mean! We were brought down to earth by the practicalities of a coal discharge - all of us going around like colliers (or pit men, depending from whence you come). The true course of love doesn't run smoothly, with typhoon 'Irving' fast approaching the colony, I decided to put to sea rather than risk being trapped up the Pearl River - particularly in view of the attention and publicity Tectus had generated. Concurrently, Joan and I had received news that her mother was unwell, so she decided to leave. She was last seen by me disappearing down the Pearl River in a sampan, on her way to Hong Kong and a flight to London. We returned to Castle Peak after a three day period, hove to off the port, to complete cargo. Tectus finally set sail for Vancouver on September 23rd. We loaded at Roberts Island - nothing more than a coal heap - returning to Hong Kong where I was relieved for furlough.

The final ship in this miscellany was Isomeria. A new experience for me in that she transported liquid petroleum gas - an entirely different kettle of fish from natural gas. I'll not bore the reader with technical differences between the two types of gas nor ship design. I joined her at Cartagena in Spain on February 14th 1983, relieving Byron Davies. We went on to complete discharge at Tarragona. From Spain we went to Falmouth to gas-free prior to moving to Belfast for an extensive refit, arriving on the 23rd. We spent 50 days in this benighted city at the height of the emergency. Although none of our staff or crew came to harm, one had to be very tactful and wary in the strange and threatening atmosphere that pervaded the Province at that time. To enter the down town area one had to pass through security gates and police checks, each shop was locked to casual entry - one had to show identity before the doors opened to admit the customer. The inhabitants were so used to the situation that they didn't feel much was untoward - but, to the first-time visitor, the attitude was almost bizarre. Difficult to believe this was part of the United Kingdom. There were explosions and casualties within a small radius of Harland and Wolff's, the world famous shipyard, where we lay.

On completion of the repair period Isomeria went north to the Shetland Isles to load at Sullom Voe, the first of three loading ports. After completion of our operation at Sullom Voe we went to anchor at Colgrave Sound, a remote bay to the north east of Sullom Voe, east of Yell. Here we conducted a hush hush anti-terrorist exercise with the Royal Marines Special Boat Squadron. We were constrained by the Official Secrets Act, and I suppose I still am! However it was most interesting and I guess the SAS have an equal in the SBS - a tough bunch of fellows if ever there was! We continued our loading sequence at Teesport and Flushing before setting sail for South Korea - now that's some trip, all of thirty days taking in the English Channel, the Mediterranean, Suez Canal, Malacca Straits, Singapore Strait (and pirates once more!) and the South China Sea. We arrived at Yosu, on the southern coast on June 17th 1983. Byron Davies took over once more and I left the ship the following day. I had one of the most hair raising drives of my life between Yosu to Seoul - talk about French drivers, they're amateurs compared with the Koreans! Flew to Tokyo, thence to London, arriving home on June 20th.

That's that of this and that!

CHAPTER TWENTY

ENERGY

Isomeria's funnel pecten, Shell's familiar symbol, was the final one for me. For the remainder of my seafaring days I served under the Islamic star of Malaysia - the star being part of the Malaysian International Shipping Corporation ships' funnel livery. I had sailed with funnels of many hues and insignia, ranging from battleship grey to the striking MISC design. Those in between included: the Anglo-Saxon buff; Eagle Oil's smart bird; Shell Tankers' red pecten on a buff background and their yellow pecten on a red backdrop; the British Gas black with white horizontal stripes; Tectus's buff then black stack and finally Heogh's blue and grey livery.

As I mentioned at the end of the last chapter, I arrived home in Merthyr on June 20th 1983. Joan and I had a wonderful summer furlough. Rhiannon and Lloyd flew from Canada to spend their summer vacation in Britain. We enjoyed a magnificent holiday in the West Country, renting a luxury apartment in Torquay which we used as a base. Most of our time was spent touring Devon, Dorset and Cornwall stopping at many beautiful fishing villages. We called on Dorothy and Alec Howe at Brixham - he, a much admired mentor of Arianta days. We visited the lovely village of North Bovey where the Shears family had once resided - a family related to Rhiannon and me and who had emigrated to Australia at the beginning of the century (and whom I visited whilst serving aboard Hemiglypta in 1961). We, all four, got along famously! We had a hilarious time despite the dreaded generation gap. We used to fool around the swimming pool, much, incidentally, to the entertainment of the famous comedian Michael Barrymore, who was staying at the apartment building whilst doing theatre at Torquay - so we must have been pretty amusing to have made a funny man laugh! Lloyd drank copious quaffs of scrumpy and still wasn't much good at arm wrestling. All good things come to an end, and that happened with the young people returning to Canada at the beginning of September.

I now began my final career phase. In 1983 a new liner trade was inaugurated, between Sarawak in East Malaysia and Tokyo, in the transport of liquid natural gas (LNG). The fleet consisted of five ships owned by MISC with names consisting of the Malay prefix for Energy - Tenaga followed by a number, 'one' through to 'five', thus: "Tenaga Satu" to "Tenaga Lima". This was perhaps an even more 'international' enterprise than the Brunei/Japan venture of a decade earlier. The ships were chartered by Malaysian LNG (a company jointly owned by the Malaysian Government [Petronas], Shell Gas BV and the Mitsubishi Corporation). As with the other scheme, all the ships were built at French shipyards - who were now preeminent in the construction of this type of ship. There was a joint management/manning contract between MISC and Shell Tankers(UK)Ltd for the initial years of the ships' operation. Basically the agreement called for all senior staff plus middle rank officers to be appointed by STUK with junior officers, cadets and crew being supplied by MISC. As experience was gained, Malaysian officers would replace their British counterparts from the lower ranks upwards. The management of the ships was controlled by MISC head office in Kuala Lumpur, headed by an American (Dick Eddy), Director of LNG, and a Malaysian manager (Captain Mohd.Suhaimi Bin Shamsuddin), A liaison office was established at Yokohama manned by two Frenchmen (Messieurs Vaudolon and Giraud) and a senior STUK operations superintendent (Captain Peter Liddell) who were responsible for the 'nuts and bolts' operation of the fleet. A truly cosmopolitan set-up, you'll agree.

Prior to being appointed to a ship. I headed up a team to inspect one of the Tenaga ships at Canvey, to familiarize ourselves and to form an assessment for STUK management. The ship was at Canvey undergoing cryogenic trials before lay-up at Stavanger in Norway. As with any new scheme, the trade between Sarawak and Tokyo Bay had to be developed gradually. Although in the planning stage it had been hoped to introduce the ships on a systematic basis, in step with the shore installation and reception facility progress, matters didn't work out as anticipated - the ship building progress outstripped the manufacturing undertaking at Bintulu (the loading port) and therefore ships were laid up, in waiting, whilst one, then two ships followed by a third 'developed' the trade over the first two years of the scheme.

The Maritime Department of the University of Wales, Cardiff, had constructed a dedicated building housing a ship simulator facility in the City. One of the programmes which had been installed was the pilotage passage and berthing operation at Bintulu. I and a few others spent a week at the simulator, gaining valuable 'hands-on' experience at manoeuvring a Tenaga ship in and out of the port. It was quite uncanny in its realism! When, in reality, one arrived off the port for the first time, it felt as if one had visited the place numerous times before. The only thing absent at Bintulu was the sound of the Merthyr train thundering past - the simulator was adjacent to the Valley Line!

I flew to Japan during the last week of October 1983. I was interviewed by the people in the MISC liaison office at Yokohama before crossing Tokyo Bay to join Tenaga Empat (four) at Sodegaura (Chiba). It was part of the acclimatisation process that newly appointed masters carried out a familiarization voyage to Bintulu before assuming command. I accompanied the urbane Colin Oxley, as my mentor, for the voyage from Tokyo Bay to Sarawak. I thoroughly enjoyed his company, and received grounding in the ways of MISC and their crewing system. I assumed command on arrival at Bintulu on November 1st 1983.

The Tenaga ships were absolute crackers! At that time they were the biggest LNG ships in service. Modern, sophisticated, beautifully appointed and powerful, they were wonderful ships to operate. The ships were a little less than twice the size of the 'G' class carriers with a cargo carrying capacity of 130,000 cubic metres, propelled by a steam turbine developing 45,000 shaft horse power (compare with the 36,000 ship of a 'L' class ship of 320,000 tons) giving a sea speed of 21 knots - fast for a merchant ship. The Shell policy of giving parity to masters' and chief engineers' facilities was not the case aboard MISC ships. I occupied a palatial apartment on the top deck, in lofty isolation- not so my colleague! The Chief had a sumptuously appointed, but smaller suite, and, it was on a lower deck! Didn't go down too famously with some of my colleagues!

The singular difference in managing a Tenaga ship, apart from the contrast in shore management, was dealing with Malaysian officers, petty officers and crew members. Although primarily Muslim, there were nevertheless people of Hindu, Buddhist and Christian persuasions. The sensibilities of these religious and racial groups had to be understood and tactfully respected. The Muslims were, even at this juncture, showing increased leanings to orthodoxy and to fundamentalism - so discretion became paramount. Newly joining British officers were issued with notes outlining taboos concerning the racial groups, so that embarrassment could be kept to a minimum. As examples: one did not point at people with one's forefinger or use one's foot to point at an object; due respect had to be accorded Malaysian Royalty; one never discussed anything relating to Islam. There was, therefore, considerable attuning to accomplish. A room was set aside as a prayer room (Surau), cooking was carried out in separate galleys - therefore in the Officers' Saloon, diners sitting alongside one another would often be eating entirely different dishes which occasionally led to logistic difficulties. Strict segregation of meat had to be maintained in the refrigerated rooms, with one cold room exclusively used to store Halal meat (carcases slaughtered according to Islamic law), such meat had to be certified as Halal when taken on board in Japan. The Malaysian crew were well educated, typically to 'O' level standard. They were youthful, cheerful, bright and smart, and, hard working - an altogether interesting ambience that I hadn't experienced aboard any previous ship.

The trade was similar to that of the Brunei/Japan scheme in that Tenagas discharged at Sodegaura (Chiba) with the occasional visit to Kawasaki on the western side of Tokyo Bay. During my sojourn aboard Empat we refitted at Yokohama in December, which gave everyone the opportunity to go ashore in this 'sailors" port. The senior staff were royally entertained at the Liddell residence in Yokohama. Peter had, and probably still has, a vast model railway set-up which appealed to the 'little boy' in all of us! We returned to trading just before Christmas.

I left Tenaga Empat on March 10th 1984 at Bintulu, having had the lively company of Janet and Jack Beaumont for the southbound voyage from Japan. An old and valued friend and colleague, the genial Jack made the six day hand-over a pleasure. I arrived back in Merthyr only to learn that an uncle of mine was to be buried the following day - in fact the funeral had been delayed in order that I could attend. My final year as a seafarer, 1984, was to be one of mixed emotions. It had been my fondest hope that Joan could have accompanied me on my last voyage, however fate intervened in that Ethel, my dear mother-in-law, became seriously ill and required Joan's continuing care - which upset any plans we may have had.

My final ship was Tenaga Dua (Energy Two). I assumed command at Bintulu on June 28th and spent my last months performing what I was most used to doing - carrying cargoes of LNG to Tokyo Bay. At the conclusion of my service I had delivered a total of seventy two such cargoes to Japan. In company with every other master on their final assignment, I had to battle with a gnawing anxiety that no catastrophic incident would happen during this last tenure. From that aspect, I was fortunate - perhaps because I subscribed to the adage that accidents don't happen, they result as a consequence of lack of care and attention. However, I suffered a grievous personal loss which marred the satisfaction of completing a career.

The reader will have noticed throughout this narrative that I have made frequent reference to my brother, Tom. Tom and I were so alike, despite his being three years my junior, we could have been taken for twins. He was a much more likable fellow than I! At first a regular army officer, who was shattered by the loss of his platoon during the Emergency in Malaya in the nineteen fifties, he pursued a lonely bachelor life thereafter. At the time of my impending retirement, Joan and I were so looking forward to re-establishing our relationship with Tom. There were never three people more friendly than we - indeed, in our younger days, our happiest times were spent as a trio. He was such a wit and so generous - he, was the brother that Joan never had. At the time I write of, he was a manager with Manpower in Oakville, Ontario. He enjoyed a quiet, if sophisticated lifestyle, indulging in theatre, concert going and good reading in Toronto where he had his home and each year seeing different parts of the world. On October 13th 1984, I received an instruction from Shell that I was to contact

Joan. We had satellite communication equipment, so I was able to speak to her almost immediately. I feared the worst regarding her mother. However, I was devastated and initially uncomprehending, when she told me that Tom had died in the early hours of that morning. It was the biggest shock of my life. Apparently he suffered a heart attack whilst feeding his dog. He was just 53 years old. We, as a family, have never really recovered from that blow.

Life goes on. There was no room for grief or privacy when operating a ship. Just one voyage after this happened, Peter Liddell, our Marine Superintendent, sailed with us on a voyage of inspection. I never quite knew what this shrewd, quiet Gloucestershire man really thought of us - one thing's for sure, there was no way in which bull...t was going to baffle brains in his case! His visit concentrated the mind.

In October, the ship's officers threw a magnificent retirement party for me. I shall never forget the occasion nor the gifts I received to mark the end of my seafaring. When the actual day arrived to go down the gangway for the very last time, and by odd coincidence, precisely thirty nine years to the day that I climbed aboard my first ship, Neocardia, I was nearly overcome by emotion. For all its hardships, for all the suffering I had inflicted upon the innocents in my family, I loved every minute of my shipboard days. Wasn't I lucky?

CHAPTER TWENTY ONE

MERTHYR TYDFIL AND ELORA

I am writing the final chapter of my 'recollections' in Elora, Ontario. It is January 1999, the last year of the 20th Century, and, it seems to me an appropriate time to complete the record of my life, thus far. I have been uncommonly fortunate to have enjoyed fifteen years of deep fulfilment as a retiree. Joan and I have savoured the years we've been given together both in Elora and Merthyr.

I left Tenaga Dua on December 4th 1984. After a farewell party given by the manager of the Bintulu plant, I flew to London via Kuala Lumpur to spend my final furlough before beginning my retirement the following March. Retirement, for some, is contemplated with apprehension because of the loss of importance and direction, not to mention the problem of inactivity. Strangely and fortunately I was never thus afflicted. Rather, I regarded being pensioned-off at 57 years of age as a gift! A wise friend of mine told me that we should divide our lives into three distinct and separate phases: education, work and retirement, and never to pine for the former. An axiom I have embraced.

During this furlough I and a number of other would-be retirees were invited to Shell Centre for a farewell dinner, hosted by the then MD, John Rendell CBE, together with other directors and guests of our choosing. It was a stylish and emotional finish and in keeping with the enlightened managerial attitude that we, in the Fleet, had enjoyed. Shell was a class act. I was, and remain, fiercely loyal to this fine enterprise.

One of the major sources of strength throughout my seafaring days, apart from my family ties and support, had been my love for my home town and the friends who lived there. Every time I returned, I recharged my batteries and derived a strength from the place and its people. For me, the humour and humanity one experienced within this blighted borough were quite priceless. For example, it didn't do to have any pretensions because they would be swiftly and often cruelly debunked (it was known colloquially as being a 'bit of madam'!) I once mistakenly went to a dance in uniform, I was called 'Admiral', 'Steward' and 'Captain Birdseye' - so that put pay to any further wearing of braid! The fact was - Merthyr was always there, and it didn't change. Whilst I was Chief Officer of Borus in 1959, we were refitting in Singapore. During our stay, we invited the Anglican Bishop to lunch. During the pre-lunch jollification he enquired from whence I came, I replied, somewhat facetiously, "From the hub of the universe!" "And that is ?" he responded. "Merthyr Tydfil" said I . "Ah, yes" said he "I thought as much" with the wriest of smiles! As I wrote in the Preface, Merthyr is situated in an area of great beauty and is, arguably, one of the most conveniently placed towns within the Principality - I used to say it was two and a half hours from anywhere worthwhile. Were it not for the ugly scars of the Industrial Revolution (which are fast disappearing) Merthyr would be an excellent tourist and heritage centre - the very first steam locomotive to carry a payload of cargo and passengers by rail, invented by Richard Trevithick, ran from Merthyr to Abercynon in 1804 - predating Stephenson's 'Rocket' by a quarter of a century. The polyglot population of the 19th Century left a rich legacy. In my youth, there were, in addition to the indigenous Welsh people, sizable communities of Irish, Italian, Spanish and Jewish people - living in an atmosphere of amity and tolerance. It was such an interesting town despite the dreadful deprivation that existed

Joan and I had a lovely house perched on almost a promontory, exactly on the 1000 feet contour line, overlooking the Taff Fawr Valley and with an ever changing panoramic view of the Brecon Beacons. This was our dream home and during subsequent years we added and improved both inside and out. I became a gardener of sorts and together we created a garden we were proud of.

Any ambitious plans I may have had, such as taking up golf, had to be shelved in the initial stages because Ethel, my mother-in-law, who lived with us, was now showing the distressing symptoms of senility. It was as well I retired when I did because I was able to share the work of caring with Joan and this became our loving responsibility until the old lady slipped away in May 1986. I honoured her for her staunch support and love during many difficult times and for her boundless enthusiasm for what her daughter had undertaken in life.

Our first Christmas was enlivened by a visit from Rhiannon and Lloyd which made it not only enjoyable, but memorable. The following summer, in 1985, we went to Canada for a month. On our return we acquired a handsome beagle puppy called Bosun. I mention this little character because he coloured our lives vividly for the rest of his life. We were told by friends who owned a beagle, that the easiest way to suffer a nervous breakdown was to let one into your family. They were nearly right! Certainly in the first months the mutt nearly sent me round the twist, but with perseverance and establishing the fact that I was the undisputed leader of our pack, he became our dearest companion.

Immediately prior to my retirement, Joan, who was a committee member of the local branch of the Royal National Lifeboat Institution, proffered my services as honorary secretary - quite unbeknownst to me - as they needed someone to replace the incumbent when she left the town. This became a major involvement for the next nine years. I just loved it! Together with Joan and a committee of wonderfully committed volunteers, we literally put Merthyr on the RNLI map. In this period I must have walked scores of miles in house to house collections, stood on numerous street corners during flag days, often chased down house driveways by rottweillers or alsatians. We used to organize coffee mornings, car boot (trunk) sales, fabric sales, trolley (cart) dashes at supermarkets, sell souvenirs at stalls all around South Wales, orchestrate sponsorships - you name it, we did it! Inevitably, the committee members largely consisted of ladies - which, I found, needed a somewhat different approach from that in dealing with Jolly Jack! In the nine years that Joan and I worked together with all these great people who comprised the Merthyr RNLI team, we sent in excess of fifty thousand pounds to HQ - not bad, considering we were twenty five miles from the nearest coastline. I also became involved in the marine community in South Wales. I was already a longstanding member in the Royal Institute of

Navigation and the Nautical Institute, additionally I became a member of a liveried company in the City of London, the Honourable Company of Master Mariners. I became a committee member in the Bristol Channel Branch of the Royal Institute of Navigation and served as Chairman for two years. So for a number of years I kept myself reasonably informed about things maritime. Three BP masters and three Shell masters who retired at about the time I did, together with wives, formed an association known as the Retired Master Mariners' Club. This was strictly an eating, drinking and arguing fraternity! It was a most enjoyable idea in the early days. For the time that we belonged to the 'gang' we really enjoyed their company - inevitably, seafarers speak the same language.

A further joy to me was the annual meeting of the Shell Fleet Retired Staff Association, held every April. On that day we would home in on Shell Centre for the AGM followed by a superb meal in the executive dining room and complimentary refreshments. It was such a happy get-together, one's whole life was relived meeting many of one's ex-shipmates and recalling episodes from one's past. Of course 'complimentary refreshments' meant an almost total disappearance of inhibitions with resulting thick heads the following morning!

Joan and I travelled widely through England and Wales, going wherever, whenever. We enjoyed opera and classical music so we made full use of the two fine concert halls in Cardiff and Swansea. We indulged in dining out as often as we could afford to - South Wales possesses many fine eating places.

I cannot conclude my musings on my early retirement days without reference to my twice weekly visits to the Merthyr Rugby Club. Whereas Joan busied herself with the Women's Royal Voluntary Service, 'Antiques' and 'Family Tree' classes, I enjoyed the company of my good friends from Merthyr. Three retired head masters, two university lecturers, an industrial artist and two others made for some of the liveliest conversation I can remember. Nor can I fail to recall happy nights spent with the Royal Naval Association. I was allowed to join as an associate member, because I wasn't regarded as a 'real' sailor! Still, they were ex seafarers and in my book, the salt of the earth. In both these social activities I was accompanied by my very best friend, Lyn Perkins (who had spent one year aboard a naval ship and had more tales to tell than I could muster in forty years!), I miss him more than anyone - he has been such a stalwart to both Joan and myself.

Nothing in life is perfect. Although you may think that Joan and I were happily settled in retirement, we lacked one very important dimension - being near our family. This became particularly onerous as grandchildren appeared on the scene. Whereas we would meet at least once a year, it just wasn't enough. Our first grandchild, Caitlin, was born in 1988 and our second, Owen, in 1992. Joan and I visited Canada in the summer of 1992 when Owen was a few months old and we decided that we had to contemplate a move across the pond at some time after our 65th birthdays. We were both 65 in 1993, so we put the wheels in motion in May. We thought it would take many months, if not years, before we achieved our goal because of emigration formalities and the selling of our house. From the time we applied to emigrate until we arrived as immigrants in Canada took just six months! Nobody expected such a swift resolution - but it happened. Prior to our leaving for Canada, the family came over to spend one last glorious holiday in Britain - this time we made Tenby our resort of choice.

Joan and I arrived in Canada on November 13th 1993, Bosun joined us five days later and our furniture was delivered within two weeks of our arrival. I have to tell this tale about our little mutt. As soon as the removers arrived at our Merthyr home, a pet delivery van took Bosun to an animal transit place near Heathrow to await transshipment to Toronto. Because our finances were haemorrhaging we chose the cheapest possible flight to Canada - which happened to be Air India, whereas our beagle travelled in style with British Airways! His transportation costs were 40% more than both Joan's and mine combined! We never regretted one penny we spent upon him - he helped us so much to settle in the new country. It didn't matter to him where he was so long as he had his daily square meal, two decent walks each day and his mistress's lap in the nights! He succumbed to cancer in March 1998 - he is sorely missed.

It was no easy matter to uproot ourselves at 65 years of age! We were, however, at long last with our family. It goes without saying that being near Rhiannon was a comfort to both of us and the prospect of watching our grandchildren grow up was exciting. Nevertheless, if we hadn't had such a fine, caring, gentlemanly son-in-law as Lloyd, I doubt we would have embarked upon the venture.

We were fortunate in that Rhiannon and Lloyd had been able to rent a house, on our behalf, for six months from November 1993 until the end of April 1994. The house was ideal for our purposes, particularly as the owners, who were in Mexico, gave permission for us to store our furniture in the basement, and allowed us to have Bosun with us. The owners, Peggy and Dick Nightingale, have since become very good friends of ours. Joan and I look back on our time in Ariss, during the coldest winter that Ontario had experienced in a century, with great fondness. Within weeks of our arrival in Canada we negotiated the purchase of a house in Elora and took possession at the beginning of March. The couple of months' breathing space enabled us to alter and decorate our new home before we moved in at the end of April.

Elora - Ontario's Beautiful Village. This is Elora's self description and one which is justifiable in Ontario terms. Founded by one Captain William Gilkinson, in 1832 and named after The Ellora caves in the Indian province of Andhra Pradesh (interestingly enough Joan has just read about John Betjeman's wife's [Penelope Chetwode] article on the 'cave temples of Ellora').

There are so many reasons why I would recommend this little town. Elora is situated near Guelph, the Royal City, lies on the River Grand (which empties into Lake Erie and eventually goes over the Niagara Falls) which, together with the River Irvine - a tributary that joins the Grand in Elora - form two spectacular gorges. Extending along both sides of the Gorge is one of Ontario's oldest conservation parks, which is a Mecca for campers, embracing 500 camp sites. The population in the area derives from many European back-grounds, with perhaps a preponderance of people of Scottish inher-itance. Perhaps the most interesting group would be the nearby Mennonite communities - a religious sect that espouses nineteenth century lifestyle and values, originating in Germany then forming colonies in Pennsylvania and finally settling in this part of Ontario. Mostly involved with farming, these people, dressed in black and moving from place to place by horse and buggy, create a fascinating dimension rarely seen elsewhere.

238

When we were in the process of emigrating, we resigned ourselves to the inevitability of the loss of culture we enjoyed living in Merthyr Tydfil, or more generally in Britain. We had a shock! This area is a vibrant centre of culture in all its forms. In fact Canada, as a whole, is a cultured country - contrary to popular belief in Europe.

We were impressed when we attended St.John The Evangelist Church in Elora. I doubt if there is better choral singing anywhere in Christendom - and I include the British cathedral choirs. The parish choir is professional - an innovation we had not met before. The Church is, I would estimate, eighty percent full on most Sundays. Wisely, there is a service for the modernists, so all tastes are catered for. The urbane Rector, Robert Hulse, manages that Church with skilful and tasteful efficiency. However the source of the musical quality is a young man, one Noel Edison, the Choirmaster. Coincidentally, he is also the artistic director of the Elora Festival and the conductor of the famed Toronto Mendelssohn Choir. It's a fulfilling musical event as well as a religious experience every Sunday.

The Elora Festival extends over a three week period from mid July each year. It is one of Canada's major musical events and provides a rich panoply of music to suit almost everyone's tastes - events being held in the village churches, and, in the most unusual venues, viz., a salt barn and a quarry! In addition we hear world class chamber music, during a fall series, at an octagonal church (with superb acoustics) nearby at Speedside. Joan and I occasionally hear opera and orchestral concerts in Kitchener and Toronto - so our tastes are eminently satisfied.

Joan and I are happy in Elora. We are 'naturally' involved with our family - as opposed to the frenetic three week annual visitations we enjoyed whilst apart. I don't suppose I would ever have experienced the magical moment when, some years ago, Caitlin sat on my lap whilst we were looking at a full moon and said, "Taid, is there really a man in the moon ?" I said that of course there was and she mused "I wonder, does he like peanut butter sandwiches?" (Taid, is the Welsh for Grandpa). Or when Owen said to his mother " Mum, is Taid's name Dick? ", "Yes" said Rhiannon, " I don't like it - it's a sex word", said he! These things are beyond value.

I miss many things. My friends in Merthyr, the annual 'thrash' with my fellow retirees and ex shipmates. I occasionally see a ship - in fact I purposely go out of my way to see a laker on one of the Great Lakes. However the compensations far outweigh any passing regrets I may have. The people in Elora are friendly and welcoming and the Fall colours create one of Nature's most vivid tapestries. I believe we are content.

A POST SCRIPT FROM JOAN

I feel a slight embarrassment - all the tributes to me are for all the Merchant Navy wives who have lived similar lives and have enjoyed the 'feast and the famine' with dedicated and committed seafaring partners.

Dick and I are fortunate to be together to enjoy the "Twilight Years" - though I often say " Get back to sea"!!

APPENDIX

NEOCARDIA
MOTOR VESSEL. 8,211 GRT   465' X 59'
BUILT 1943 BLYTHSWOOD SB CO. GLASGOW
APPRENTICE: FROM DECEMBER 4TH 1945
TO OCTOBER 30TH 1946.

SAN VIRGILIO
MOTOR VESSEL. NO DETAILS.
DISTRESSED BRITISH SEAMAN (DBS): FROM
NOVEMBER 11TH 1946 TO NOVEMBER 27TH 1946.

MIRALDA
MOTOR VESSEL. 8,069 GRT   465' X 59'
BUILT 1936.NETHERLANDS SB CO. AMSTERDAM
APPRENTICE: FROM JANUARY 27TH 1947
TO NOVEMBER 22ND 1947.

ALEXIA
MOTOR VESSEL 8,069 GRT 465' X 59'
BUILT 1935 BREMER VULCAN, VEGESACK.
APPRENTICE: FROM DECEMBER 22ND 1947
TO JUNE 6TH 1948.

DORCASIA
MOTOR VESSEL. 8,053 GRT 465' X 59'
BUILT 1938. LITHGOWS LTD. PORT GLASGOW
APPRENTICE: JUNE 8TH 1948 TO JULY 9TH 1948
AND ACTING THIRD OFFICER: JULY 10TH 1948
TO FEBRUARY 28TH 1949

HYALINA
TURBO-ELECTRIC SHIP 12,287 GRT 583' X70'
BUILT 1948. SWAN HUNTER'S WALLSEND
APPRENTICE: JUNE 3RD 1949
TO OCTOBER 18TH1949.

DROMUS
MOTOR VESSEL 8,036 GRT 465' X 59'
BUILT 1938. HARLAND AND WOLFF, BELFAST
THIRD OFFICER: MARCH 25TH 1950
TO JUNE 26TH 1950.

THELLEPUS
TURBO-ELECTRIC SHIP. 10,693 GRT 506' X 68'
BUILT 1945. KAISER INC. PORTLAND OREGON
THIRD OFFICER: JUNE 27TH 1950 TO JUNE 7TH 1951.

NASSARIUS
MOTOR VESSEL 8,246 GRT   465' X 59'
BUILT 1944. HARLAND AND WOLFF. BELFAST
SECOND OFFICER: AUGUST 21ST 1951
TO JUNE 14TH 1952.

TENAGODUS
TURBO-ELECTRIC SHIP. 10,644 GRT 506' X 68'
BUILT 1944. ALABAMA DD & SB CO. MOBILE
SECOND OFFICER: JANUARY 25TH 1953
TO MARCH 1ST 1953.

TRIGONOSEMUS
TURBO-ELECTRIC SHIP. 10,693 GRT 506' X 68'
BUILT 1944, KAISER INC. PORTLAND OREGON
SECOND OFFICER: MARCH 1ST 1953
TO MARCH 12TH 1953.

OPALIA (1)
MOTOR VESSEL 6,195 GRT 430' X 54'
BUILT 1938. NETHERLANDS DOCK CO. AMSTERDAM.
SECOND OFFICER:MAY 1ST 1953 TO JULY 16TH 1953.

KELLIA
MOTOR VESSEL 5,666 GRT   410' X 53'
BUILT 1929. SWAN HUNTER'S WALLSEND
SECOND OFFICER: JULY 16TH 1953
TO AUGUST 8TH 1953.

NACELLA
MOTOR VESSEL 8,196 GRT 465' X 59'
BUILT 1943. SWAN HUNTER'S, WALLSEND
SECOND OFFICER: OCTOBER 5TH 1953
TO OCTOBER 26TH 1954.

SELADANG
MOTOR VESSEL 401 GRT 142' X 27'
BUILT 1944. BUILDERS UNKNOWN
CHIEF OFFICER: JANUARY 26TH 1955
TO MARCH 24TH 1956.

TRIBULUS
TURBO-ELECTRIC SHIP. 10,699 GRT 506'X68'
BUILT 1945. KAISER INC.PORTLAND ORE.
CHIEF OFFICER: OCTOBER 2ND 1956
TO JANUARY 28TH 1958.

DILOMA
MOTOR VESSEL. 8,146 GRT 465' X 59'
BUILT 1939. CAMMELL LAIRD'S, BIRKENHEAD.
CHIEF OFFICER: JANUARY 28TH 1958
TO FEBRUARY 22ND 1958.

BORUS
MOTOR VESSEL 3,735 GRT 343' X 48'
BUILT 1945. SIR J. LAING'S SUNDERLAND
CHIEF OFFICER: JULY 23RD 1958 TO JULY 26TH'59.

ARIANTA
STEAM TURBINE SHIP 13,148 GRT 560' X 72'
BUILT 1959 . J.L.THOMPSON 'S, SUNDERLAND
CHIEF OFFICER: NOVEMBER 4TH 1959
TO NOVEMBER 8TH 1960.

HEMIGLYPTA
STEAM TURBINE SHIP 12,180 GRT 555' X 69'
BUILT 1955. CAMMELL LAIRD'S, BIRKENHEAD.
CHIEF OFFICER: MARCH 8TH 1961
TO FEBRUARY 23RD 1962.

SAN EDMUNDO
STEAM TURBINE SHIP. 10,711 GRT 525' X 77'
BUILT 1955. FURNESS SB. HAVERTON HILL
CHIEF OFFICER: JUNE 6TH 1962
TO SEPTEMBER 5TH 1962.

SAN FERNANDO
STEAM TURBINE SHIP. 12,215 GRT. 555' X 69'
BUILT 1953 CAMMELL LAIRD'S, BIRKENHEAD
CHIEF OFFICER: OCTOBER 9TH 1962
TO OCTOBER 21ST 1963.

METHANE PROGRESS
STEAM TURBINE SHIP 21,875 GRT 621' X 81'
BUILT 1964 HARLAND AND WOLFF, BELFAST.
CHIEF OFFICER: AUGUST 30TH 1964
TO JANUARY 6TH 1965
AND MARCH 5TH 1966 TO JULY 11TH 1966.
MASTER: SEPTEMBER 1ST 1979
TO DECEMBER 14TH 1979.

METHANE PRINCESS
STEAM TURBINE SHIP 21,867 GRT 621' X 81'.
BUILT 1964. VICKERS ARMSTRONG, BARROW-
IN-FURNESS.
CHIEF OFFICER: FEBRUARY 12TH 1965 TO
MAY 18TH 1965 AND JULY 19TH 1965 TO JANUARY 6TH
1966. MASTER: MAY 23RD 1981 TO JULY 27TH 1981.

PALLIUM
STEAM TURBINE SHIP 13,607 GRT 560' X 72'.
BUILT 1959. DEUTSCHE WERFT AG HAMBURG.
MASTER: AUGUST 26TH 1966
TO FEBRUARY 20TH 1967.

ASPRELLA
STEAM TURBINE SHIP. 12,321 GRT 560' X 69'
BUILT 1959. KIELER HOWALDTSWERK AG
KIEL. MASTER: APRIL 8TH 1967
TO OCTOBER 28TH 1967.

244

HEMICARDIUM
STEAM TURBINE SHIP 12,215 GRT 555' X 60'
BUILT 1953. CAMMELL LAIRD'S BIRKENHEAD
MASTER: JAN.3RD 1968 TO 21ST JULY 1968.

AMASTRA
MOTOR VESSEL 12,273 GRT 559' X 69'
BUILT 1958. SMITH'S DOCK MIDDLESBOROUGH.
MASTER: OCTOBER 10TH 1968
TO JANUARY 15TH 1969.

DONACILLA
MOTOR VESSEL 40,170 GRT 800' X 110'.
BUILT 1966. THOMPSON'S, SUNDERLAND
MASTER: MARCH 5TH TO 1ST AUGUST 1969

OPALIA (2)
STEAM TURBINE SHIP 32,122 GRT 748' X 102'
BUILT 1963. CAMMELL LAIRD'S, BIRKENHEAD.
MASTER: OCTOBER 7TH 1969 TO APRIL 9TH 1970.
AS THE CADET TRAINING SHIP:
JANUARY 24TH 1975 TO MAY 30TH 1975
OCTOBER 12TH 1975 TO FEBRUARY 1ST 1976
MAY 13TH 1976 TO JULY 12TH 1976
NOVEMBER 17TH 1976 TO JUNE 3RD 1977.

DAPHNELLA
MOTOR VESSEL 39,929 GRT 800' X 110'
BUILT 1966 THOMPSON'S, SUNDERLAND.
MASTER: JUNE 18TH TO DECEMBER 1ST 1970.

MARISA
STEAM TURBINE SHIP 105,495 GRT 1067' X 155'
BUILT 1968. HITACHI ZOSEN, SAKAI.
MASTER: JANUARY 23RD TO JULY 16TH 1971.

MELANIA
STEAM TURBINE SHIP. 104,561 GRT 1067' X 155'
BUILT 1969. NETHERLANDS SB, AMSTERDAM.
MASTER: OCTOBER 9TH 1971 TO MARCH 3RD '72.

MELO
TEAM TURBINE SHIP. 105,138 GRT 1067' X 155'
BUILT 1969. KAWASAKI HI, SAKAIDE.
MASTER: JUNE 6TH - OCTOBER 22ND 1972.

MANGELIA
STEAM TURBINE SHIP. 105,138 GRT 1067' X 155'
BUILT 1968. KAWASAKI DOCKYARD, KOBE.
MASTER: JANUARY 16TH TO JULY 3RD 1973.

GADINIA
STEAM TURBINE SHIP 48,612 GRT 843' X 115'
BUILT 1972. CHANTIERS DE L'ATLANTIQUE,
ST.NAZAIRE. MASTER:
MAY 10TH 1973 TO MARCH 3RD 1974
JULY 11TH 1974 TO NOVEMBER 5TH 1974
FEBRUARY 28TH 1980 TO JUNE 19TH 1980.

GARI
STEAM TURBINE SHIP 48,612 GRT 1102' X 115'
BUILT 1973 CHANTIERS DE L'ATLANTIQUE
ST. NAZAIRE. MASTER:
AUGUST 11TH 1975 TO OCTOBER 3RD 1975
GARI (CONT'D)
SEPTEMBER 22ND 1980 TO JANUARY 24TH 1981.

LEPETA
STEAM TURBINE SHIP 161,632 GRT 1102' X 181'
BUILT 1976. HARLAND & WOLFF. BELFAST.
MASTER: AUGUST 22ND TO OCTOBER 13TH 976.

ERINNA
MOTOR VESSEL. 19,656 GRT 556' X 85'
BUILT 1977 SAINT JOHN, NEW BRUNSWICK.
MASTER: OCTOBER 21ST TO DECEMBER 9TH 1977

GENOTA
STEAM TURBINE SHIP. 52,708 GRT. 850' X 115'
BUILT 1975 CNIM, MARSEILLES.
MASTER: FEBRUARY 25TH TO JUNE 28TH 1978.

TECTUS
MOTOR VESSEL. 65,134 GRT 858' X 138'
BUILT 1974. HARLAND & WOLFF, BELFAST.
MASTER:
SEPTEMBER 5TH 1978 TO JANUARY 7TH 1979.
JULY 20TH 1982 TO NOVEMBER 11TH 1982.

VEGA SEAL
MOTOR VESSEL. 57,462 GRT
NO OTHER DETAILS AVAILABLE,
MASTER: MARCH 3RD TO JUNE 12TH 1979.

GADILA
STEAM TURBINE SHIP. 48,612 GRT 843' X 115'
BUILT 1973. CHANTIERS DE L'ATLANTIQUE
ST.NAZAIRE. MASTER:OCTOBER 12TH 1981
TO FEBRUARY 2ND 1982.

ISOMERIA
MOTOR VESSEL. 39,932 GRT 688' X 103'
BUILT 1982. HARLAND & WOLFF, BELFAST.
MASTER: FEBRUARY 14TH TO JUNE 6TH 1983.

TENAGA EMPAT
STEAM TURBINE SHIP. 68,085 GRT 922 X 138'
BUILT 1981 CNIM LA SEYNE.
MASTER: OCT. 25TH 1983 TO MARCH 10TH 1984.

TENAGA DUA
STEAM TURBINE SHIP.68,085 GRT 922' X 138'
BUILT 1981. SOC.M&N, DUNKIRK.
MASTER: JUNE 28TH TO DECEMBER 4TH 1984.